THE NEW BATTLE OVER WORKPLACE PRIVACY

THE NEW BATTLE OVER WORKPLACE PRIVACY

- How far can management go?
- What rights do employees have?

Safe Practices to Minimize Conflict, Confusion, and Litigation

William S. Hubbartt

AMACOM
American Management Association
New York · Atlanta · Boston · Chicago · Kansas City · San Francisco · Washington, D.C.
Brussels · Mexico City · Tokyo · Toronto

This publication is designed to provide accurate and authori-
tative information in regard to the subject matter covered. It
is sold with the understanding that the publisher is not engaged in rendering legal, accounting, or other professional
service. If legal advice or other expert assistance is required,
the services of a competent professional person should be
sought.

Library of Congress Cataloging-in-Publication Data

Hubbartt, William S.
     The new battle over workplace privacy : how far can management go?
what rights do employees have? : safe practices to minimize conflict,
confusion, and litigation / William S. Hubbartt.
     p. cm.
  Includes bibliographical references and index.
  ISBN 0-8144-0357-3
  1. Labor laws and legislation—United States. 2. Employee rights—United
States. 3. Privacy, Right of—United States. I. Title.
  KF3455.H83 1997
  344.7301—dc21   97-38669
                                                              CIP

Printing number

10 9 8 7 6 5 4 3 2 1

To Gloria, the love of my life

Contents

Preface

In *The New Battle Over Workplace Privacy,* we take a look at the emerging conflict between an employer's right to manage and an employee's perceived right to privacy in the workplace.

As we enter a new millennium, the issue of workplace privacy has become a raging legal battleground of conflicting expectations. On the one hand, employees assert that their privacy rights are being trampled upon by ruthless, prying employers. Employers, on the other hand, claim the need to protect business assets from employee theft, accidents caused by employees, drug abuse, and other problems as justification for employment practices that may threaten an employee's perceived privacy right.

The workplace privacy battleground covers a wide variety of employment practices. Individuals seeking employment are subjected to a variety of inquiries, investigations, and background checks. Businesses collect and maintain a wide range of data on employees. Drug testing is now a major screening tool used by a majority of large and small firms alike. Employees on the job are increasingly likely to be subject to performance monitoring, drug/alcohol testing, searches, and other kinds of employer surveillance. Employee computer files, E-mail, voice mail, and telephone calls are often subject to employer monitoring. Even employee activity off the job has been subject to employer scrutiny and corrective action.

Some privacy issues are addressed by various state or federal laws. And there is a constitutional foundation for our belief that we have a right to privacy. But few workers realize the limited extent of privacy protection for employees in the private workplace. As a result, many invasion of privacy issues arise from disputed employment practices and end up being settled in private law suits brought by individuals against their employers.

The New Battle Over Workplace Privacy examines the various privacy issues confronting employers in the workplace. Relevant laws on privacy issues are identified, together with numerous illustrative case examples that show the human side of the workplace privacy battleground. Then, to aid the reader in dealing with privacy issues in the workplace, the book identifies critical issues to consider and suggests management guidelines for minimizing liability and developing effective employment policies. In addition, the book includes sample policies, forms, checklists, charts, highlights of employee rights, and suggested notices to employees.

The legal environment of workplace privacy is continually changing. New laws have been proposed or are being passed in various states to prevent abuses of employer regulation of off-duty conduct, surveillance, and electronic monitoring in the workplace. Often, these laws provide only limited protection for the employee in the private workplace. Meanwhile, the tug-of-war between employee privacy rights and employer management rights rages on. *The New Battle Over Workplace Privacy* is intended to help the reader to better navigate this treacherous ground.

Acknowledgments: I want to acknowledge the assistance and suggestions offered by the following individuals during the research, writing, and editing of this book: Gloria D. Kwasniewski for content suggestions and countless hours of keyboarding; Anne Basye for editorial advice, assistance, and organization; and editors Adrienne Hickey, Nancy Brandwein, and David Follmer for editorial suggestions.

THE NEW BATTLE OVER WORKPLACE PRIVACY

1

Privacy Rights: The New Employee Relations Battlefield

Can an employee be dismissed for dating a fellow employee?

Can a manager monitor conversations in his employees' break room?

Does a drug test invade privacy, or is it a reasonable safeguard against accidents on the job?

Is E-mail private correspondence?

These and other questions strike at the heart of the conflict between an employer's concern for managing the safety and security of the workplace and an employee's privacy interest.

The news media are filled with reports of employers who routinely conduct locker searches, monitor telephone calls, mount video cameras that watch employees on the job, and monitor computers and electronic mail systems. Many of these stories emerge when a lawsuit is filed by an outraged employee seeking redress for a perceived violation of his or her privacy.

I say "perceived" because an employee's right to privacy in the private-sector workplace is *not* fundamentally guaranteed by the Constitution or federal laws, even though many employees believe this to be the case. On the other hand, employers do not have carte blanche. Some federal and state laws do afford certain limited privacy protections for employees. But in their desire to control their businesses, some employers clearly cross the boundary between reasonable management practices and outrageous personal violations.

Why are conflicts over privacy increasing?

Companies don't set out to spy on employees or break into desks and lockers. But as companies have watched losses caused by theft and drug abuse soar, they have responded by instituting controls to protect their assets and interests. Such common deterrents as drug testing and workplace surveillance are extremely sensitive and can offend employees if they are not explained adequately and implemented with care.

Another "hot spot" is workplace technology. Sophisticated computer and communications technology allows managers to monitor performance by monitoring conversations or counting keystrokes. Again, if such procedures are instituted with little explanation or respect, employees will have strong negative reactions.

Their reactions are understandable. Most of us regard the right to privacy as one of the fundamental freedoms of a democratic society. Our history lessons taught us that the American colonists sought privacy protections and freedom from colonial rule of the English government. Our founding fathers sought to include privacy protections in our Constitution and our government. We grew up believing that individuals should be protected from unwanted prying into their personal lives and activities and that information about one's private life should not be subject to scrutiny by others, by the government, or by one's employer.

With these expectations, it's natural that both employers and employees wonder whether there are laws against employer spying and just what privacy rights employees are entitled to on the job. In truth, there *is* no comprehensive privacy statute. Yes, there is a constitutional provision that limits certain search and seizure actions by the government. And yes, there are laws that limit certain forms of monitoring and specify how an employer can use or release private information. But most of the constitutional protections we enjoy as private citizens vanish when we go to work. While the government, as an employer, is subject to constitutional privacy limitations, laws impose few limitations on the private employer.

Our privacy rights on the job are much more limited than most of us believe. The Constitution affords only limited privacy protections, which are outlined in chapter 3. Local laws vary from state to state and, like federal laws, are subject to judicial interpretation. Many areas of privacy are new and have yet to be legislated. Other laws are so recent that cases that hinge on their interpretation are only now making their way through the court system, so it may be months or years before an employer can see the significance of a ruling. In the meantime, employers and employees find themselves clashing on privacy in a number of areas, as the following summary reveals.

Preemployment Tests

Arlene Kurtz learned that workplace privacy concerns begin at the start of the employment process when she applied for a job as a clerk typist with the city of North Miami, Florida. The city had developed a policy that all job applicants must sign an affidavit stating that they had not used tobacco products for one year before seeking city employment. The city had implemented a no-smoking policy in 1990, claiming that smokers create higher health costs, as much as $4,611 per year more than nonsmokers. When Kurtz refused to sign the affidavit, she was not hired. She then filed suit against the city alleging that the no-smoking rule was an invasion of privacy.

In her suit, Kurtz claimed that the rule interfered with an aspect of her personal life in which she had a legitimate expectation of privacy. She alleged that if the city's ban against the hiring of smokers was permitted, it would allow employers to further regulate personal lives of employees on other matters, such as when to go to bed at night, what to drink on weekends, where to take vacations, or what hobbies to engage in. In evaluating the facts of the case, the courts sided with the city, indicating that the city's concern for protecting employees' health and for controlling health care costs justified the no-smoking rule.[1]

In *Kurtz*, the city was able to justify its preemployment smoking rule. But other kinds of preemployment tests also have been subject to privacy invasion or other legal claims:

Physical exams. Many firms use physical exams in prehire placement and during employment. Improper use of this information can result in a privacy invasion or violate employment laws.

Drug/alcohol screening. Record numbers of firms are conducting drug/alcohol screening tests. The intrusive nature of these tests prompts many privacy invasion claims.

Background checks. Improper handling or disclosure of information gathered from education, credentials, credit, driving, or criminal records can result in privacy claims or other labor law violations.

---

1. *Kurtz v City of North Miami*, 11 IER Cases 480, US, No. 95-545 (1996).

Reference checks. Resume fraud and other employee relations problems have led employers to seek verification of employment information provided by job candidates. Careless use of this information can result in privacy or defamation claims.

Testing. Employer use of psychological testing, polygraph testing, and other kinds of paper-and-pencil measuring instruments are subject to legal restrictions. Improper inquiries or handling of test results can lead to privacy invasion claims.

How much of an individual's private life can an employer probe into when evaluating candidacy for employment? What information is private, and what information does the employer have a legitimate interest in learning about to evaluate suitability for the job? Can an employer request private medical information before hiring? Is an individual's credit record fair game for an employer's preemployment inquiry? Do psychological or honesty tests invade the privacy of our minds? These questions, which arise during the screening and selection of potential employees, will be discussed in chapters 4 and 5.

New Information Technologies

New information technologies raise new questions and concerns. The privacy of E-mail has been the subject of debates and legal claims. Likewise, Internet access raises new workplace issues. As more and more firms go on-line, questions like these arise: Can an employee expect privacy in E-mail communications? Should an employer monitor E-mail use? Can "erased" E-mail messages be retrieved? Can an employee use company Internet access for personal research? Does use of a password when accessing an E-mail box or when creating computer files provide privacy for the employee?

What privacy rights does an employee have when using E-mail? Ann Miller learned the answer to this question the hard way.

Miller, a human resources manager for USF&G Corporation, received E-mail messages from Alan Lucas, another employee of the firm. Lucas was dissatisfied with his job and his company's salary guidelines. In his messages to Miller, Lucas used a numerical code list that had circulated around the office containing extensive profanity and vulgar terms. When company management discovered the E-mail messages, both employees were discharged.

Miller sued USF&G charging that the firm disciplined her more severely than if she had been a man and that she was therefore a victim of sex discrimination. Further, she claimed that she was out sick when the messages were sent. The company claimed that Miller's acquiescence to the use of the code undermined management authority and that her conduct was inappropriate as a human resources manager. The U.S. District Court in Maryland upheld USF&G's firing of Miller and dismissed her claim.[2] One significant aspect of this case is the court's support of the employer's interception of employee E-mail messages.

Privacy issues surrounding E-mail and other new technologies are discussed in chapter 7.

Release of Private Information

In business, information is power. Information lets managers determine what products or services to offer, how these products or services should be designed and priced, and which customer groups or regions should be targeted for marketing or sales efforts. Information on costs, materials, equipment, and inventory is used to plan, organize, and control the business enterprise.

Information about employees is used to administer salary, government-required benefits such as social security and unemployment insurance, and employer-provided benefits such as health insurance. Employees freely provide information for the employment application, insurance enrollment cards, and numerous other forms, but they expect the employer to exercise reasonable care in protecting the information so that confidential or embarrassing information is not released to fellow employees or others. Employee and employer workplace privacy concerns collide when the employer inappropriately seeks, uses, or releases private information about an employee, former employee, or applicant for employment. A privacy invasion may occur when an employer inappropriately releases private information, as was alleged in a lawsuit filed by an employee using the pseudonym John Doe.

John Doe sued the Southeastern Pennsylvania Transportation Authority for breach of a constitutional privacy right when the employee's use of

2. *Miller v USF&G*, DC Md, No. 93-1968 (1994).

an HIV antiviral drug became known to fellow employees conducting an audit of prescription drug plan records. The information leak occurred during an audit of the Authority's prescription drug plan records when an individual who came across Doe's prescription records and recognized that claims had been paid for prescription drugs used to treat AIDS shared that information with others involved in the audit. Doe learned of the leak of information and that it had occurred because of the auditor's concern about potential HIV exposure. Doe filed a lawsuit claiming a privacy invasion. During the trial, Doe argued that the employee who had sought the information was not seeking the records for legitimate purposes but rather was motivated by fear of persons with AIDS.

But the law of privacy is complex. The courts weigh the private information released and the manner of release against the employer's needs or use for the information. Whether a privacy invasion occurs depends on the law of the state and the facts of the case. In this case, the court noted that Doe suffered no adverse employment action and that the release of information occurred only within the context of a prescription plan audit and was limited to individuals involved in the audit. The audit of plan records, said the court, was a legitimate business activity, and disclosure within this context outweighs an employee's interest in keeping his prescription purchases confidential.[3]

What liability is there when an employer provides a bad employment reference? What must an employer do to protect confidentiality of medical records? Is it best to obtain an employee's authorization before releasing data from personnel records? These and other questions about medical and personnel records will be explored in chapter 8.

Monitoring Employees and Their Performance

Workplace privacy concerns also cover performance monitoring, workplace investigations, and their influence on employee terminations. In addition, searches or surveillance often results in privacy claims, prompting questions like these: Can an employer search desks or lockers? Are searches of personal

3. *Doe v Southeastern Pennsylvania Transportation Authority*, 11 IER Cases 417, CA3, No. 95-1559 (1995).

property or vehicles lawful? Are there legal limits on monitoring telephone use? How far can an investigator go to catch a workers' compensation cheat? See chapter 9 for answers.

After-Hours Activities

What an employee does off the job is his or her business—or is it? Employer intrusions into personal lives of employees create many questions. Can an employer regulate or prevent employees from taking a second job? Can an employee be fired because he was arrested off the job? What should an employer do if an employee refuses to work because of religious beliefs? Is it lawful for an employer to regulate an employee's drinking or smoking off the job? Is it a privacy invasion when the employer limits dating between employees? These kinds of issues have created many privacy invasion claims.

Consider the case of Robin Joy Brown, who applied to the State of Georgia for a position as a state's attorney.

> Brown had all the prerequisites: a Phi Beta Kappa undergraduate, she had received a law scholarship, edited the law review, received her law degree, and completed law clerk experience. After being offered a job by the Georgia state's attorney's office, she accepted. But prior to starting her employment she advised a deputy state's attorney of her plans for an upcoming wedding and that she would be changing her name from Brown to Shahar. She did not tell the deputy that she planned to marry another woman.
>
> When Georgia Attorney General Bowers learned that the planned wedding was to another woman, he withdrew the job offer stating in a letter that the purported marriage would "jeopardize the proper function of this office." Brown went ahead with her marriage plans, changed her name to Shahar, and filed suit for loss of job. In her suit, Shahar alleged that she was "fired" because of her participation in a private religious ceremony of marriage. The U.S. Court of Appeals ultimately heard the case and found that the employer's action violated the Shahars' constitutional right of intimate association.[4]

Employer involvement in off-the-job conduct usually occurs in one of the following areas:

4. *Shahar v Bowers*, 11 IER Cases 521 (1994).

Criminal and other off-duty misconduct. Some individuals just can't seem to stay out of trouble. Inappropriate collection or release of this information can lead to privacy claims and other liabilities.

Secondary employment. Employees may feel that secondary employment is a private affair, but when it affects the employer's business, the employer may have a say.

Smoking and use of other lawful products off the job. Off-the-job use of lawful products is generally the employee's business. On some issues, an employer may have justification to regulate off-duty conduct, but privacy claims frequently occur when employers try to control this kind of conduct.

Employee dating. Regulation of dating may seem beyond the employer's purview, but sexual harassment claims as well as privacy invasion claims make this a sensitive subject.

Personal beliefs and lifestyles. Employee beliefs and lifestyles may be related to religion, marital status, or sexual preference. These issues are highly personal, and improper handling of them can lead to privacy invasion or other legal claims.

Issues related to employer regulation of off-duty conduct are covered in chapter 10.

Privacy Law and Company Policy

How much privacy can an employee expect? How far can management pry into an employee's private life? Where does the employer's right to manage end and the employee's right to privacy begin? I first grew interested in these questions when I heard the story of Robert Ruffalo, an operations manager at a pharmaceutical distribution company in suburban Chicago. Finding a bullet on the floor of his office, he reasoned that there was a gun on the premises and ordered a search of lockers and other work spaces. When no gun turned up, Ruffalo checked employee purses and personal belongings. Then, according to news reports, Ruffalo allegedly blocked the front door and announced that each employee would be frisked before being allowed to leave. News reports stated that he ordered employees to raise their arms and proceeded to physically touch employees on the arms, stomachs, ribs, backs, thighs, and calves. No gun was found, and employees were permitted to leave.[5]

5. "Workers Sue over Search," *Chicago Tribune*, May 24, 1996, p. 1.

The search, however, prompted a lawsuit seeking $240,000 in compensatory and punitive damages for each of seven female employees of the firm. Defending the manager's actions, company executives asserted that "one of our objectives is to maintain a safe and secure work environment. Any time that is in jeopardy, there is a need for immediate action."

My interest was piqued when I learned that legal experts believed the outcome of the employees' claim would hinge on the company's policy for dealing with workplace searches. As a consultant, I have helped many companies develop employee handbooks and company policies. In my experience, I have found that a fair, consistent policy that is administered equitably can head off many misunderstandings and keep people out of trouble. This case clearly demonstrates my belief that a company's policy can determine its ability to fend off a lawsuit or avoid paying a fine.

Tracking workplace privacy court cases confirmed my conviction. A well-drafted company policy will help minimize the potential for conflict over workplace privacy. A well-drafted policy coupled with a climate of respect for employees is even more powerful. All companies function better when relations between employers and employees are positive. A company that deals with employees respectfully, practices open and honest communication, and treats people as adults will have a climate that encourages trust and discourages litigation.

A firm's employee handbook or personnel policy manual should let employees know that the company will respect the private lives of its employees unless they become involved in actions that may adversely affect the company or its customers. In that case, the company has the obligation to protect itself and its customers from harm and can undertake the measures indicated in the policy.

When you draft your policy, make sure it complies with your state's laws regarding privacy. Outline clearly your policies regarding searches, telephone monitoring, drug testing, and other potentially controversial controls. If you communicate that policy to everyone in the company and uniformly and fairly follow that policy, you will minimize conflicts with your employees about privacy and maximize your chances of a favorable ruling if you end up in court.

For example, if your policy outlines the circumstances under which workplace areas will be searched and employees tested for drugs or alcohol, then searches and tests you conduct that comply with your policy will probably survive a legal challenge. If your policy indicates that the company reserves the right to control the use of company-provided equipment and gain access to it, then an employee's privacy expectation is reduced. This reduces the likelihood of a privacy invasion claim if management finds it necessary to search a desk, locker, or computer file.

But let's say you don't have a policy on searches and seizures. Furthermore, you let employees secure their lockers with their own locks. By doing so, you create an expectation of privacy. If you conduct a search in which an employee's lock is broken, your employee may well have a claim.

Two additional policy elements can help increase your ability to successfully fend off a privacy invasion or discrimination claim.

First, it is important to *notify your employees* of your policy. Your policies will not withstand a legal challenge if no employees know about them. That is why it is important to make sure that your employees actually read your policies. Policies can be communicated to employees in a letter, bulletin board posting, employee handbook, management policy guide, or policy statement to employees with a signed acknowledgment of receipt.

Second, it is important to *have a clear business justification* for your policies. Whether you monitor employee telephone conversations, impose a dress code, or review E-mail messages, you must justify your policy on business grounds. For example, drug tests may be conducted in order to promote safety or investigate an accident. Dress codes may be specified for safety reasons or to convey a professional image to the customer. Surveillance may be justified in order to protect against workplace violence or guard against theft.

Supervisors: A Critical Link

To make your policy a success, your company's management and supervisors must be familiar with its contents and willing to abide by its guidelines. Even companies that are famous for positive employee relations can find themselves in trouble if a supervisor chooses to ignore company policy. Consider the case of IBM employee Virginia Roulon-Miller.

> After joining the company's Philadelphia data center as a receptionist, Roulon-Miller obtained a college degree, was promoted several times, and was placed into IBM's Accelerated Career Development Program. She received top performance ratings and pay increases and was eventually promoted to marketing manager at IBM's San Francisco office.
>
> During her career, Roulon-Miller met and began dating a fellow IBM employee, account manager Matt Blum. Blum left IBM to join a competing office products company called QYX. Blum and Roulon-

Miller had dated on and off for several years, and IBM management was aware of their relationship.

Shortly after receiving a $4,000 raise, Roulon-Miller was called in to supervisor Phil Callahan's office. Callahan confronted her about whether she was dating Blum, stating that the dating relationship created a conflict of interest. Callahan told Roulon-Miller to stop dating Blum. When Roulon-Miller protested against the company's intrusion into her private life, Callahan dismissed her. Roulon-Miller sued IBM, claiming that the company's action was an invasion of privacy and that she was wrongfully discharged because of a social relationship.

A jury found the supervisor's actions outrageous and atrocious conduct, a flagrant disregard of company policies. The jury determined that the company's actions were an invasion of Roulon-Miller's right to privacy and awarded her a $200,000 judgment.[6]

IBM has a reputation for openness and dignity in employee relationships. The company prides itself on its progressive human resources practices and for providing career opportunities for employees. Yet even IBM found itself in trouble, thanks to a renegade supervisor who ignored company policy.

Privacy: An Individual Perception

Even companies with top-quality policies can find themselves in court. That's because different people have different levels of tolerance on privacy issues. One individual may be highly offended by an employer's action while another may be unconcerned. But just because an employee feels that his or her privacy was invaded does not mean that a legally recognized privacy invasion occurred.

For example, two employees were fired for drinking on the job. The employer, which had recently distributed a no-drinking/no-drugs workplace policy, promptly fired the pair when a supervisor caught them with alcohol on company property. To reinforce the message to other workers, the employer announced the firings at a supervisor's meeting. The two employees reacted differently upon learning that the reason for their firing was communicated to the firm's supervisory employees.

One employee, a heavy drinker, had been through this before. He moved on and sought other employment. But the second fired employee was vitally

6. *Roulon-Miller v IBM*, 1 IER Cases 405 (1984).

concerned about his reputation. He felt that the announcement to the firm's supervisors about his firing was defamation and a privacy invasion. If he files a privacy invasion claim, he may learn whether the law in his state recognizes a privacy claim on the matter presented and what actions must be present for his case to win.

How can a firm minimize or prevent these claims? The answer is the same: by clearly defining a policy, communicating that policy to employees and supervisors, and continually striving to administer the policy fairly and uniformly.

Case Examples Illustrate Lessons Learned

A company policy will do no good if it exists on paper only. In order to protect the rights of employer and employees alike, it must be vigilantly monitored and, when necessary, enforced. Throughout this book, you will find court cases whose decisions hinged on company policy.

If you're reading this book, you probably are in the thick of the controversy surrounding workplace privacy. This book has a number of features that will help you find your way through the complex issue. First, it acquaints you with workplace privacy laws and principles you must know before you draft or implement a policy. Second, it delves into many very sensitive areas of workplace privacy and recommends ways to implement fair, defensible policies and procedures that respect your employees while protecting your corporate interests.

Just a note about cases before we start: This book contains many cases that show how privacy laws apply to the workplace. In some cases, the employer's conduct was clearly outrageous and directly contrary to a particular law, leading to a finding of privacy invasion. In other cases, however, the court's decision contradicts our expectations of what is a privacy invasion. In some cases that seem similar, courts appear to reach conflicting decisions. There are several reasons why this may occur:

- Privacy statutes differ from one state to the next.
- Historical common-law concepts differ from one state to the next.
- The law under which the employee has made his claim differs from one case to another.
- Employer policies or procedures differ from firm to firm.
- The employee may have failed to prove his or her case.

When considering privacy cases, the courts seek to balance an employee's privacy rights against the employer's right to manage the business. In some cases, the court found the employer's actions to be an outrageous unlawful invasion of privacy. In others, the court recognized the employee's privacy expectation but determined that the employer's purpose for the action was justified and outweighed the employee's privacy right.

For these reasons, the cases selected and used in this book are illustrative only; court decisions described here may not represent the current state of the law in every state or jurisdiction. That's why it's imperative to consult a personnel policy specialist *before* you release your company policy or employee handbook. A thousand dollars of legal advice may save you hundreds of thousands in litigation.

Conclusion

In all aspects of our lives, certain individual freedoms are given up in order to accommodate the greater needs of the public, the government, or an organization such as a employer. Because of terrorism and hijacking, our society readily submits to use of metal detector screens and searches of personal belongings when boarding commercial aircraft at the airport. Upon return from overseas trips, travelers customarily accept luggage searches because of the recognized need to control the unauthorized influx of drugs into the country.

Freedom of speech does not protect the calling out of "fire" in a crowded theater. As a society, we tolerate the increased presence of security cameras at banks, retail stores, and other places where cash is handled because we recognize that the use of these devices to deter crime is more important than the loss of certain aspects of our privacy. But privacy rights seem to be diminishing, and employer prying seems to be growing. In chapter 2, we take a detailed look at why employers pry.

2

Why Employers Pry

A business exists in order to develop, manufacture, and sell its product or to provide service. IBM markets business machines and computers. Motorola manufacturers communications equipment. Dayton Hudson operates retail department stores. UPS delivers parcels. Unlike spy organizations such as the American CIA or the Soviet KGB, these prominent firms were not created for the purpose of spying on or invading the privacy of their employees. How is it, then, that these firms and many other employers become embroiled in privacy invasion claims?

Problems Facing Employers

Job applicants who lie on resumes. Employees who falsify accident reports in order to obtain workers' compensation benefits, or commit crimes on the job. Troubled employees who experience job performance problems and frequent absences. Drug and alcohol abuse. Customer complaints and inventory losses.

Every business has the right to exercise reasonable control of business operations. And when problems like these occur, managers are justified in implementing procedures to prevent or correct them.

Some employers react to these situations by creating loss control policies and procedures. Other firms take action to control and prevent problems before a crisis occurs. Security systems and surveillance may be developed to combat property or inventory losses. Employee performance may be monitored to prevent customer relations problems. Reference checks and other background-checking procedures may be instituted to verify data provided by job candidates.

Some of the control measures set up by employers may infringe on an employee's expectation of privacy. Firms that do not experience these problems are less likely to set up procedures that may conflict with an employee's privacy on the job. Either way, a close look at the problems employers face reveals the areas in which privacy conflicts take root and flourish.

Theft

According to the U.S. Commerce Department, theft of business assets costs employers an estimated $40 billion annually, a figure that rises every year. While shoplifting and holdups account for some of the theft, business security experts say that the majority of theft is done by employees.[1]

Some thefts are petty, like stealing office supplies to provide pens and pencils for kids when school starts. Firms that use expensive tools and machines, particularly portable tools, find that these items are targets of theft if proper security measures are not in place. Retail and distribution organizations report that big ticket inventory items such as electronics and clothes are frequent targets of theft.

One security professional says that 10 percent of employees are likely to steal from their employer, while another 10 percent of employees will never steal. The remaining 80 percent are likely to stay honest if the employer creates an environment that discourages and detects theft. The best theft prevention measure is an open, trustworthy workplace culture. Employees who feel valued and trusted will have no need to steal to "get back" at their employer. Security professionals also recommend that employers develop a comprehensive program to discourage theft, including a formal antitheft policy, inventory systems and financial controls, various tests to screen job candidates for trustworthiness, and security measures to prevent theft.

Is a job candidate likely to steal, or has the candidate stolen from past employers? Job candidates can be scrutinized through some form of honesty test, reference checking, background checks, or criminal record checks. Are current employees stealing from the firm? To find out who is responsible for a current theft problem, employers may institute surveillance of the work area, polygraph testing, and workplace searches.

Drug Abuse

As drug abuse has escalated and its consequences in the workplace have grown more serious, a record 81 percent of major corporations now test new

1. Samuel Greensguard, "Theft Control Starts with HR Strategies," *Personnel Journal*, April 1993, p. 81.

hires and employees for drug use, according to a 1996 survey conducted by the American Management Association (AMA).[2] A similar AMA study conducted in 1986 revealed that only 22 percent of responding employers conducted drug testing, primarily due to concern about employee privacy.[3] Rising drug abuse rates caused many companies to reconsider their position in the intervening ten years.

Consider the case of a medium-sized midwestern metal fabricator who supplied parts to the automobile industry.

> To meet customer demand the firm ran production on two shifts. The day shift was well supervised because most management and support personnel were on the premises. But the night shift operated with fewer management personnel. The night supervisor reported some quality problems and need for rework. Over the course of several months, some thefts were noted also. Management began to pay closer attention to second-shift operations and then discovered evidence of drug use on company premises.
>
> Fearing a widespread problem, management announced and conducted a drug testing sweep. A testing service was called to the premises, and all employees were subjected to the testing procedures. Over 10 percent of the employer's workforce were found to have a positive test result showing the employees were working with drugs in their bodies. All those testing positive were dismissed.
>
> Originally reluctant to start a practice of drug testing, the employer ultimately decided that the need for safety, security, and productivity of operations outweighed employee privacy concerns. While some employees were upset about the drug testing, their concern faded when they learned that fifteen coworkers were on the job with drugs in their system.

Today, drug/alcohol testing is viewed as a necessary means to control workplace problems caused by drug and alcohol abuse. Drug testing now occurs during preemployment screening, following accidents or other workplace incidents, and on a random basis. Employers in certain transportation indus-

2. "Drug Testing of Employees, New Hires on the Increase," *Policy & Practice Update*, May 2, 1996.
3. "Drug Testing Grows—AMA Study Finds," *Managing Office Technology*, July 1996, p. 23.

tries are subject to drug testing rules in federal regulations. Some firms also offer referral and treatment through drug treatment programs for current employees.

Alcohol Abuse

Employee alcohol abuse has long been recognized as a costly problem affecting individual and company productivity. According to the National Council of Alcoholism, some six million alcoholics are on the payrolls of American businesses. Drug and alcohol abuse affects an estimated 10 to 20 percent of the working population. In other words, an organization of one hundred employees is likely to have between ten and twenty individuals who are personally dealing with a drug or alcohol problem or coping with a family member's drug or alcohol problems.

Alcoholism is often a hidden problem. Alcoholics are often able to maintain a "normal" front at work, hiding their drinking problems from the boss and coworkers while family members suffer from abusive behavior at home. Alcoholics tend to hold onto work at all costs, letting the rest of their life activities center on the drinking. But sooner or later, drinking takes its toll on work activities. The toll? More than $30 billion a year in sick leave, absenteeism, accidents, poor performance, insurance payments, and other hidden costs.

A Minneapolis manufacturing firm recognized the potential problem of alcoholism and implemented a program of confidential assistance and referral for employees seeking help with chemical dependency. The human resources manager received training on recognizing and responding to employees in need of assistance. When the new policy was introduced to employees, company management emphasized the importance of protecting the confidentiality of an individual's situation and providing confidential treatment or counseling as needed.

During meetings to announce the policy, several employees approached the human resources manager and acknowledged that they were recovering alcoholics. In the weeks that followed, three employees and an employee's spouse sought help through the firm's chemical dependency program. One of the employees, whose problem had been hidden for years, had been involved in a domestic dispute that resulted in costly surgery and lost time as he recuperated from the injuries. After another weekend binge, the employee's spouse called the human resources manager seeking assistance. As arrangements were

being made to place the employee into a chemical dependency treatment program, the employee's spouse sighed, "You don't know what
kind of hell we've been going through. Thank God there's help."

Companies fight alcohol abuse in many ways. Many use reference checks
and driving record checks to carefully screen applicants and drug/alcohol
screens and psychological testing of new employees. When an employee's job
performance suffers because of drinking, employers are more likely to carefully
monitor an individual's performance or to refer the employee for alcohol abuse
testing. Many also offer employee assistance plans that provide confidential
assessment and referral for medical assistance.

Workplace Violence

Violence in the workplace is increasing at an alarming rate. According to a
report from the National Institute for Occupational Safety and Health, over
one million workers a year are victims of workplace violence. The U.S. Labor
Department says that job-related homicides accounted for one of every six fatal
work injuries occurring in 1995. In that year, homicides were the second leading cause of job deaths for men and women combined, but the leading cause
of on-the-job death for women alone. In a survey conducted by the Society of
Human Resource Management (SHRM), nearly half of the human resources
management professionals surveyed reported that one or more incidents of
violence had occurred in their workplace since January 1, 1994. In a similar
survey conducted by the society in 1993, by comparison, 33 percent of respondents reported acts of workplace violence.[4]

Standard Gravure of Louisville, Kentucky, came face to face with workplace violence on September 14, 1989, when an employee of the firm
on long-term disability entered the printing plant's reception area carrying an AK 47 assault rifle. The employee made his way through the
building's offices, up to the third floor, and then down into the lower
levels of the press room, randomly shooting employees. All told, seven
people were killed, and twelve were wounded. Following his ram-
page, the employee committed suicide.

4. "Workplace Violence on Rise, According to SHRM Survey," *HR News*, July 1996, p. 16.

Years later, company officials still do not know what set this employee off. The man was treated like any other employee on long-term disability. But after the carnage, the company improved security systems, hired full-time guards, and began a visitor sign-in policy. Nevertheless, officials acknowledge that if someone is intent on causing harm, no workplace can be made completely safe.[5]

Human resources specialists agree that the best way to prevent workplace violence is to create an atmosphere in which individuals are treated with dignity and respect. For example, supervisory personnel should discipline employees calmly yet firmly, avoiding emotional or personal attacks in front of others. But violent acts still occur among employees and between employees and supervisors. To prevent them, companies are increasing surveillance of workplace premises, installing video monitor systems, increasing or forming security staffs, and installing more sophisticated locking and entry systems. They are also conducting background investigations, criminal checks, reference checks, and psychological testing of potential hires in an effort to avoid hiring potentially violent employees.

Employee Turnover

Employee turnover is created by a number of factors. A company's workforce grows or shrinks as work levels fluctuate. Individuals may leave one job for another, seeking better pay, career advancement, better opportunity, or more suitable working conditions. A certain amount of turnover is normal and even healthy for an organization. But when turnover and employee separations become excessive, the firm incurs greater costs in recruiting, hiring, training, increased overtime work, and lost productivity as employees fill in during periods of short staffing.

Where turnover becomes a significant problem, some firms undertake a study of the reasons that employees are leaving. If a study points to separations due to drug or alcohol problems, the firm may begin screening new employees more carefully, using reference checks, drug/alcohol screens, psychological testing, and driving record checks. Similar screens may help identify workers who have a high potential to quit.

---

5. Linda Thornberg, "When Violence Hits Business," *HR Magazine*, July 1993, p. 40.

Poor Work Performance

Performance monitoring and appraisal is a customary and reasonable prerogative of management. After all, how can a business function properly if it cannot
manage the performance of its employees? According to a Commerce Clearing
House (CCH) publication *Performance Appraisal Manual for Managers and Supervisors*, over 80 percent of large firms conduct performance appraisals of employees.[6] Traditional performance appraisals are not generally considered an
invasion of privacy, but many employers are monitoring performance more ag-
gressively.

New technology is one reason employers can monitor performance more
closely. Computers can count keystrokes, orders, transactions, errors, and other
productivity and quality measures for employees whose jobs are largely performed on a computer. Telemarketing employees and telephone customer service agents are accustomed to management monitoring their telephone calls
with customers, once customers are duly notified that their conversations may
be recorded. At Duke Power's customer service center, for example, supervisors monitor four calls a month for each representative. The employees are
then rated and given verbal feedback on their performance.[7] Surveillance cameras are used to monitor employees as well as prevent robbery in banks, conve-
nience stores, and other jobs involving the handling of cash.

Employee Misconduct

Misconduct is any employee behavior that deliberately violates company policy or disregards guidelines for conduct on the job, such as lateness, absentee-
ism, inappropriate dress or appearance, poor attitude, disregard for a policy
or rule, or failure to follow a supervisor's instruction. It may also involve possession or use of drugs or alcoholic beverages on the job, theft, or misuse of
company property.

Employers customarily have dealt with employee misconduct by conducting an internal investigation and imposing such disciplinary actions as warnings, suspension without pay, or discharge. Maintaining order in the workplace
and dealing with misconduct is viewed as a normal employer prerogative.

6. William S. Hubbartt, *Performance Appraisal Manual for Managers and Supervisors* (Chicago: CCH, 1992), 10.
7. Jennifer J. Laabs, "Surveillance: Tool or Trap?" *Personnel Journal*, June 1992, p. 104.

Employers seek to prevent misconduct by conducting reference and driving record checks, drug/alcohol screens, and psychological testing on new employees. Surveillance systems such as video cameras are also used in monitoring employee misconduct as well as monitoring work performance and workplace security.

Negligent Hiring Liability

Employers are held liable for the acts of their employees while performing job duties. When an employee causes an accident, damages customer property, or commits a criminal act, the employer generally will be held liable. For example, if a day care center or school district hired a known child sex offender for a teaching position, the employer's lack of diligence in screening out an obviously unfit employee most likely would result in a costly liability claim.

> A midwestern industrial gases distributor operated a store and warehouse selling flammable and nonflammable compressed gases used for welding and other industrial processes. The firm needed to hire a truck driver to load the truck, make deliveries to businesses throughout the community, unload tanks at the customer site, and pick up empty tanks for return to the store. A middle-aged driver who had worked for another firm in the community for over fifteen years applied for the job.
>
> In a small town, personal relationships are common; the driver was a friend of the owner, who was aware of the man's reputation as a drinker. The applicant insisted that the drinking was not a problem and that he had a good driving record. The owner hired the individual. Within three months, the driver was involved in a serious accident, causing injury to another individual and major property damage from an explosion of one of the flammable gas canisters being delivered on the truck. An investigation revealed that alcohol was a contributing factor to the accident and that the driver in fact had a prior DUI offense in another state. When these facts surfaced, the industrial gas company was subject to a negligent hiring lawsuit for failing to adequately check the driving record and for hiring an obviously unqualified driver.

When the stakes are high, employers are right to screen new hires carefully. Reference checks, drug/alcohol screens, background checks, criminal record checks, psychological testing, and driving record checks are some methods used to screen out unfit or dangerous employees.

Government Requirements

Many employers delve into employees' backgrounds and behaviors in order to satisfy government regulations. Employers involved in truck, rail, and air transportation, for example, are subject to U.S. Department of Transportation (DOT) regulations that specify requirements for drug testing, define administrative procedures to manage the program, and require referral for treatment and training for supervisors. To comply with the regulations, transportation companies must set up a drug testing program and test new drivers.

For example, a highway materials company specializing in providing gravel, concrete, and other materials used in highway construction employs over one hundred drivers and equipment operators who are subject to the DOT regulations. New employees seeking jobs as drivers must present a commercial driver's license and satisfactorily complete a preemployment drug test. A positive drug test showing presence of drugs in the body means that the driver is unqualified and cannot be hired until a subsequent test shows an negative result.

DOT-regulated employers are likely to use other employee screening techniques such as reference checks, background checks, criminal record checks, and driving record checks to make sure their employees meet workplace safety criteria.

Resume Fraud

Human resources managers report growing incidence of misrepresentation of credentials by job seekers trying to distinguish themselves from other candidates. Sometimes referred to as "resume fraud," this practice may include exaggeration or outright falsification of some aspect of a person's work history, job experience, dates of employment, education, degrees, or salary. Undetected resume fraud can lead a company to hire unqualified workers. This in turn may lead to performance or service problems caused by an unqualified worker who cannot handle the job. If the unqualified employee's actions cause harm to another, a negligent hiring or negligent retention lawsuit may result.

To prevent resume fraud, employers may check references closely; verify education or degrees; require proof of professional licenses; check driving records, criminal records, and background; and conduct psychological testing.

Workers' Compensation Fraud

The workers' compensation system is designed to provide limited income maintenance and medical insurance for employees who are injured or become ill in the course of employment. It is intended to provide a fair and equitable benefit for the employee by simplifying the liability determination and claim payment process on behalf of the employer. In most areas, the workers' compensation system is a state-run adjudication system with benefits for employees provided through mandatory insurance coverage paid by the employer.

Unfortunately, the system can be abused. An employee may become injured at home over the weekend and then on Monday morning report the injury as a work injury occurring on the job. Some employees falsify claims of job injuries because the workers' compensation insurance plan pays 100 percent compared to the group health plan, which may require payment of deductible amounts or specified copayments.

> For example, an employee at a metal fabricating firm reported that he sustained a back injury while moving some product on Friday. The employee, however, neglected to report the alleged injury to management until the following week. On learning of the employee's injury, the supervisor referred the employee to the local occupational clinic. Although the employee complained that his back was still sore, the X-rays and examination were inconclusive. The doctor recommended that the employee be transferred to a light duty assignment.
>
> Because this small firm had no available light duty work, the employee was released on a medical leave. For a number of weeks, the employee received disability pay and continued to complain of back soreness. Follow-up visits to the clinic continued to be inconclusive. The employee's supervisor reported that he had heard rumors of the employee playing golf while on disability leave, but nothing was confirmed or proved.
>
> Eventually, the workers' compensation insurance paid a settlement to the employee, who returned to work. A few weeks later, the employee was driving a new car to work. Management's suspicions about a fraudulent claim were never confirmed, and in the following month, two other employees reported back injuries.

In response to incidents like this one, firms are conducting thorough and detailed accident investigations. Where fraud may be suspected, some firms are increasing surveillance of workplace premises, installing video monitor systems, and using private investigators to conduct surveillance of "disabled" employees as they engage in regular activities at their homes. To avoid hiring potentially dishonest employees, firms are undertaking more thorough screening of job candidates. Screening may include background investigations, criminal checks, reference checks, and psychological testing.

Unauthorized Use of Company Property

Everyone makes the occasional personal phone call or uses the office copier to copy a map for the neighborhood golf outing. But when unauthorized use of telephones, fax machines, copiers, and other company property gets out of hand, employers are forced to institute controls.

The use of company computers to play computer games is one area that is beginning to draw attention. Computer experts note that there are three concerns with employee use of game software on company computers: loss of productivity, software piracy, and viruses. Certainly, employees playing computer games on the job are nonproductive. Except for the lucky guy or gal who has the job of quality control tester at the video game company, employers generally do not want to pay employees for playing computer games on the job. Further, when an employee copies a computer game or other software to the company's computers on a nonlicensed basis, the employee has violated the copyright law. The company could be held liable for pirated use of software on its premises. Finally, the introduction of "shareware" or other downloaded software from bulletin boards may actually introduce computer viruses into the company's computer system.

So far, employers do not appear to be overly concerned with the widespread practice of copying and using games and other software on company computers. According to one survey of large corporations conducted by CIMI Corp., a strategic planning consulting firm, only 11 percent of surveyed firms had policies prohibiting use of game programs on company computers. Of the surveyed firms, only 4 percent acknowledged reprimanding or terminating employees for playing games.[8] But some companies are beginning to take corrective action.

The owner of a manufacturer of custom marine canvas purchased a special software program that displayed a memo on the computer screens of employees using the company computers to play games. In 1995, the use of

8. Ibid.

computer games on state computers was so widespread that Virginia Governor George Allen ordered that software games be deleted from all state-owned computers.[9]

Employers who are taking action declare that nonwork activity is not permitted, limit computer use to business purposes, and prohibit the copying of software or begin to more closely monitor how telephones are used. Employers may undertake increased surveillance of the workplace, monitoring employee use of computers or other company property.

Taking Care of Business

Every business enterprise is concerned with producing its product or providing its service. Businesses in the private sector must operate at a profit. Likewise, organizations in the not-for-profit and governmental sectors must provide their services within established budget or funding limits.

An employer's management decisions are subject to many influences: political, personal, economic, legal, and organizational. A manager's decision may be based on self-interest, or it may be for the good of the organization. We would like to believe that most managers make reasonable decisions to select and direct employees to do their part in helping the organization make its product or provide its service. Ideally, this should be done in a way that respects employees as individuals and recognizes an individual's privacy rights.

For the most part, employers are concerned with profits rather than prying, with sales rather than surveillance, and with reducing costs rather than detecting drugs. But when an employee does something that interferes with the organization's purpose, management will deal with the matter.

The bottom line is this: An employer will take action as needed to improve profits, raise efficiency, control costs, and effectively manage the business. Management's actions, however, should be consistent with good principles of human resources management and within the spirit and the letter of various laws that affect privacy issues.

9. Lin Grensing Pophal, "Computers at Work, Fair Game?" *HR News*, June 1995, p. 1.

3

Privacy Law Primer

Before you can draft and implement fair and defensible employee policies regarding drug testing, performance monitoring, and other potentially sensitive areas, you need to know the pertinent laws regarding workplace privacy.

Remember, even though no single law governs workplace privacy, employees expect certain privacy rights. When an employer directs an employee to participate in a drug test or conducts a search of a locker or desk, employees may feel that privacy rights have been violated. But the employee in the private workplace simply does not have the sweeping privacy protections that he or she may assume.

Yes, there are laws that deal with privacy issues. Yes, the U.S. Constitution includes a provision that provides certain privacy protections. But an individual's privacy rights are protected by a patchwork of safeguards in the Constitution, in our common law, and in federal and state laws that define conduct in this area. These laws are interpreted by the courts to determine whether an action violates a person's privacy. In deciding whether a claim is justified, the court examines the facts of the case, the law, and related court decisions to make its determination.

Whether you are a human resources specialist or a plant manager or supervisor, a working knowledge of these laws is essential. So is access to a publication or an expert who can keep you abreast of current changes in laws and their interpretation. Sadly, I have seen companies write employment policies that run afoul of labor law. Instead of keeping them out of legal trouble, these policies have put them squarely in the middle of it!

A working knowledge of the law is so important that I believe any human resources specialist who is frequently involved in policy issues should subscribe to a publication that reports on current labor legislation. Published by business law publishers, these newsletters and digests can inform subscribers of important legal issues that affect employment decisions, explain laws and regulations, and alert the reader to emerging issues. Some are written for lawyers, accountants, consultants, and human resources specialists. Others are tailored to better meet the interests of supervisors and managers whose responsibility is to administer employee policies. (But if you are interested, by all means subscribe.) A number of very good sources of labor law information are listed in the appendix.

To determine which actions are legal and which are not, supervisors and managers should develop a rapport with an expert, turning to the expert for answers whenever questions about personnel policy or employment or labor law issues arise. In addition, every proposed employment policy should be reviewed by a specialist before being published. No newsletter can substitute for the opinion of an expert!

The Hierarchy of Laws

Our Constitution is the foundation of the democratic form of government that shapes society in the United States. Besides defining the executive, legislative, and judicial branches of our federal government, the Constitution contains a number of amendments dealing with matters such as freedom of speech, freedom of religion, and the right to bear arms. The federal government, through the U.S. Congress, passes laws on employment and various other matters. Federal governmental agencies define administrative regulations to interpret and implement the laws.

The states, through their legislatures, define certain state laws on employment and other matters. Likewise, state government agencies define administrative regulations to interpret and to administer the state laws. Federal laws and administrative regulations generally take precedence over state laws and state regulations. Court decisions interpret the laws and regulations. Counties and municipalities and other units of government continue in this descending hierarchy of laws and regulations. (See figure 3-1 for a flowchart of this hierarchy.) Special governmental units such as transportation authorities, school districts, and library districts define certain rules and procedures for operation of their mandated activities.

The foundation of our legal system rests on common law, the set of legal concepts and precedents brought to the United States by English colonists three centuries ago. While the principles of common law are modified by state or federal statutes, in the absence of a statute on a particular issue, such as privacy, the courts follow common-law concepts. These common-law concepts may vary from state to state.

Figure 3-1 Hierarchy of Laws

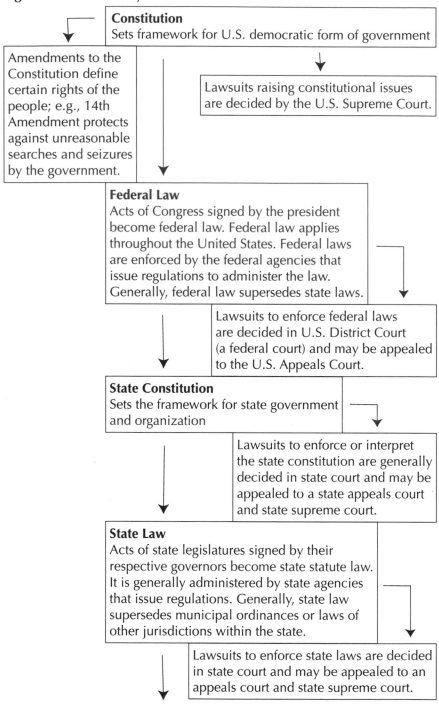

Constitution
Sets framework for U.S. democratic form of government

Amendments to the Constitution define certain rights of the people; e.g., 14th Amendment protects against unreasonable searches and seizures by the government.

Lawsuits raising constitutional issues are decided by the U.S. Supreme Court.

Federal Law
Acts of Congress signed by the president become federal law. Federal law applies throughout the United States. Federal laws are enforced by the federal agencies that issue regulations to administer the law. Generally, federal law supersedes state laws.

Lawsuits to enforce federal laws are decided in U.S. District Court (a federal court) and may be appealed to the U.S. Appeals Court.

State Constitution
Sets the framework for state government and organization

Lawsuits to enforce or interpret the state constitution are generally decided in state court and may be appealed to a state appeals court and state supreme court.

State Law
Acts of state legislatures signed by their respective governors become state statute law. It is generally administered by state agencies that issue regulations. Generally, state law supersedes municipal ordinances or laws of other jurisdictions within the state.

Lawsuits to enforce state laws are decided in state court and may be appealed to an appeals court and state supreme court.

Figure 3-1 continued

Common Law
Common law is a series of legal concepts
that came over from England. Often referred
to as "judge-made" law, common law evolves
from court decisions. Common-law concepts
generally apply in the absence of a statute law
and may be unique from state to state.
Common-law privacy issues include intrusion
upon seclusion, public disclosure of private facts,
false-light publicity, and the appropriation
of name or likeness.

Lawsuits to enforce or interpret
common law are generally brought
in state court and may be appealed
to an appeals court and the state
supreme court. If the issue involves
a federal law, the matter may be
brought in a federal district court.

Municipal Ordinances
Cities and counties create local ordinances
and laws. These laws apply only within the
municipality or jurisdiction. They are
generally enforced by a local governmental
department, agency, or police department.

Lawsuits to enforce municipal ordinances
are generally decided in state court and
may be appealed to a state appeals court
and state supreme court.

Special Governmental Units
Government units such as transportation
authorities, school districts, or library
districts define rules and procedures for
operation of their specific activities.

Lawsuits to interpret or enforce
special government unit procedures
are generally decided in state court
and may be appealed to an appeals
court and state supreme court.

According to Kent D. Stuckey's book *The Internet and On-Line Law,* the concept of privacy was first identified by legal theorist Louis Brandeis in a *Harvard
Law Review* article in 1890. Brandeis was writing about journalistic invasions of
a person's right to be left alone. As time passed, the right to privacy was defined by other legal writers and became embodied in the common law as the
right to live one's life in seclusion without being subjected to unwanted and
undesired publicity. A violation of one's privacy rights was considered to be a
wrongful intrusion into one's private activities in a manner to cause outrage
or to cause mental suffering, shame, or humiliation to a person of ordinary
sensibilities. A violation of the right to privacy was an actionable "tort": a civil
wrong in which an individual is negligently or willfully harmed in some way
and for which the injured person is entitled to recover financial damages or
receive a court order directing the unwanted activity to stop.[1]

This common law of privacy was defined through a series of court cases
in which individuals sought legal redress against others for invasion of privacy.
The courts generally applied the law of the state where the matter was tried.
Because laws developed differently in different regions of the country,
common-law concepts vary from state to state. For example, Texas and Illinois
courts reached different conclusions about a supervisor's release of private
medical information to coworkers. (See chapter 8 and compare how employees
Ellenwood and Miller were treated.)

In considering the various cases, the courts also determined that certain
actions are not invasions of privacy. Courts have stated that an individual is
not entitled to complete isolation under his right of privacy. Rather, individual
rights must be construed in the light of duties and other actions of individuals
in a free country. For example, an employee has no action for a violation of a
right of privacy against his or her employer because the employer received
information on the employee's debts from a creditor, even though the information passed through the hands of the creditor and the employer.[2]

Common-Law Privacy Invasion

When we refer to the right to privacy, we are talking about our right to be left
alone. A claim of privacy invasion expresses a feeling that the right to be left

1. *Abernathy v Thornton,* 83 So 2d 235.
2. *Patton v Jacobs,* Ind App 78 NE 2d 789.

alone has been violated. Individuals do have certain common-law privacy rights that are recognized in every state. These common-law rights are based on court decisions that apply the facts of the particular case compared to other similar preceding cases. Referred to as "judge-made law," each case further interprets and sometimes modifies the law.

Under common law, a privacy invasion is generally claimed based on one of four legal concepts. These concepts, applied to workplace issues, are summarized here.

1. *Intrusion upon seclusion.* When an employer's actions intrude upon the private affairs of an employee in a manner that would be highly offensive to a reasonable person. The courts look at the facts of the case to determine whether the employer's action was reasonable and based on a specific need. If the employer's actions are outrageous and highly offensive, intruding upon an employee's private matters, as judged by a reasonable person, the employee's privacy has been invaded. As an example, a private detective's surveillance of an employee's activities with a girlfriend in a motel room was an unlawful privacy invasion.

2. *Public disclosure of private facts.* When an employer gives unwarranted publicity to private facts about an employee's life in a matter that is of no concern to the public. For a claim to succeed, the release must be of information that is truly private or embarrassing and for which there is no public interest or need to know, and the release must be widely disseminated. An inappropriate disclosure of an employee's mastectomy to coworkers was held by the court to be a privacy invasion. By contrast, disclosure of information to management about reasons for an employee's termination was held reasonable and not a privacy invasion.

3. *Publicity placing a person in a false light.* When an employer provides information to others that falsely portrays an employee's conduct or characteristics in a way that is widely disseminated. As an example, a jury felt that an employer's announcement of an employee's discharge for theft, when the employee's offense was removal of $5.00 worth of scrap material, was too severe and constituted a false-light privacy invasion.

4. *Appropriation of employee's name or likeness.* When an employer appropriates an employee's name or likeness without the employee's consent. An employee who willingly poses for a company publicity photo would not likely succeed in a privacy invasion claim. However, an employer's use of vivid pic-

tures of an employee's injury taken without permission and then shown to fellow employees in a safety training session was found by the court to be a wrongful likeness appropriation privacy invasion.

Specific legal standards to determine these issues vary from state to state. Further, not all states recognize all forms of privacy invasion.

In order to understand the outcome of various court cases regarding privacy invasion—and in order to develop fair and defensible employee policies—it is essential to understand these common-law principles of privacy. If the facts of an employee's privacy invasion claim fail to meet the requirements of the statute law or the common-law privacy principles of the state, the court will find that a privacy invasion did not occur. An incident on the job may be upsetting to the individual making the claim as well as to the reader of the case, but unless the facts of the case meet the legal guidelines of the state, there is no privacy invasion in the eyes of the law.

The following two cases show how attorneys cited state common law to build common-law privacy invasion cases and how the court sorted through conflicting statutes and concepts to make its decision.

It's Your Turn to Pee in the Cup

Bob Gilmore was hired as an engineer for a gas pipeline company in Oklahoma. Several years later, his company was acquired by another private employer. The new employer announced a policy of random drug testing. Before long, Gilmore was summoned to participate in a urinalysis test. Gilmore objected, claiming that the test was an invasion of his privacy. Because of Gilmore's resistance, the company relaxed its policy standard requiring employees to provide an observed urine sample and told Gilmore that he would be permitted to provide an unobserved sample. Gilmore still refused. In line with its policy, the company fired Gilmore for refusing to participate in the drug test.

Gilmore sued the company for wrongful discharge. His attorneys filed the lawsuit on several bases, one being that the random drug test was an invasion of his right of privacy. In support of their claim, the lawsuit cited portions of the Oklahoma State Constitution and certain state laws and contended that the company's action created a common-law invasion of privacy.

The court, however, disagreed. Although conceding that the constitutional right of privacy affords protection against governmental intrusions, the court held that privacy protections are not enforceable against private corporations. Further, the court explained that at the time of Gilmore's dismissal, the Oklahoma legislature had not enacted a state statute regulating or limiting drug testing by private employers. Regarding Gilmore's claim of a common-law invasion of privacy, the court held that Gilmore failed to prove that the drug test was a privacy invasion. The court acknowledged that when Gilmore's privacy concerns are balanced against the company's legitimate interest in providing a drug-free workplace in this case, the company needs prevail.[3]

The Boss Is Watching My House

Fayard, a security guard for Guardsmark, a security company, was assigned to guard a Shell Oil Company refinery. During the period of this assignment, she met and began dating a Shell employee. Fayard claimed that she had received clearance from a Shell supervisor to date the Shell employee when off duty. When Fayard's employer, Guardsmark, learned that she was dating an employee of a client, it began an investigation that included surveillance of Fayard's house and running license checks on cars and persons who visited Fayard at her house. Ultimately, Guardsmark fired Fayard for fraternization in violation of company policy.

In evaluating the case, the court applied Louisiana common-law privacy standards. The court's reasoning went like this: To succeed in a privacy invasion claim, Fayard must show that her privacy was invaded in one of four ways, such as by her employer's unreasonable intrusion into her physical solitude or seclusion. Further, she must show that the employer's action was unreasonable and seriously interfered with her privacy interest. According to Fayard's claim, however, the only surveillance that took place was of activities in the public view, and there was no physical intrusion into the employee's house by the employer. For these reasons, said the court, there was no unreasonable intrusion on Fayard's privacy and judgment was granted for Guardsmark to dismiss her privacy claim.[4]

---

3. *Gilmore v Enogex*, 9 IER Cases 1295 (1994).
4. *Fayard v Guardsmark*, 5 IER Cases 516 (1989).

Constitutional Privacy Protections

The so-called constitutional privacy right is embodied in the Fourth Amendment to the Constitution, which defines an individual's right to be free from unreasonable search and seizure by the government. The Fourth Amendment reads:

> The right of the people to be secure in their persons, houses, papers and effects, against unreasonable searches and seizures, shall not be violated, and no warrants shall issue but upon probable cause, supported by oath or affirmation, and particularly describing the place to be searched, and the persons or things to be seized.[5]

This amendment reflected the colonists' abhorrence for the so-called general warrants used by the colonial government to conduct searches of an individual and his or her belongings or property. The Fourth Amendment to the Constitution limits *governmental* searches and seizures only. Because these constitutional guarantees pertain only to searches by agents of government, private citizens, including private employers conducting a search of the workplace, do not commit an unreasonable search and seizure within the meaning of the Fourth Amendment. This means that an employee working for a private employer does not have a "constitutional" privacy protection from acts by his or her employer. There are, however, other privacy protections for employees, described in this chapter.

Public-Sector Privacy Limitations

Federal, state, local, and other public-sector organizations are subject to Fourth Amendment limitations regarding search, surveillance, and other workplace privacy issues. This means that administrators of governmental facilities making employment decisions relating to workplace privacy may have their actions challenged on the basis of a violation of an individual's Fourth Amendment rights.

For example, a government employee claimed an unreasonable search violating the Fourth Amendment when the agency administrator obtained information about the employee's use of prescription drugs for treatment of HIV.

5. Harold W. Chase and Craig R. Ducat, *The Constitution and What It Means Today* (Princeton, NJ: Princeton University Press, 1978), 341.

Likewise, a state corrections department employee alleged a constitutional privacy invasion when an investigator allegedly forced her to reveal facts about her sexual history while investigating her complaint that a coworker had sexually molested her.[6]

Although government workers may claim that an employer's action is a constitutional privacy violation, the courts will weigh the individual's privacy rights against other compelling interests. For example, a teacher who was ordered to submit to a psychiatric examination following her altercation with a coworker failed to prove constitutional privacy violation. The court held that the government's interest in determining an individual's fitness to teach outweighs the teacher's privacy expectations. Likewise, when a government agency searched motor vehicle records for an employee's address, the court held that employee's claim of a constitutional privacy invasion lacked merit because the information obtained was a matter of public record under Pennsylvania law.[7]

Do You Have a Search Warrant?

One leading public-sector privacy issue is whether government employers must obtain a warrant to search a government employee's office or locker. Dr. Magno Ortega was a physician and psychiatrist for seventeen years at the Napa State Hospital in California. As chief of professional education, he was responsible for training young physicians in the psychiatric residency program. Hospital officials, including the executive director, became concerned about possible improprieties in the management of the residency program. Management began to investigate the improper acquisition of a computer and complaints that Ortega had sexually harassed two female hospital employees and taken inappropriate disciplinary action against a resident.

After Ortega was placed on administrative leave, the administrator conducting the investigation decided to enter Ortega's office to secure state property. Investigators entered the office on several occasions, seizing personal items as well as state property from the doctor's desk and file cabinets. An investigator later acknowledged that there was no inventory of the material seized and that no effort had been made to sort state from personal property. Evidence turned up in the

6. IERM 509:707, No. 134 (March 1995), 9.
7. Ibid., 10.

investigation was used in an administrative hearing that lead to the doctor's discharge.

Ortega filed suit in federal court claiming that the search violated Fourth Amendment rights. Ultimately heard by the U.S. Supreme Court, *O'Connor v. Ortega* is viewed as a leading case in privacy rights issues. The Court held that, while a government employee may have a reasonable expectation of privacy extending to his desk and file cabinets, the individual's expectation of privacy is balanced against the government's need for supervision and control of the workplace. According to the Court, public employers have wide latitude to search the offices, desks, and files of their employees without being subject to search warrant procedures required under the Fourth Amendment.

In this case, the bottom line was this: The Court refused to impose unwieldy warrant procedures. The Court found that a warrant requirement would be unduly burdensome and would seriously disrupt the routine conduct of business. Further, the Court declined to require the government employer to have "probable cause" for its search. The Court stated:

> [P]ublic employer intrusion on the constitutional protected privacy interests of government employees . . . should be judged by the standard of reasonableness. . . . Ordinarily, a search of an . . . office by a supervisor will be justified at its inception when there are reasonable grounds for suspecting that the search will turn up evidence . . . of work related misconduct, or that the search is necessary for work related purpose such as to retrieve a needed file.[8]

In other cases involving lockers, courts have held that a public-sector employer's search of employee lockers did not violate Fourth Amendment rights where agency policies or union agreements contained stipulations that lockers might by subject to searches by the employer.

Unions and Workplace Privacy Issues

For the 18 percent of the American workforce that is unionized, many issues of workplace privacy are likely to be subjects of collective bargaining between

---

8. *O'Connor v Ortega*, 1 IER Cases 1617 (1981).

the union and the employer. The court has defined drug testing of current employees, for example, as a mandatory subject for bargaining. However, drug testing as a condition of employment for new hires was determined not to be a mandatory subject of bargaining because the job applicants were not yet in the union.

In the collective bargaining process, information is exchanged. In administering the law, courts have heard various cases dealing with information that must be provided to the other party in negotiations. Courts have held that it is permissible for an employer to provide employee names and addresses to the union during an organizing drive so that the union may contact employees about union membership. The National Labor Relations Board (NLRB), the federal agency that oversees union and employer relations, has ruled that unions are entitled to any health, safety, and chemical records that are in the employer's possession. But where the employer has an established privacy policy, the employer did not act unlawfully by refusing to turn over an employee's tardiness record to the union without the employee's consent, according to the NLRB. In another case, the NLRB determined that the employer was not required to provide information about questions and answers to psychological aptitude tests used to determine workers' fitness for particular job classifications.

A Crash Course in Federal Privacy Laws

In the absence of a comprehensive federal privacy statute, attorneys for employees claiming privacy invasion select from a variety of statutes to file their privacy claims. The following is a summary of the highlights of the federal laws that relate to privacy and other personnel issues. Also, see table 3-1 for a summary chart of these laws.

Equal Employment Opportunity:
Title VII of the Civil Rights Act of 1964

Privacy issues relating to employee dating, dress and appearance, sexual orientation or preference, and religious beliefs have resulted in legal claims under this law. The 1964 Civil Rights Act prohibits discrimination against individuals on the basis of race, sex, color, religion, and national origin. Affecting employers with fifteen employees or more, the law provides protection for covered individuals on employment matters such as recruitment, hiring, training,

Table 3-1   Summary of Federal Laws Relating to Workplace Privacy Issues

Law	Coverage	Highlights
Title VII of the Civil Rights Act of 1964	Private employers	Prohibits discrimination in employment on basis of sex, race, color, national origin, or religion
Freedom of Information Act of 1966	General public	Makes government documents available for public disclosure unless exempted
Title III of the Omnibus Crime Control and Safe Streets Act of 1968	Private employers	Limits interception and disclosure of telephone communications
Fair Credit Reporting Act of 1970	General public	Defines procedures for release of credit information and disclosure to individuals
Privacy Act of 1974	Federal government employees	Provides certain privacy protections, limiting disclosure of information on individuals
Electronic Communications Privacy Act of 1986	Public and private employers	Limits employer access to electronic communications
Immigration Reform and Control Act of 1986	Private employees	Defines document requirements to establish employment eligibility
Drug-Free Workplace Act of 1988	Federal government contractors and grants	Requires establishment of policy to promote drug-free workplace
Employee Polygraph Protection Act of 1988	Private employers and employees	Prohibits use of polygraph in preemployment screening, defines procedures for investigations
Americans with Disabilities Act of 1990	Private employers and handicapped individuals	Prohibits discrimination on basis of handicap, limits medical inquiries, and use of medical records

Table 3-1 continued

Law	Coverage	Highlights
Omnibus Transportation Employee Testing Act of 1991	Transportation employees	Requires drug testing of certain employees
Health Insurance Portability and Accountability Act of 1996	Private employers	Defines procedure for insurance continuation and medical record privacy

transfers, promotions, discipline, separations, and other terms and conditions of employment.

Title VII of the Civil Rights Act is enforced by the U.S. Equal Employment Opportunity Commission (EEOC). An employer found in violation of the act may be required to provide employment, reinstatement, promotion, back pay, front pay, punitive damages, court costs, and attorneys' fees to the individual(s) who is a victim of discrimination.

Records Access Law: Freedom of Information Act of 1966

The Freedom of Information Act requires that, except for certain exempt records, all federal government agency documents be available for public disclosure. The law defines certain procedures for requesting public records. It also protects the privacy of government workers by classifying their personnel records and medical files as secret.

An agency must determine within ten days whether it will honor an individual's request for information. A denied request may be appealed to the head of the agency. Further, a complainant may petition (file suit) in federal district court to seek a court order to produce records.

Wire Tap Law: Title III of the Omnibus Crime Control and Safe Streets Act of 1968

Often referred to as the federal wire tap law, this law provides certain privacy protections relating to use of the telephone. Generally, individuals claiming telephone monitoring privacy invasion bring actions under this law. Title III of this law prohibits the willful interception and disclosure of communications over a telephone and makes such action a criminal offense. However, it is not a criminal offense when one of the parties to the communication has given prior consent to the interception, provided the interception is not for a criminal or other injurious purpose. It also permits a telephone user in the ordinary course of business to intercept another's phone call by listening in on an extension phone.

Federal Communications Commission (FCC) regulations require that when telephone conversations are recorded, all parties to the conversation give their consent prior to the recording. Or alternatively, a beep tone must be sounded at frequent intervals during the recorded phone conversation. Government prosecutors who seek to try criminal cases using evidence obtained in violation of wire tap laws will have illegal evidence barred from their case.

Credit Reporting Law: Fair Credit Reporting Act of 1970

This law details procedures relating to privacy of an individual's credit records. The Fair Credit Reporting Act (FCRA) defines requirements for consumer credit reporting agencies and for users of credit information. It requires an employer requesting a credit report to disclose its request in writing to the job applicant. If the applicant is denied employment based on information in the report, the employer must advise the applicant of the decision and provide the address of the credit reporting agency. The applicant is entitled to request information about the nature and scope of the credit investigation and to receive a copy of the credit report.

The FCRA is enforced by the Federal Trade Commission. Violations of the FCRA may result in lawsuits seeking actual damages, punitive damages, court costs, and reasonable attorney's fees. In addition, an individual who knowingly and willfully obtains information under false pretenses may be subject to a fine of up to $50,000, imprisonment for up to one year, or both.

Federal Privacy Law: Privacy Act of 1974

The Privacy Act regulates information about individuals collected and used by federal agencies. It requires individual consent and specifies procedures for disclosure of information about the individual. A person whose private records or information are inappropriately released by the federal government may file suit in federal court. The act provides criminal penalties and fines of up to $5,000 against employers who disclose records in violation of the act.

Don't Call My Current Employer

Sullivan was employed by Lewis General Tires in New York when he interviewed for work with the postal service. On his job application with the postal service, Sullivan had checked "No" in answer to the question, "May we contact your current employer for employment verification?" However, the postal service interviewer called Lewis General Tires to check references. Sullivan claimed that, because of the inquiry, he was fired by Lewis General Tires. Further, Sullivan did not get the postal service job. As a result, Sullivan filed suit against the postal service claiming that his privacy rights were violated. In a preliminary proceeding, the U.S. District Court judge held that Sullivan's application for employment was a government record subject to Privacy Act protections that prohibit federal agencies from disclosing private records without written consent.[9]

Computer Privacy Law: Electronic Communications Privacy Act of 1986

The Electronic Communications Privacy Act (ECPA) extends federal privacy protections to electronic and computer communications. It protects all electronic communication systems, including E-mail, from unauthorized access and protects the privacy of messages transmitted over public service E-mail systems. This means that a public E-mail provider, such as America Online, is prohibited from monitoring or disclosing the contents of stored communications, with three exceptions:

1. Disclosure authorized by the sender or receiver
2. Disclosure necessary for the efficient operation of the system
3. Disclosure to the government

The law does not, however, prohibit employers from monitoring the E-mail of their employees. An exception in the law allows private employers to intercept business communications such as employee E-mail and other computer communications.[10] An individual or communications service provider may seek to

9. "Court Clears Job Applicant's Suit over Contact with Current Employer," *Employee Relations Weekly* (BNA), Dec. 2, 1996, p. 1305.
10. Kent D. Stuckey, *The Internet and On-Line Law* (New York: Law Journal Seminars Press, 1996), 5-17.

enforce the ECPA by filing a civil lawsuit in federal court. Damages for a violation of the law may be $1,000 or more.

New Hire Documents Law: Immigration Reform and Control Act of 1986

An employer's request to view documents of identity and employment eligibility is not a privacy invasion but rather action in compliance with this law. The Immigration Reform and Control Act (IRCA) is designed to control unlawful entry and employment of illegal immigrants. The law states that employers should hire only U.S. citizens and aliens who are authorized to work in the United States. The employer is required to verify the employment eligibility of every employee hired after November 6, 1986. The IRCA is enforced by the Immigration and Naturalization Service (INS), part of the U.S. Justice Department. Illegal immigrants can be deported to their countries of origin. An employer found in violation of record keeping or employment provisions of the law may be subject to civil fines and cease and desist orders. In addition, an employer may be charged with discrimination for refusing to hire or otherwise discriminating against an individual because of his or her citizenship status.

Drug Use Law: Drug-Free Workplace Act of 1988

The Drug-Free Workplace Act (DFWA) requires employers receiving federal grants or federal contracts of $25,000 or more to be performed in the United States to maintain a drug-free workplace. Covered employers are required to develop and distribute policies that prohibit possession, use, manufacture, and distribution of controlled substances in the workplace. Further, the employer must set up an awareness program to inform employees about the dangers of drug use, the employer's policy, available counseling, and penalties for violation of the policy. If an employee is convicted on a drug violation that occurs in the workplace, the employer must notify the government and take corrective actions. The DFWA is enforced by the agency administering the government contract. Penalties for violation can include contract suspension and debarment proceedings. But take note: Employer enforcement of drug testing or drug policies can result in privacy invasion claims.

Lie Detector Law: Employee Polygraph Protection Act of 1988

Passed to control privacy invasions or improper inquiries using the polygraph, the Employee Polygraph Protection Act generally prohibits use of lie detectors or polygraph exams in preemployment screening and defines specific procedures for use of polygraphs in investigations. Use of a polygraph must be limited only to the following guidelines:

- The test must be administered in connection with an economic loss.
- The employee must have had access to the property under investigation.
- The employer must have reasonable suspicion that the employee was involved.
- The employer must provide a written statement to the employee describing the incident under investigation.

The employer is prohibited from taking any form of retaliation against an employee for refusing to take a polygraph test, filing a complaint, or being a party to legal action relating to the investigation. The law is enforced by the U.S. Labor Department. Relief may include reinstatement, promotion, lost wages, benefits, and attorneys' fees. An employer found in violation of the law may be assessed a civil penalty of up to $10,000.

Employing People with Disabilities Law: Americans with Disabilities Act of 1990

This law provides certain privacy protections relating to an employer's inappropriate use of medical records or an employee's medical condition. The Americans with Disabilities Act (ADA) prohibits discrimination against individuals with a physical or mental disability in matters related to employment, public services, public accommodations, and telecommunications. The employer or service provider must make a reasonable accommodation for qualified handicapped individuals. Affecting employers with fifteen employees or more, the law prohibits preemployment medical inquiries except when certain requirements are met. Any preemployment medical inquiries must be limited to job-related criteria and must be made after a job offer has been extended. All new hires must be subject to the exam regardless of disability. The ADA requires employers to keep medical records confidential in medical files stored separately from other personnel records.

Employment-related portions of the ADA are enforced by the EEOC. An employer found in violation of the ADA may be required to provide employment, reinstatement, promotion, back pay, front pay, punitive damages, court costs, and attorneys' fees to the individual(s) who is the victim of discrimination.

Driver Drug Test Law: Omnibus Transportation Employee Testing Act of 1991

This law requires employers in aviation, motor carrier, rail, and transit industries to set up programs to test employees for drug use on the job. It imposes requirements for testing drivers prior to employment, on a periodic and random basis, pursuant to reasonable cause, and after accidents. The carrier is required to define a drug testing program, designate any driver who tests positive as unqualified to drive until the driver subsequently tests negative, appoint a medical review officer as custodian of test results, and establish an educational and training program for employees and supervisors.

Insurance Continuation Law: Health Insurance Portability and Accountability Act of 1996

The Health Insurance Portability and Accountability Act (HIPAA) was passed by Congress with the intent of increasing the "portability" of health care coverage as employees change jobs from one employer to another. It also limits the length of preexisting conditions exclusions and defines requirements for medical information privacy. The law specifies penalties for those who use a health identifier or a system of classifying individuals based on health information, obtain individually identifiable health information, or otherwise disclose individual health information to another in violation of the law. Violations are punishable by a fine of up to $250,000, imprisonment for up to ten years, or both. The HIPAA is enforced by the U.S. Labor Department.

State Privacy Laws

Laws and provisions concerning workplace privacy vary widely from state to state. The state laws range from nondiscrimination issues to smoker's rights to limits on blacklisting, AIDS testing, and employer use of personnel records. An employer whose business operates in more than one state must comply with the labor and employment laws of each state where the business operates. Of course, it must also comply with all pertinent federal laws.

Where laws conflict, federal law generally takes precedence over state laws. However, when a state law provides greater protection for the employee, the employer generally is subject to both the federal law and the greater coverage of the state law. To aid reader understanding, I have grouped state privacy-related laws into a number of broad categories, described below. These are summarized in figure 3-2 in the appendix.

Consumer Reports Protection Laws

Consumer reports protection laws limit employer use of consumer reports in employment decisions and prohibit employers from discriminatory action against an individual because of information obtained from a consumer credit report. A privacy invasion claim may occur if an employer requests consumer report data for an inappropriate reason or allows inappropriate release of such data. Eight states have a law that limits employer use of consumer credit information.

Smoking Laws

Smoking laws tend to fall into one of two categories: a clean air law, or a smokers' rights law. Twenty-two states have smokers' rights laws. The smokers' rights laws generally prohibit discrimination against an employee because he or she is a smoker. As an example, the state of Illinois has a smokers' rights law prohibiting discrimination against an employee for off-the-job use of lawful products such as cigarettes. Further, Illinois has a clean air law requiring businesses that are open to the public to designate certain areas as nonsmoking areas. Employer action that adversely affects an employee because of use of smoking materials may result in a privacy invasion or other claim under a smokers' rights law.

Lawful Off-Duty Conduct

Laws that deal with lawful off-duty conduct are generally similar to smokers' rights laws but extend employee protections to other forms of conduct off the job. Such laws have the effect of limiting or preventing the employer from establishing policies that prevent an employee from engaging in lawful activities off the job. Examples of such activities are dating fellow employees, smoking, consumption of alcoholic beverages, or accepting part-time employment. Nine states have laws limiting employer regulation of off-duty conduct.

Off-duty conduct laws have resulted in litigation when an employee was fired or disciplined for off-duty conduct. The New York law received considerable publicity when Wal-Mart Stores fired two employees for dating each other in violation of a company policy. The discharge resulted in a lawsuit alleging that the firm's policy violated New York's off-duty conduct law.

Reference-Checking Immunity Laws

A generation ago, employers freely gave detailed references on former employees. But in the wake of lawsuits filed by individuals charging former employers with defamation for providing poor references, employer attitudes have changed. Some employers no longer give references. Others limit information to job title, dates of employment, and verification of pay.

In response, at least twenty state legislatures have passed reference-checking immunity laws that provide some degree of protection for an employer who provides truthful employment references in good faith when requested by another employer. For example, Illinois's law protects employers who provide truthful, performance-related references from civil law suits related to those references. The law presumes that an employer providing reference information has acted in good faith and is therefore immune from liability. However, if it can be shown that an employer knowingly disclosed false information or violated the individual's civil rights, the liability shield is lost.

Two variations of reference-checking immunity laws prohibit blacklisting and require the employer to issue a service letter to the employee summarizing employment and reason for separation. Twenty-eight states have blacklisting laws, designed to prohibit employers from taking deliberate action to prevent an individual from obtaining employment in the area or industry.

Bad Reference Bodes Big Bucks

When he was let go, project manager Kenneth Stanbury was told that the reason for his layoff was lack of work. But when another employer considering Stanbury for employment contacted his former employer, Sigal Construction, for a reference, Sigal executive Paul Littman stated that Stanbury seemed "detail oriented to the point of losing sight of the big picture," and that "obviously he no longer worked for us and that might say enough." Stanbury sued Sigal, claiming that the reference constituted defamation. The court found that Littman did not personally know about Stanbury's work and that the comments formed the basis of defamation, and the court awarded Stanbury $250,000 in compensatory damages.[11]

11. *Sigal Construction v Stanbury,* 8 IER Cases 201 (1991).

Personnel Records Laws

State laws regarding personnel records provide guidelines on which employment records an employer may maintain, which should not be maintained, and how an employee may access his or her personnel file. Thirty-four states have laws that relate to personnel records access. Oregon, for example, permits an employee to request to inspect his or her own personnel file at the place of employment, and to view and request copies of records relating to employment qualifications, promotion, compensation, discipline, and termination. Improper release of private information from personnel records can result in a privacy invasion claim.

Antibias Laws

All but two states prohibit employment discrimination on the basis of race, color, age, sex, religion, or national origin. (Alabama and Arkansas are the exceptions.[12]) Some state laws also cover ancestry, marital status, physical or mental disability, sexual orientation, or military service. These laws prohibit employment discrimination in hiring, recruiting, selection, testing, training, pay, promotions, transfers, discipline, layoff, discharge, and other areas of employment. Antibias laws have resulted in litigation when an employee was not hired, or was fired or otherwise discriminated against, because he or she was a member of a protected class and was treated differently. Privacy-related issues presented under antibias laws have dealt with employee dating, dress and appearance, religious beliefs, and sexual orientation.

Polygraph Testing Laws

Many states have laws against the use of polygraphs or lie tests in employment. Some of these laws were passed prior to the Federal Polygraph Protection Act, which applies to all covered employers. A state law may also apply to covered employers in the state, and if it provides a greater degree of protection for the employee, the employee will receive the protection of both laws.

For example, Connecticut polygraph testing law states,

> No person, firm, corporation, association or the state or any political subdivision thereof shall request or require any prospective em-

12. Ronald M. Green, William A. Carmell, and Jerrold F. Goldberg, *State-by-State Guide to Human Resources Law* (New York: Panel Publishers, 1993), table 1.2–1.

ployee or any employee to submit to, or take, a polygraph examination a condition of obtaining employment or of continuing employment with such employer or dismiss or discipline in any manner an employee for failing, refusing or declining to submit to or take a polygraph examination.

The law also states, "Any person, firm, corporation or association which violates any provision of this section shall be fined not less than two hundred and fifty dollars nor more than one thousand dollars for each violation." The law excludes state or local government.[13]

State polygraph protection laws have resulted in litigation when an employee was not hired, or was fired or otherwise discriminated against, because he or she was subjected to a polygraph test or an improper procedure related to a polygraph test.

Right-to-Privacy Laws

Fourteen states have right-to-privacy laws that place limits on employer collection or use of non–job-related information about an employee or other employer actions that may affect the employee's activities off the job. The Massachusetts Privacy Act, for example, protects an individual's privacy from "unreasonable, substantial, or serious" interference. The law grants to the Massachusetts court the power to enforce privacy rights and to award damages. State right-to-privacy laws have resulted in litigation when an employee was not hired or was fired or otherwise discriminated against because the employer obtained or used non–job-related information about the employees.

Drug Test Determination Different for Driver and Desk Jockey

An example of a state privacy invasion claim occurred when two employees of Motorola alleged privacy invasion as a result of being selected for participation in the company drug testing program. One employee, James Webster, was an account executive who traveled in excess of 20,000 miles a year. He participated in the test under protest rather than face termination. The other employee, Michael Joyce, was employed by a Motorola subsidiary as a technical editor. Both employees sued their employer claiming that the drug test violated their civil

---

13. Connecticut General Statutes, Annotated Sec. 31–51g.

rights and violated their statutory right to privacy as outlined in the Massachusetts Privacy Act.

The court held that the company's drug testing program and the manner in which it was administered were allowable under state laws. It concluded that the testing program was allowable for account executive Webster because he operated a motor vehicle on the job, but that in the case of technical editor Joyce the drug test was unreasonable in relation to his privacy interests because his office job did not present a danger to others.[14]

Drug/Alcohol Use and Testing Laws

Thirty states require firms to maintain a drug-free workplace, or limit employer practices relating to drug/alcohol testing. In some states, drug/alcohol testing requirements are limited to certain sectors, such as workers in safety-sensitive jobs, transportation drivers, and police officers or transit workers. Drug-free workplace requirements may be limited to state government contractors and patterned after the federal drug-free workplace law. For example, North Carolina's law is intended to protect individuals from unreliable and inadequate examinations and screening for controlled substances. It establishes procedural requirements for the administration of controlled substance examinations. Requirements are defined for collection of samples, use of approved labs, retention of samples, chain of custody procedures, and penalties for violations.[15]

State drug/alcohol use or testing laws have resulted in litigation when an employee was not hired or was fired or otherwise discriminated against because the employee was involved in an incident in which drug or alcohol abuse became part of the picture.

Urine, or You're Out!

Darryl Kise's claim against his former employer, Product Design and Engineering, Inc., is a good example of an employee's claim under a state drug testing law. Kise, a lift truck driver, was injured on the job. He previously had been treated for chemical dependency, and he admitted working under the influence of drugs and alcohol in the past. As a result of the accident, Kise was requested to take a drug test. He refused and was discharged. Kise sued his former employer, alleging

14. *Webster v Motorola,* 9 IER Cases 1527 (1994).
15. North Carolina General Statutes, Sec. 95-230 to 95-234, Chap. 687.L.

that the company's actions were arbitrary and capricious, in violation of the Minnesota Drug and Alcohol Testing in the Workplace Act. Upon examination of the facts, the court found that the company's requirement for a postaccident drug test was not arbitrary or capricious and that the policy met the minimum requirements of the act. As a result, the court upheld the employer's discharge of Kise.[16]

Whistle-Blowing Protection

State whistle-blowing laws provide protection for individuals who report information about employer wrongdoing to the government or media. An individual who goes public with an issue against the wishes of his or her employer is typically subjected to some form of discrimination, adverse job action, discharge, or even threats of harm. Whistle-blowing laws are intended to provide a degree of protection so that individuals will not fear reprisals when reporting some sort of inappropriate behavior. Forty-two states have laws providing protection for whistle-blowers.

Nepotism Laws

Nepotism laws control or prevent employer use of policies that limit or prohibit employment decisions based on the hiring of relatives. Depending on the focus of the law, it may prohibit giving preference to relatives or it may prohibit denial of employment because of family relationship. Fifteen states and a number of cities have nepotism laws.

Arrest Records Laws

Twenty-three states have passed laws that prohibit the use or consideration of an individual's arrest record in employment decisions. Such laws were passed for two reasons. First, an arrest does not mean conviction or guilt, and therefore arrest records should not be considered in hiring or other employment decisions. Second, minorities are more likely to be arrested and therefore adversely affected if arrest records are considered in employment decisions. State arrest records laws have resulted in litigation when an employee was not hired or was fired or otherwise discriminated against because of an arrest record, in violation of the law.

16. *Kise v Product Design and Engineering*, 5 IER Cases 385 (1990).

Workers' Compensation Retaliation

A state workers' compensation retaliation law prohibits employers from retaliating against or discharging an employee because he or she has filed a workers' compensation claim. State workers' compensation retaliation laws have resulted in litigation when an employee was not hired or was fired in violation of the law or otherwise discriminated against because of filing a workers' compensation claim. Twenty-nine states have provisions in workers' compensation laws or another law against workers' compensation retaliation.

No Way, Says Safeway

Linda Stoker, a price checker for Safeway Stores in Texas, was injured on the job and received workers' compensation benefits. Her claim was still pending when Furr's, Inc., purchased the Texas Safeway store. Furr's refused to hire Stoker, claiming that she was unable to perform the job as checker. Stoker sued, claiming wrongful discharge and discrimination under the Texas Workers' Compensation Act. Furr's argued, however, that as a successor company, it had not hired Stokes, and therefore she was not an employee who could make a claim of discrimination under the law. The court agreed, holding that an employment relationship must exist for an employee to file a discrimination claim under the Texas Workers' Compensation Act.[17]

Appendix

Sources of Labor Law Information[18]

Government Agencies

Government agencies responsible for enforcing the law are a good source of information. Most will provide—at little or no cost—literature, booklets, copies of the law, or information on administrative regulations that affect employers. The EEOC, for example, offers publications on avoiding discrimination, dealing with sexual harassment, and developing affirmative action plans. OSHA offers a variety of booklets on safety guidelines and lists of its many safety regulations.

17. *Stoker v Furr's*, 6 IER Cases 151 (1991).
18. William S. Hubbartt, *Personnel Policy Handbook: How to Develop a Manual That Works* (New York: McGraw-Hill, 1993).

To obtain this information, an employer need only contact each agency for information on its laws. (Be sure to update your file periodically to keep abreast of changes.) No need to fear that contacting an agency will inspire a visit from its representatives. These agencies are eager to provide information and to respond to an employer's sincere effort to comply with the law.

The Federal Register

This enormous publication, issued daily, details the regulatory requirements of many federal agencies. Don't buy an annual subscription unless your company wants information about everything from agriculture to zoology. Better to learn the dates when major workplace laws or regulations appear and then request or purchase copies of the specific regulations from the Government Printing Office, government bookstore, or agency.

Topical Law Reporters

These subscription services keep subscribers up to date on national laws, regulations, and court decisions. Some also cover state labor law developments. A key benefit of these services is that you can subscribe to the specific topical law reporting services that relate to your interest. They also offer a large binder of background information, interpretive comments, copies of regulations, periodic updates, and a newsletter subscription.

The following is a partial list of companies that publish topical law reports and information on privacy or human resources issues.

Bureau of National Affairs
1231 25th Street NW
Washington, DC 20037

Business and Legal Reports
39 Academy Street
Madison, CT 06443

Warren Gorham & Lamont
31 St. James Avenue
Boston, MA 02116

Commerce Clearing House
4025 West Peterson Avenue
Chicago, IL 60640

Magazines and Trade Journals

HR Magazine
HR News
1800 Duke Street
Alexandria, VA 22314

Human Resources Bulletin
Bureau of Business Practice
24 Pope Ferry Road
Waterford, CT 06381

HR Focus
1601 Broadway
New York, NY 10019

Personnel Journal
245 Fischer Avenue
Costa Mesa, CA 92626

What's the Law in Your State?

Figure 3-2 shows fourteen categories of state privacy laws and identifies states that have passed laws dealing with that topic. However, the list is by no means comprehensive. Each state has other laws that may relate to privacy issues. Use this chart as a starting point in checking privacy laws in your state, but be sure to investigate *all* state laws that may affect your employment policies.

Q & A: U.S. Laws and Employee Rights to Privacy

Q   *Is there a constitutional right to privacy in the United States?*

A   The Fourth Amendment to the U.S. Constitution defines an individual's right to be free from unreasonable search and seizure by the government. It requires the government to obtain a search warrant when searching an individual's private property. Fourth Amendment protections have been applied to government employers in their dealings with government employees. But an employee working for a private employer *does not* have a constitutional privacy protection from his or her employer. Some state constitutions define certain privacy protections.

Q   *Is a search warrant needed for an employer to search an employee's office, desk, computer, or locker?*

A   In a case that was decided by the U.S. Supreme Court, the court held that public employers in the routine conduct of employment matters have wide latitude to search offices, desks, and files of employees without being subject to warrant procedures required by the Fourth Amendment. Likewise, private employers have similar latitude if there is a valid business reason for the search and the employer has communicated a policy that minimizes an individual's expectation of privacy.

Q   *But isn't it an invasion of privacy when an employer probes too deeply into a person's private life?*

A   In each state, certain common-law privacy rights have evolved based on various court decisions. A violation of those privacy rights may be a privacy invasion. A privacy invasion is generally claimed based on one of the following issues:

- Intrusion upon seclusion
- Public disclosure of private facts
- False-light publicity
- Unauthorized use of an individual's name or likeness

If an employer's actions have the effect of harming an individual in one of the ways described above, the individual may bring suit in state court claiming a privacy invasion.

Figure 3-2   Summary of State Privacy Laws[19]

State	Smokers' Rights	Lawful Off-Duty Conduct	Antibias	Blacklisting Prohibited	Reference-Checking Immunity	Personnel Records	Polygraph Testing Limits	Right to Privacy	Drug/Alcohol Use and Testing	Whistle-Blowing Protection	Nepotism	Arrest Records	Workers' Compensation Retaliation	Consumer Reports Protection
Alabama				x			x[a]			x[a]			x	
Alaska					x		x	x	x[a]	x[a]				
Arizona	x			x	x	x[a]		x	x[a]	x[a]	x	x[a]		x
Arkansas				x		x			x		x		x	
California				x	x	x	x	x	x	x		x	x	x
Colorado		x	x	x	x	x[a]				x[a]	x	x		
Connecticut	x		x	x		x	x		x	x		x	x	
Delaware			x			x	x		x[a]	x			x	
District of Columbia	x		x			x	x						x	
Florida			x	x	x			x	x	x			x	
Georgia			x		x				x[a]	x[a]		x		
Hawaii			x				x	x	x	x		x	x	
Idaho			x	x			x			x[a]	x[a]			
Illinois	x	x	x		x	x		x	x[a]	x		x	x	
Indiana	x		x	x	x	x[a]				x			x	
Iowa			x	x		x	x		x	x				
Kansas			x	x	x	x[a]	x		x	x		x		
Kentucky	x		x			x[a]		x		x	x	x[a]	x	
Louisiana			x	x	x	x		x	x	x		x	x	
Maine	x		x	x	x	x			x	x				x
Maryland			x				x		x	x[a]			x	
Massachusetts			x			x		x		x[a]		x	x	x
Michigan			x		x	x	x			x		x	x	
Minnesota	x		x	x		x	x		x	x		x		x
Mississippi		x		x					x	x		x		

19. IERM 541 (1996).

Figure 3-2 continued

State	Smokers' Rights	Lawful Off-Duty Conduct	Antibias	Blacklisting Prohibited	Reference-Checking Immunity	Personnel Records	Polygraph Testing Limits	Right to Privacy	Drug/Alcohol Use and Testing	Whistle-Blowing Protection	Nepotism	Arrest Records	Workers' Compensation Retaliation	Consumer Reports Protection
Missouri		x	x						x[a]	x			x	
Montana		x	x	x			x	x			x			
Nebraska			x		x[a]	x			x		x[a]			
Nevada		x	x	x		x	x		x[a]	x[a]	x[a]			
New Hampshire	x		x	x		x				x				x
New Jersey	x		x				x						x	
New Mexico	x		x	x	x	x							x	x
New York	x	x	x				x			x		x	x	
North Carolina		x	x	x		x[a]				x	x	x		
North Dakota		x	x	x		x[a]				x	x	x		
Ohio		x								x		x		
Oklahoma	x	x	x	x	x	x			x	x[a]	x	x	x	
Oregon	x	x	x	x	x	x	x		x	x[a]	x	x	x	
Pennsylvania			x			x	x			x		x		
Puerto Rico		x	x											
Rhode Island	x		x			x	x	x	x	x		x		
South Carolina	x		x		x	x[a]			x[a]	x				
South Dakota	x		x		x	x[a]			x[a]	x[a]				
Tennessee			x		x	x			x	x	x[a]		x	

Figure 3-2   continued

State	Smokers' Rights	Lawful Off-Duty Conduct	Antibias	Blacklisting Prohibited	Reference-Checking Immunity	Personnel Records	Polygraph Testing Limits	Right to Privacy	Drug/Alcohol Use and Testing	Whistle-Blowing Protection	Nepotism	Arrest Records	Workers' Compensation Retaliation	Consumer Reports Protection
Texas			x	x	x	x	x		x	x	x		x	
Utah	x		x	x	x	x[a]			x	x	x[a]	x		
Vermont	x		x				x		x					
Virginia	x		x	x			x					x	x	
Washington			x	x			x	x	x		x			x
West Virginia	x		x				x			x[a]			x	
Wisconsin		x	x	x	x	x	x	x		x	x			
Wyoming	x		x											

[a]Law applies to public sector only.

Q   *How are employee privacy rights affected if there is a union collective bargaining agreement?*

A   Where there is a union in the employment relationship, the union and employer are responsible for bargaining over matters relating to pay, benefits, and conditions of employment, including privacy issues such as searches and drug/alcohol testing. When a union is seeking to organize an employer, courts have held that it is permissible for the union to receive employee names and addresses so that employees may be contacted about union membership. But it is an unfair labor practice for an employer to conduct surveillance of employees engaged in union organizing activities.

Q   *What federal laws deal with workplace privacy?*

A   There is no comprehensive federal law that deals with workplace privacy. Certain laws deal with specific issues that may relate to privacy. A federal civil rights law prohibits discrimination on the basis of race, sex, color, religion, or national origin. A freedom of information act permits disclosure of federal government documents except for certain documents that are exempted. A federal wire tap law limits monitoring of telephone calls. A federal privacy law limits certain privacy protections for government records on government employees. A computer privacy law defines certain limits on monitoring of E-mail systems. A lie detector law limits employer use of polygraph exams. A disability discrimination law prohibits discrimination because of disability and defines limits on use of medical information, storage of medical records, and use of physical exams. Drug testing laws define requirements for drug testing of transportation workers in safety-sensitive positions. A new insurance continuation law defines requirements for medical information privacy.

Q   *What state laws deal with workplace privacy?*

A   State laws vary from state to state. Consumer reports protection laws limit use of consumer credit information in employment decisions. Clean air laws prohibit use of smoking materials in certain public places. Smokers' rights laws prohibit discrimination against smokers. Lawful off-duty conduct laws prohibit discrimination against individuals for lawful conduct off the job. Reference-checking immunity laws give employers immunity from legal claims when providing truthful employment information in a reference check. Personnel records laws detail what records should be maintained or define guidelines for employee access to their personnel files. State polygraph testing laws limit or prohibit use of polygraph tests. State right-to-privacy laws limit employer collection or use of private information. State drug or alcohol laws define limits on drug/alcohol testing or require drug-free workplaces. Whistle-blowing protection laws provide protection for individuals who report employer wrongdoing to the government or media. Nepotism laws control or prevent employer use of policies that limit the hiring of relatives. Arrest records laws limit consideration of arrest records in employment decisions. Workers' compensation laws prohibit retaliation against an individual filing a workers' compensation claim.

Late breaking news: Amendments to the Federal Credit Reporting Act, effective in 1997, help protect personal privacy and place new obligations on employers using credit reports in employment decisions. Under revisions to the law, credit bureaus can only release financial information to those with a legitimate need to know. An employer must provide written notice to the employee if a credit check will occur. Also, an individual's written authorization is needed before financial information may be released. An employer making an employment decision based on the credit report must provide an adverse action notice to the employee and provide a summary of employee rights under the FCRA. The law also streamlines procedures for removing mistakes from credit reports and holds creditors responsible for the information which they report on individuals.

4

Don't Judge the Book by Its Cover: Preemployment Inquiries, Background Checks, and Nepotism Policies

While Kelley Larason was employed by Logan Consumer Discount Company, fellow employee Mark Shoulberg ordered her credit report and placed it in her personnel file. After Larason complained to Logan president Jerry Utz, she was terminated. Larason filed suit against Logan, complaining of wrongful discharge and violation of the Fair Credit Reporting Act. In Larason's complaint, she alleged: "When I asked the president of Logan why Mark Shoulberg obtained the said report, he replied, 'he was just curious.'" She alleged that the president acknowledged that the report was unauthorized and inappropriate.

In its defense, the company claimed that Larason had a loan from the company that was delinquent, and the credit report was obtained to evaluate Larason's credit status, a permissible purpose under the act. The court found that Larason may have a basis for a claim because of the questions about the purpose of the inquiry.[1]

Because selecting and hiring good workers is critical to the future success of an organization, managers continually seek better ways to hire and promote employees. The traditional process of screening and interviewing applicants,

---

1. *Larason v Logan Consumer Discount*, 6 IER Cases 1439 (1991).

evaluating qualifications, and selecting a good applicant often leaves managers wondering whether they have actually selected the candidate who will best fit the position and the company. That's why many companies supplement the traditional hiring and promotion process by thoroughly checking the applicant's references, educational and public records, and credit record.

However, background checking to screen applicants or evaluate current employees' qualifications for promotion and new assignments can land a company in hot water when tests are used inappropriately or test data are improperly released, as the following situations illustrate:

- Failure to check a candidate's references resulted in a negligent hiring claim.
- Refusal to hire job applicants because of arrest records violated the law.
- Preferential hiring of relatives adversely affected minority workers.
- Refusal to hire individuals because of poor credit records was found discriminatory.
- Denial of employment to unwed mothers was improper.

In a variety of legal forums, employees have claimed that certain kinds of background testing are an invasion of privacy. This chapter will provide guidelines to help employers avoid privacy invasion and other legal claims when screening and selecting applicants. It covers:

- Checking references from previous employers and credentials from educational institutions
- Using public records to obtain, verify, or evaluate facts in an individual's educational or employment history, including driver's records, court records, fingerprints, and arrest and conviction records
- Checking an applicant's credit

Two other issues that relate to screening and hiring employees are also covered:

- Examining workplace documents
- Devising and enforcing nepotism or antinepotism policies

Let's start by looking at preemployment inquiries—the kinds of questions an employer can and can't ask during an interview.

What Form of Birth Control Do You Use? and Other Inappropriate Preemployment Inquiries

Are you married?
Do you plan to have children?
Are you pregnant?
Do you have a health condition that would prevent you from performing job duties?

Most working women can recall a job interview in which the interviewer—most likely male—probed into personal matters relating to birth control, pregnancy, or child care. Likewise, most individuals with a disability have had to face probing inquiries about their health or disability.

In years past, many of these same questions appeared on employment applications. Today they have largely been banished, thanks to equal employment opportunity laws. But even though personal and private questions have no place in the job interview, some employers continue to ask inappropriate questions in job interviews.

Do questions like these constitute an invasion of privacy? An individual who revealed this information during an interview because of coercion or an implied threat may have a privacy invasion claim; an individual who provides this information voluntarily in an interview may not. Either way, he or she probably would have grounds for a claim under equal employment laws. The EEOC and the courts have held that preemployment inquiries directed solely to women and not to men constitute sex discrimination.

In the dynamics of a job interview, the employer has the power to offer or deny a job opportunity. The applicant who wants the job is likely to say or do whatever he or she thinks the employer wants in order to gain acceptance and land the job. In the final analysis, however, the applicant has the power to walk away and seek work elsewhere if he or she is uncomfortable with the questions being asked. An applicant or employee most likely would not win an invasion of privacy claim when he or she is the source of publicity relating to a private matter.[2]

Critical Issues in Use of Preemployment Inquiries

The legality or illegality of preemployment inquiries has been determined by government enforcement of Title VII of the Civil Rights Act of 1964 and the

2. Alfred G. Feliu, *Primer on Individual Rights* (Washington, DC: BNA, 1993), 218.

various state antibias laws. Generally, preemployment inquiries on employment applications and during job interviews have been declared illegal if there is an adverse discriminatory effect on protected-class individuals.

Inquiries about age or birth date should be avoided due to potential for age discrimination. Questions about birthplace or citizenship may be a basis for national origin discrimination and therefore should be avoided. Inquiries about pregnancy, birth control, or plans for children are typically asked only of women and therefore constitute sex discrimination. Questions about religion, religious beliefs, or working on the Sabbath amount to religious discrimination.

In summary, inquiries that directly or indirectly focus on an individual's race, color, religion, age, sex, national origin, or disability are improper inquir-

---

Sample Policy: Preemployment Inquiries

It is the policy of XYZ Company to limit preemployment inquiries to job-related issues that aid in determining applicant qualifications, as summarized in the procedures below:

1. All preemployment inquiries and hiring decisions shall be made without regard to race, sex, age, religion, national origin, color, disability, or other status prohibited by law.

2. All managers are required to conduct preemployment inquiries in a manner consistent with this policy.

3. All employment inquiries should focus on eliciting information to evaluate the candidates' job knowledge, skills, abilities, and experience.

4. Avoid non–job-related inquiries.

5. The human resources manager is responsible for evaluating and selecting an employment application that complies with this policy.

6. The human resources manager is responsible for instructing other managers on proper interview techniques to avoid improper preemployment inquiries.

Sample Employee Notice:
Notice to Applicants and Employees

XYZ Company is an equal employment opportunity employer. All employment decisions are made without regard to race, sex, age, color, national origin, religion, or disability.

ies under federal law. Some states and municipalities define other protected class categories, such as marital status, source of income, residence, veteran/ military status, type of military discharge, or sexual orientation. See the interviewing checklist in the appendix for dos and don'ts of conducting preemployment inquiries.

What Former Employers Say:
A Look at Reference Checking

Asking for references is a time-honored part of the employment selection process. Most employment applications include a section asking the job seeker to list several references who may be contacted for information about the job seeker's character and experience. Many managers contact the applicant's former employer(s) to verify information listed in the application. According to a 1995 survey of 5,000 members of SHRM, 80 percent of human resources managers conduct reference checks of candidates for executive, professional, administrative, and technical positions. Of this group, 89 percent require candidates to sign a waiver granting permission to conduct a reference check.

Eighty-one percent of survey respondents reported that they conduct reference-checking inquiries by telephone. However, less than 50 percent provide reference information over the telephone. Salary information, in particular, was more likely to be released in response to a written inquiry, primarily out of fear of litigation from former employees. In fact, 17 percent of the respondents had been challenged by disgruntled former employees.[3]

3. Jennifer Click, "SHRM Survey Highlights Dilemmas of Reference Checks," *HR News*, July 1995, p. 13.

Employers ask for references from prior employers, educational institutions, and others to learn more about a job candidate and to verify information provided on the resume and application. Unfortunately, applicants sometimes exaggerate or falsify experience or educational information, erroneously report dates of employment to show a more continuous job history, inflate salary information in order to get a higher pay level on the next job, or falsify reason for separation to cover up a firing. According to a study conducted by St. Louis–based Reference Checking Services, 34 percent of 1,200 job applicants admitted lying on their resumes. Likewise, a college admission director suggests that over a third of individuals were hired with exaggerated credentials.[4] Because applicants who misrepresent educational or work achievements may not be qualified to perform the job, it's easy to see why many firms insist on checking job references closely.

Liability for *failing* to check references closely is an even more compelling reason for conducting a thorough reference check. Generally, the employer is responsible for the on-the-job conduct of employees. When an employee engages in criminal conduct and has had a history of such conduct, employers have been held liable for negligent hiring. There are two aspects to the concept of negligent hiring: negligent hiring and negligent retention. Negligent hiring may occur when an employer failed to make reasonable efforts to uncover an applicant's incompetence or unfitness. Negligent retention may occur when an employer becomes aware of an employee's unfitness and fails to take corrective action such as reassignment, training, or discharge.[5]

> An example of negligent hiring occurred when KMS Investments, a real estate management company, hired a resident manager for its apartment complex in Minnesota. When hiring the resident manager, KMS failed to learn that the individual had a history of convictions for violent crime. The resident manager raped a tenant living in the complex. The tenant then sued KMS for negligently hiring someone with a violent past. The court agreed that this hiring was negligent and ruled that the apartment management firm had a duty to exercise reasonable care to avoid hiring persons who could pose a threat of injury.[6]

But getting a candid assessment of an applicant can be tough these days. Ideally, an employer should seek to obtain first-hand information about perfor-

4. Marlene Brown, "Checking the Facts of a Resume," *Personnel Journal Supplement*, Jan. 1993, p. 6.
5. "Checking References," in *Personnel Practices/Communications* (Chicago: CCH, 1991), Par. 331.
6. *Pontica v KMS Investments*, Minn 331 NW 2d 90 (1983).

mance, attendance, and work habits from the candidate's former supervisor. However, the potential for defamation suits by former employees makes companies reluctant to provide such detailed information. Many companies refer reference-checking inquiries to the human resources department, respond only to written inquiries, and limit information to confirming job title, dates of employment, and salary. Release of any other information, it is feared, could result in legal claims. Such fears are not totally without merit, as chapter 8 will show.

You may be able to get greater employer cooperation on reference checks if your company operates in one of the twenty-two states with reference-checking immunity laws that protect employers from liability for providing good-faith job references on former employees. You can facilitate the reference-checking process by including a line on your application form that authorizes former employers to provide information about the candidate's employment and releases the employer from liability for providing truthful information.

States with Reference-Checking Immunity Laws

Alaska	Illinois	New Mexico	Tennessee
Arizona	Indiana	Oklahoma	Texas
California	Kansas	Oregon	Utah
Colorado	Louisiana	South Carolina	Washington
Florida	Maine	South Dakota	Wisconsin
Georgia	Michigan		

Critical Issues in Reference Checking

Reference checking is a useful procedure to detect resume fraud. Further, failure to check references can lead to hiring employees who perform poorly or individuals whose criminal conduct injures others, resulting in a claim of negligent hiring. However, employers have been sued for defamation by former employees who received negative references. Chapter 8 will discuss problems and precautions on the release of employment information on former employees in response to reference-checking inquiries.

Sample Policy: Reference Checking

XYZ Company conducts preemployment reference checks as part of its screening and hiring process to help assure the hiring of the most qualified candidates. The following procedures apply:

1. All job candidates are responsible for completing a detailed employment application listing prior employer, dates of employment, job duties, pay, and employment references.

2. The application shall include an applicant's certification that all employment, educational, and other information provided on the application and during the interview process is true, complete, and accurate; and that falsification of information is grounds to deny or withdraw a job offer or to terminate employment.

3. The application shall include an applicant's certification authorizing prior employers and educational institutions to release employment or educational information and waiving any claims against these organizations for providing any information.

4. Prior to making a job offer, the hiring manager is responsible for contacting the candidate's prior employers and/or educational institutions to verify information provided.

5. If an employee is currently employed, the hiring manager will contact all prior employers and make any job offer contingent upon a satisfactory employment verification from the current employer, to be completed after the individual has separated from the most recent employer.

Sample Policy: Reference Checking

6. In the event of discrepancies, incorrect or falsified information is sufficient grounds to deny or withdraw a job
offer. If discrepancies are minor in nature, the hiring
manager may schedule a subsequent interview to probe
for more information and to clarify the discrepancies.

7. All reference-checking information shall be treated as
confidential information. Reference-checking information shall be stored with employment applications in the
human resources department.

Is There a Skeleton in the Closet?
Find Out with Background Checks

While traditional reference-checking procedures are helpful, they often do not
provide enough details to verify an individual's background or experience.
Some human resources specialists and recruiters conduct a more detailed
background check to obtain additional information about a candidate. Background screening firms or private investigators also conduct detailed background checks on individuals.

A background check can include interviews with neighbors or other ac-
quaintances and a thorough check of the following public and private records.

• *Criminal records* can be examined to find out an individual's arrest or
conviction record. Obtain records from a state's central repository of criminal
convictions or from individual counties. Evaluation of a candidate's criminal
convictions should be limited to job-related issues. Further details on arrests
and convictions are covered later in this chapter.

• *Driving records* offer an opportunity to verify whether the candidate has
a valid driver's license appropriate for the vehicle to be operated on the job
and identify the frequency or severity of traffic violations. A license suspension
due to repeated citations or a DUI conviction may be reasonable cause to deny

Sample Employee Notice:
Applicant's Certification (on an employment application)

1. I certify that the information provided in this application is true, accurate, and complete to the best of my knowledge. I understand that submission of false information on this application or in an employment interview is grounds for withdrawal of a job offer or for dismissal of employment.

2. I authorize release of employment, salary, education, and other related records to the company for the purpose of checking my references and verifying my employment and educational history. Further, I release former employers and other organizations providing information from any liability for providing information.

3. In consideration of my employment, I agree to conform to the rules and regulations of the company, and my employment and compensation can be terminated with or without cause and with or without notice at any time at the option of the company or myself.

_____

Signature of Applicant   Date

Copyright 1991, Hubbartt & Associates. Reprinted with permission.

employment as a driver. While a driver's authorization for release of driving records is not needed in most areas, it is recommended that applicants be notified that employment is subject to a driving record check.

■ *Workers' compensation claims* are filed with a state's workers' compensation agency. Denial of employment due to prior workers' compensation claims may be a violation of the state workers' compensation law or other law that prohibits retaliation or other discrimination for filing a claim. Further, preemployment medical inquiries are a violation of the ADA, as chapter 5 shows.

For these reasons, this information should be used only if you have a very compelling business necessity that justifies making employment decisions based on prior workers' compensation claims.

- *Federal court records* can be checked to determine whether the candidate was involved in any criminal, civil, or bankruptcy matters, or whether the individual has legal, financial, or criminal problems. The federal Bankruptcy Act prohibits discrimination against an individual because he or she has filed for bankruptcy.

- *Educational records* can be verified by telephone when sufficient identifying information is provided. Although educational records are not public, one background checking services firm estimates that 97 percent of colleges and universities will verify a job applicant's degree or attendance at that institution.

- *Fingerprint records* are a foolproof means of identification often included in background checks for government, public safety, and security occupations. Use of fingerprints is permitted in certain states for school and child care workers, private detectives and security guards, police or public safety officers, workers at gambling facilities or in gaming positions, and employees in banking or securities trading. In some states, use of fingerprinting in the private sector is prohibited. In order to use fingerprinting in background checking, an organization must have access to government files where fingerprints are stored.

- *Credit records* can provide important information about an individual who is applying for a job handling funds.

One useful resource for individuals conducting background investigations is *The Guide to Background Investigations,* published by National Employment Screening Services of Tulsa, Oklahoma. This comprehensive publication provides information on how to access public records to conduct background investigations. The book outlines federal and state records depositories to obtain information on criminal records, driving records, professional licensing boards, and other public records.[7]

---

7. *The Guide to Background Investigation* (Tulsa, OK: National Employment Screening Services, 1994).

Critical Issues in Use of Background Checks

Because government records are considered to be in the public domain, a background check involving access to government or other public information is not likely to result in a privacy invasion claim. But to avoid any chance of a legal claim, it is best to have a statement or notice to the applicant that such records will be checked or verified in the employment process and to identify a job-related reason for the background check. Further, take care to protect confidentiality of the information obtained in the background check. Inappropriate disclosure of information about an individual could result in a privacy invasion claim.

Doin' Time on the Rock: How Employers Consider Arrest and Conviction Records

Many employers seek to check an individual's arrest or conviction records in order to avoid hiring persons with a criminal record. Claims about use of these records in employment decisions normally are brought forth as antibias discrimination claims rather than privacy invasion claims because minorities are more likely to be affected by arrests. Federal employment law does not specifically prohibit inquiries into arrest or conviction records. In fact, in the landmark *Paul v Davis* case, the U.S. Supreme Court stated that the use of criminal records does not violate the right to privacy. Rather, these inquiries have been the subject of various discrimination cases considered by the EEOC and the courts.[8] The EEOC has held that denial of employment because of arrest records is illegal and a violation of the federal Civil Rights Act. The reason, according to the EEOC, is that blacks and Hispanics are arrested in greater proportions than whites, and arrest record inquiries, therefore, have an adverse impact on this population.

An employer's use of conviction records to screen out candidates is more likely to withstand legal challenge when there is a clear job-related correlation between the conviction and job duties. A transit authority's rule against hiring convicted narcotics users was shown to be job related because narcotics users were a safety risk on transit vehicles and a potential security threat to riders.[9] A hotel requirement that bellhops and other employees with access to guests'

8. *Paul v Davis*, 424 US 693 (1976).
9. *New York City Transit Authority v Belzer*, 19 FEP Cases 149 (1979).

Sample Policy: Background Checks

XYZ Company conducts background checks to aid in evaluating job candidates prior to hiring or placement into designated jobs.

1. Background checks may be routine background checks or detailed background checks. Routine background checks include checking of employment references and educational records. Detailed background checks include check of criminal convictions and driving records as well as the routine background checks.

2. Routine background checks are conducted as employment reference checks (all positions) and educational records checks (all professional positions requiring education beyond high school).

3. Detailed background checks are conducted as criminal conviction checks (all positions involving security, public contact, and funds management) and driving record checks (all positions involving operation of a company vehicle on the job).

4. Background checks shall be conducted by the human resources manager. Background checks should be made after a candidate has been deemed to be "qualified" based on the preliminary job interview.

5. Background information is confidential and shall be maintained with the candidate's employment application.

Sample Policy: Background Checks

6. Candidates shall be advised that, prior to being hired for the specified position, they will be subject to a background check.

7. The application shall include an applicant's certification that all employment, educational, and other information provided on the application and in the interview process is true, complete, and accurate, and that falsification of information is grounds to deny or withdraw a job offer or to terminate employment.

8. The application shall include an applicant's certification authorizing prior employers and educational institutions to release employment or educational information and waiving any claims against these organizations for providing any information.

9. In the event of discrepancies, incorrect or falsified information provided by a candidate on a job application is sufficient grounds to deny or withdraw a job offer. If discrepancies are minor in nature, the hiring manager may schedule a subsequent interview to probe for more information and to clarify the discrepancies.

property be free of a serious property-related criminal record was held by the courts to be a reasonable hiring criterion.[10] An applicant's falsification of information on a prior conviction on an employment application was a legitimate reason for the employer to refuse to hire the individual.[11] However, the seriousness of the conviction and the degree to which it is related to a particular position should be considered when making an employment decision. A railroad's rejection of an applicant because of conviction for petty larceny was held to be an improper rejection because of the minor nature of the offense.[12]

10. *Richardson v Hotel Corporation of America,* 3 FEP Cases 1031 (5th Cir 1972) (1979).
11. *Osborne v Cleland,* 22 FEP Cases 1292 (8th Cir 1980).
12. *Green v Missouri Pacific Railroad,* 10 FEP Cases 1409 (8th Cir 1975).

**Sample Employee Notice:
Background Checks**

XYZ Company takes pride in providing a high degree of professionalism in serving our customers. In order to select individuals meeting our high standards of professionalism, candidates for the jobs listed below are subject to a background check. The background check will include one or more of the following: Employment reference check, educational credentials check, criminal record check, and driving record check.

States That Limit or Prohibit Consideration of Arrest Records in Employment

Arizona	Illinois	Minnesota	Oregon
California	Kansas	Mississippi	Pennsylvania
Colorado	Kentucky	North Carolina	Rhode Island
Connecticut	Louisiana	North Dakota	Utah
Georgia	Massachusetts	Ohio	Virginia
Hawaii	Michigan	Oklahoma	

Critical Issues in Use of Arrest and Conviction Records

If a clear business necessity is present, an employer may be able to inquire about an individual's arrest record. But requirements vary from state to state. For example, the Illinois Human Rights Act, which prohibits arrest record inquiries on a job application, allows an exception permitting employers providing services to children to require job seekers or volunteers to disclose arrests or convictions for certain offenses against children. The EEOC has determined that consideration of arrest records adversely affects minorities. Convictions records, if related to the job, are a lawful selection criterion, but consider the severity. Denial of employment may be justified for a felony conviction related to the job but may not be for a misdemeanor conviction.

Sample Policy: Arrest and Convictions

It is the policy of XYZ Company not to consider an applicant's arrest record in employment decisions, but a job-related conviction may be considered. XYZ Company provides delivery services for its customers, and many employees operate company vehicles on the job. The company checks driving records of all candidates for driving positions. A conviction for driving under the influence (DUI) of alcohol or drugs or any other conviction resulting in loss of driver's license is grounds to deny employment.

**Sample Employee Notice:
Arrests and Convictions**

XYZ Company is an equal employment opportunity employer. All employment decisions are made without regard to race, sex, age, color, national origin, religion, or disability. An individual's arrest record is not considered in employment decisions. However, a criminal conviction may influence an employment decision if it is related to job responsibilities.

Pay Your Bills on Time? When Employers Conduct Credit Checks

Checking credit is an increasingly common way to conduct the background investigation of job candidates who will handle cash or manage funds for banks and other financial institutions. Controllers, investment managers, loan officers, and other financial managers are also likely to be subject to credit checks.

Credit information is generally available from consumer credit reporting agencies that receive, store, and dispense credit or financial information on individuals. An individual's credit file consists of data provided by the individual consumer when applying for credit or a loan, plus payment history or credit-related judgments provided by creditors. Credit reports from these agencies typically provide information related to an individual's address, social security number, credit standing, credit capacity, loans, child support obligations, bankruptcies, or judgments.

However, an employer must always tell an applicant that his or her credit will be evaluated, especially if that is the reason an applicant is turned down. Chicago retailer Marshall Field and Company was charged by the FTC with violating the federal FCRA when it failed to tell applicants for security positions that their credit ratings were at least part of the reason they were denied employment. Failure to provide such information to applicants together with information on the credit reporting agency is a violation of the act. Field's eventually reached a settlement with the FTC in which no violation of the law was admitted, but the retailer agreed to provide the required notification to security applicants who were denied employment and to provide notice to candidates who will be subject to the credit check.

Guidelines on handling and use of credit information are defined by the FCRA. Under this law, employers must have a permissible purpose for obtaining credit information, and any information obtained must be handled in a confidential manner. The credit law allows for two types of reports: consumer reports and investigative reports. The consumer report is information provided by a credit reporting agency that details an individual's credit standing, creditworthiness, and related data generally used by creditors to evaluate an individual's credit application. Employers may evaluate such data to determine an individual's suitability for employment. The investigative report is a more detailed investigation of an individual's background obtained through interviews of neighbors, friends, or associates.

When an employer conducts a credit investigation of a job applicant, the employment application should have a clear and conspicuous notice that the investigation will occur. While the employer is not required to advise the job applicant of the contents of the credit report obtained, the employer must notify the individual if employment is denied because of the credit report. Further, the employer must provide the individual with the name and address of the agency or individual providing the credit report.

Can an employer's investigation of credit history be viewed as a privacy invasion? While most individuals would prefer to keep personal financial information private, the fact remains that credit information is available through

Sample Policy: Use of Credit Reports

XYZ Company conducts a credit check to aid in evaluating job candidates prior to hire or placement into designated jobs.

1. The credit check is used to aid in evaluation of job candidates with responsibility for handling and/or managing large amounts of company funds. Candidates for the following jobs will be subject to credit checks: controller, accounts payable clerk, accounts receivable clerk, and cash receipts clerk.

2. Credit checks shall be administered to all final job candidates immediately prior to making a job offer.

3. Candidates shall be advised that a credit check will occur as part of the screening and selection process.

4. All credit reports must be treated as confidential documents. Credit reports are filed in the individual's personnel file.

5. In the event employment is denied in whole or in part because of the credit report, the hiring manager must so notify the employee. The notification must include the name and address of the credit agency providing the credit report.

credit agencies. Every time an individual takes out a loan, opens a new charge account, or incurs any form of legal judgment based on credit, these financial transactions end up in his or her credit record. The FCRA defines certain limits and protections on the use of this data. There is little basis for a privacy invasion or other legal action if credit information is:

- Obtained for a permissible purpose
- Properly used in a nondiscriminatory manner
- Not inappropriately released to others

> **Sample Employee Notice:**
> **Employee Credit Reports**
>
> Candidates for positions at XYZ Company involving the handling or management of funds are subject to a credit check. In the event that employment is denied in whole or in part because of the credit report, the candidate will be so advised and will receive the name and address of the credit reporting agency providing the credit report.

Inappropriate public release of credit information would be grounds for a privacy invasion claim. Take care to handle credit information confidentially. Also, the EEOC has held that the use of credit checks adversely affects women and minorities. The commission held that a bank violated the federal Civil Rights Act when it refused to hire a black computer operator in part because of a poor credit history. Take care to use this information in a nondiscriminatory fashion. Conduct credit checks only for jobs involving handling of funds or security issues, and conduct checks of all candidates for these positions.

Critical Issues in Use of Credit Reports

An employer contemplating checking an applicant's credit should consider two important issues. First, it must abide by the notification requirements imposed by the FCRA. Second, it must keep in mind that the EEOC has found civil rights violations when credit reports adversely affect employment opportunities of protected-class individuals. Be sure that there is an appropriate business justification and a job-related concern when conducting credit checks of individuals. Credit checks of candidates for jobs handling funds is a clear job-related requirement. Notify candidates if employment is denied due to the credit check.

Let's See Your I.D.:
A Look at Work Document Requirements

Have you got your papers?
Are you legally authorized to work?

While questions like these seem nosy, they are asked in order to fulfill the employee documentation requirement of the IRCA, designed to prevent the employment of individuals who are in the United States illegally. The law does this by requiring all individuals to provide documentary evidence of employment eligibility at time of hire.

Application of the law is the responsibility of all employers. Within three days of hire, the employer has five obligations:

1. Fill out the Employment Eligibility Verification Form I-9 (reproduced in figure 4-1).
2. Require every newly hired employee to provide documents establishing identity and work authorization.
3. Complete the I-9 form identifying documents provided by the employee.
4. Retain the I-9 forms for three years or until one year after the individual separates employment.
5. Provide the I-9 forms for inspection to INS or Labor Department investigators upon request.

Documents such as a U.S. passport, certificate of U.S. citizenship, or certificate of naturalization show both identity and employment authorization. Under the law, a person's identity may be established with a driver's license, government photo I.D., or voter card; employment eligibility may be established with a social security card or birth certificate.[13]

Critical Issues in Work Document Requirements

An employer's request to see these documents is not an invasion of privacy. The various documents are generally a matter of public record. Further, the law requires employers to check documents of all individuals hired, not just aliens. An employer may lawfully refuse to hire an individual who fails to provide appropriate documents at time of hire. However, an employer's refusal to hire foreign-looking or foreign-born applicants may result in a national origin discrimination claim. Further information is available in the INS *Handbook for Employers*.

13. *Handbook for Employers, Instructions for Completing Form I-9*, Publication M-274 (Washington, DC: U.S. Department of Justice, Immigration and Naturalization Service, Nov. 21, 1991).

Figure 4-1 Employment Eligibility Verification Form I-9

U.S. Department of Justice
Immigration and Naturalization Service

Employment Eligibility Verification

Please read instructions carefully before completing this form. The instructions must be available during completion of this form. ANTI-DISCRIMINATION NOTICE. It is illegal to discriminate against work eligible individuals. Employers CANNOT specify which document(s) they will accept from an employee. The refusal to hire an individual because of a future expiration date may also constitute illegal discrimination.

Section 1. Employee Information and Verification. To be completed and signed by employee at the time employment begins

Print Name: Last	First	Middle Initial	Maiden Name

Address (Street Name and Number)		Apt. #	Date of Birth (month/day/year)

City	State	Zip Code	Social Security #

I attest, under penalty of perjury, that I am (check one of the following):

☐ A citizen or national of the United States
☐ A Lawful Permanent Resident (Alien # A _____)
☐ An alien authorized to work until ___/___/___
(Alien # or Admission # _____)

I am aware that federal law provides for imprisonment and/or fines for false statements or use of false documents in connection with the completion of this form.

Employee's Signature	Date (month/day/year)

Preparer and/or Translator Certification. *(To be completed and signed if Section 1 is prepared by a person other than the employee.) I attest, under penalty of perjury, that I have assisted in the completion of this form and that to the best of my knowledge the information is true and correct.*

Preparer's/Translator's Signature	Print Name

Address (Street Name and Number, City, State, Zip Code)	Date (month/day/year)

Section 2. Employer Review and Verification. To be completed and signed by employer. **Examine one document from List A OR examine one document from List B and one document from List C** as listed on the reverse of this form and record the title, number and expiration date, if any, of the document(s)

List A	OR	List B	AND	List C

Document title: _____

Issuing authority: _____

Document #: _____

Expiration Date (if any): ___/___/___

Document #: _____

Expiration Date (if any): ___/___/___

List B: _____ ___/___/___

List C: _____ ___/___/___

CERTIFICATION - I attest, under penalty of perjury, that I have examined the document(s) presented by the above-named employee, that the above-listed document(s) appear to be genuine and to relate to the employee named, that the employee began employment on (month/day/year) ___/___/___ and that to the best of my knowledge the employee is eligible to work in the United States. (State employment agencies may omit the date the employee began employment).

Signature of Employer or Authorized Representative	Print Name	Title

Business or Organization Name	Address (Street Name and Number, City, State, Zip Code)	Date (month/day/year)

Section 3. Updating and Reverification. To be completed and signed by employer

A. New Name (if applicable)	B. Date of rehire (month/day/year) (if applicable)

C. If employee's previous grant of work authorization has expired, provide the information below for the document that establishes current employment eligibility.

Document Title: _____ Document #: _____ Expiration Date (if any): ___/___/___

I attest, under penalty of perjury, that to the best of my knowledge, this employee is eligible to work in the United States, and if the employee presented document(s), the document(s) I have examined appear to be genuine and to relate to the individual.

Signature of Employer or Authorized Representative	Date (month/day/year)

(continues)

Figure 4-1 continued

U.S. Department of Justice
Immigration and Naturalization Service

OMB No 1115-0136
Employment Eligibility Verification

INSTRUCTIONS
PLEASE READ ALL INSTRUCTIONS CAREFULLY BEFORE COMPLETING THIS FORM.

Section 1 - Employee. All employees, citizens and noncitizens, hired after November 6, 1986, must complete Section 1 of this form at the time of hire, which is the actual beginning of employment. **The employer is responsible for ensuring that Section 1 is timely and properly completed.**

Preparer/Translator Certification. The Preparer/Translator Certification must be completed if Section 1 is prepared by a person other than the employee. A preparer/translator may be used only when the employee is unable to complete Section 1 on his/her own. However, the employee must still sign Section 1 personally.

Section 2 - Employer. For the purpose of completing this form, the term "employer" includes those recruiters and referrers for a fee who are agricultural associations, agricultural employers, or farm labor contractors.

Employers must complete Section 2 by examining evidence of identity and employment eligibility within three (3) business days of the date employment begins. If employees are authorized to work, but are unable to present the required document(s) within three business days, they must present a receipt for the application of the document(s) within three business days and the actual document(s) within ninety (90) days. However, if employers hire individuals for a duration of less than three business days, Section 2 must be completed at the time employment begins. **Employers must record: 1)** document title; **2)** issuing authority, **3)** document number, **4)** expiration date, if any; and **5)** the date employment begins. Employers must sign and date the certification. Employees must present original documents. Employers may, but are not required to, photocopy the document(s) presented. These photocopies may only be used for the verification process and must be retained with the I-9. **However, employers are still responsible for completing the I-9.**

Section 3 - Updating and Reverification. Employers must complete Section 3 when updating and/or reverifying the I-9. Employers must reverify employment eligibility of their employees on or before the expiration date recorded in Section 1. Employers **CANNOT** specify which document(s) they will accept from an employee.

- If an employee's name has changed at the time this form is being updated/ reverified, complete Block A.

- If an employee is rehired within three (3) years of the date this form was originally completed and the employee is still eligible to be employed on the same basis as previously indicated on this form (updating), complete Block B and the signature block.

- If an employee is rehired within three (3) years of the date this form was originally completed and the employee's work authorization has expired or if a current employee's work authorization is about to expire (reverification), complete Block B and.
  - examine any document that reflects that the employee is authorized to work in the U.S. (see List A or C),
  - record the document title, document number and expiration date (if any) in Block C, and
  - complete the signature block.

Photocopying and Retaining Form I-9. A blank I-9 may be reproduced provided both sides are copied. The instructions must be available to all employees completing this form. Employers must retain completed I-9s for three (3) years after the date of hire **or** one (1) year after the date employment ends, whichever is later.

For more detailed information, you may refer to the INS Handbook for Employers, (Form M-274). You may obtain the handbook at your local INS office.

Privacy Act Notice. The authority for collecting this information is the Immigration Reform and Control Act of 1986, Pub. L. 99-603 (8 U.S.C. 1324a).

This information is for employers to verify the eligibility of individuals for employment to preclude the unlawful hiring, or recruiting or referring for a fee, of aliens who are not authorized to work in the United States.

This information will be used by employers as a record of their basis for determining eligibility of an employee to work in the United States. The form will be kept by the employer and made available for inspection by officials of the U.S. Immigration and Naturalization Service, the Department of Labor, and the Office of Special Counsel for Immigration Related Unfair Employment Practices.

Submission of the information required in this form is voluntary. However, an individual may not begin employment unless this form is completed since employers are subject to civil or criminal penalties if they do not comply with the Immigration Reform and Control Act of 1986.

Reporting Burden. We try to create forms and instructions that are accurate, can be easily understood, and which impose the least possible burden on you to provide us with information. Often this is difficult because some immigration laws are very complex. Accordingly, the reporting burden for this collection of information is computed as follows **1)** learning about this form, 5 minutes; **2)** completing the form, 5 minutes; and **3)** assembling and filing (recordkeeping) the form, 5 minutes, for an average of 15 minutes per response. If you have comments regarding the accuracy of this burden estimate, or suggestions for making this form simpler, you can write to both the Immigration and Naturalization Service, 425 I Street, N.W., Room 5304. Washington, D. C. 20536; and the Office of Management and Budget, Paperwork Reduction Project, OMB No. 1115-0136. Washington, D.C. 20503.

Form I-9 (Rev. 11-21-91) N

**EMPLOYERS MUST RETAIN COMPLETED I-9
PLEASE DO NOT MAIL COMPLETED I-9 TO INS**

LISTS OF ACCEPTABLE DOCUMENTS

LIST A		LIST B		LIST C
Documents that Establish Both Identity and Employment Eligibility	**OR**	**Documents that Establish Identity**	**AND**	**Documents that Establish Employment Eligibility**

LIST A — Documents that Establish Both Identity and Employment Eligibility

1. U.S. Passport (unexpired or expired)

2. Certificate of U.S. Citizenship (INS Form N-560 or N-561)

3. Certificate of Naturalization (INS Form N-550 or N-570)

4. Unexpired foreign passport, with I-551 stamp or attached INS Form I-94 indicating unexpired employment authorization

5. Alien Registration Receipt Card with photograph (INS Form I-151 or I-551)

6. Unexpired Temporary Resident Card (INS Form I-688)

7. Unexpired Employment Authorization Card (INS Form I-688A)

8. Unexpired Reentry Permit (INS Form I-327)

9. Unexpired Refugee Travel Document (INS Form I-571)

10. Unexpired Employment Authorization Document issued by the INS which contains a photograph (INS Form I-688B)

OR

LIST B — Documents that Establish Identity

1. Driver's license or ID card issued by a state or outlying possession of the United States provided it contains a photograph or information such as name, date of birth, sex, height, eye color, and address

2. ID card issued by federal, state, or local government agencies or entities provided it contains a photograph or information such as name, date of birth, sex, height, eye color, and address

3. School ID card with a photograph

4. Voter's registration card

5. U.S. Military card or draft record

6. Military dependent's ID card

7. U.S. Coast Guard Merchant Mariner Card

8. Native American tribal document

9. Driver's license issued by a Canadian government authority

For persons under age 18 who are unable to present a document listed above:

10. School record or report card

11. Clinic, doctor, or hospital record

12. Day care or nursery school record

AND

LIST C — Documents that Establish Employment Eligibility

1. U.S. social security card issued by the Social Security Administration (other than a card stating it is not valid for employment)

2. Certification of Birth Abroad issued by the Department of State (Form FS-545 or Form DS-1350)

3. Original or certified copy of a birth certificate issued by a state, county, municipal authority or outlying possession of the United States bearing an official seal

4. Native American tribal document

5. U.S. Citizen ID Card (INS Form I-197)

6. ID Card for use of Resident Citizen in the United States (INS Form I-179)

7. Unexpired employment authorization document issued by the INS (other than those listed under List A)

Illustrations of many of these documents appear in Part 8 of the Handbook for Employers (M-274)

Sample Policy: Work Document Requirements

It is the policy of XYZ Company to hire only U.S. citizens and individuals lawfully eligible for employment in the United States. The following procedures apply:

1. All employees hired by XYZ Company must be U.S. citizens or individuals who are lawfully eligible for employment in the United States.

2. The human resources manager is responsible for posting a notice in the company lobby advising job applicants that XYZ Company requires new employees to provide documented evidence of identity and employment eligibility as required by law.

3. Within three days of hire, all new employees must complete the Employment Eligibility Verification Form I-9 and provide documents showing identification and employment eligibility.

4. The human resources manager is responsible for checking documents and signing the I-9 form. I-9 forms are kept in the employment eligibility file. While it is not required by law, it is XYZ practice to make a photocopy of the sample documents provided by the employee and attach them to the I-9 form.

5. In the event that an employee fails or refuses to provide documents or to complete and sign the I-9 form, XYZ may lawfully refuse to hire the individual.

6. In the event that an individual provides falsified information or documents, XYZ Company may discharge the individual.

**Sample Employee Notice:
Work Documents**

It is the policy of XYZ Company to hire only U.S. citizens and individuals lawfully eligible for employment in the United States as defined by the Immigration Reform and Control Act of 1986. Upon hire, you are required to provide documented evidence of identity and employment eligibility as required by law.

All in the Family: Employer Attitudes toward Nepotism Policies

Employer attitudes toward nepotism vary widely from firm to firm. A Minneapolis manufacturing company employs many members of the same family because it has found that a good employee with a strong work ethic has other family members who share that attitude. A tooling and manufacturing firm located near a large midwestern city takes the opposite approach in its antinepotism policy and will not hire an individual if his or her spouse works for the firm. If two employees marry, the less senior individual must quit his or her job. Another company has a "no-spouse" rule that prohibits an employee from supervising or working in the same department as his or her spouse. These companies complain that hiring family members, or allowing them to work in the same department, creates the potential for fraud or theft or family arguments disrupting the workplace.

Family members hold all the firm's top positions in a privately owned Indiana trucking company. The firm's founder and owner serves as chairman of the board. One son is president, a second son directs all of the firm's operational activities, and a son-in-law handles administrative and financial matters.

Should an individual be forced to quit his or her job just because he or she marries another employee of the same company? Is it fair to deny employment to an individual because another family member works for the same firm? Or is it fair that a manager places his spouse in a key job even though there are other employees who may be better qualified? Do these actions represent an invasion of privacy?

States with Laws That May Affect Nepotism Issues

Arizona	Montana	North Dakota	Texas
Arkansas	Nebraska	Oklahoma	Utah
Colorado	Nevada	Oregon	Washington
Idaho	New York	Tennessee	Wisconsin
Kentucky	North Carolina		

When an employer bases an employment decision on an individual's family relationship, employees are likely to be concerned. For example, when a manager gives a job to a spouse or other family member rather than to another individual, the nepotism preference is upsetting to other employees. But nepotism issues generally do not result in a privacy invasion claim. Nepotism is a personal matter, not a private matter that has been publicized to others in an outrageous manner.

Legal claims relating to nepotism, antinepotism, and different treatment because of marital status are generally brought under marital status discrimination claims or equal employment opportunity laws. Slahoda's claim against UPS in New Jersey is an example of an issue involving an employee's private life that was presented as a marital status discrimination claim rather than a privacy invasion.

> Slahoda, a married employee, claimed he was wrongfully discharged by UPS because of an adulterous act. He alleged that the company did not fire unmarried employees for engaging in sexual relationships, and that this distinction violated state law. The court held that if an employer's discharge policy is based in significant part on an employee's marital status, such a discharge violates New Jersey law.[14]

Critical Issues in Nepotism Policies

Federal employment law does not specifically address nepotism issues. However, nepotistic practices may provoke a sex discrimination claim if the workforce is predominantly male and a female is denied employment on this basis. In states where marital status is a protected-class category under antibias laws,

14. *Slahoda v UPS*, 475 A2d 618 (NJ Supr 1984).

States That List Marital Status as a Protected-Class Category under Equal Opportunity Laws[15]

Arkansas	Massachusetts	North Dakota
California	Michigan	Oklahoma
Connecticut	Minnesota	Oregon
Delaware	Missouri	Rhode Island
District of Columbia	Montana	South Carolina
Florida	Nebraska	South Dakota
Hawaii	New Hampshire	Virginia
Illinois	New Jersey	Washington
Kansas	New Mexico	West Virginia
Maryland	New York	Wisconsin

an individual who is denied employment or otherwise subject to an employment decision because his or her spouse works for the firm would appear to have grounds for a discrimination claim based on marital status. The EEOC has held that an employer's exclusive reliance on hiring only friends or relatives of current employees, when the workforce is predominantly one race, is a discriminatory hiring practice because minorities are adversely affected. And an employer who applies an antinepotism policy to roommates of current employees may find its policy against the law in states with laws prohibiting discrimination against individuals for lawful off-duty conduct.

Summary

In the employee selection process, employers seek as much information as possible about an individual in order to evaluate the person for employment. But these inquiries go beyond an applicant's reasonable expectation of privacy when they are too probing, too detailed, or irrelevant to employment. Certain inquiries are in fact against the law, including inquiries relating to race, sex, age, religion, or national origin. Other inquiries, however, may seek publicly available information such as driving records, criminal records, or credit rec-

---

15. Ronald M. Green, William A. Carmell, and Jerrold F. Goldberg, *State-by-State Guide to Human Resources Law* (New York: Panel Publishers, 1993), table 1.2-1, pt. B.

Sample Policy: Employment of Relatives

XYZ Company maintains a merit employment policy where all employees, including relatives of current employees, are hired based upon skills, abilities, and experience.

1. All employment decisions are based on job-related criteria and objective evaluation of job candidates based on their skills and abilities.

2. XYZ employees are encouraged to refer friends and relatives for consideration for employment.

3. To avoid potential conflicts of interest, XYZ will not hire or place members of an immediate family in a direct supervisor-subordinate relationship.

4. In the event that a conflict arises with this policy, the individual with the least seniority will be reassigned to other employment if available or laid off from employment.

**Sample Employee Notice:
Employment of Relatives**

We believe that when you refer a friend for employment at XYZ, it is a reflection that XYZ is a good place to work. All individuals are considered based on merit, skills, ability, and job qualifications. Please recognize, however, that it is our practice not to place family members in a direct supervisor-subordinate relationship.

ords. When the employer has a job-related purpose for the inquiry and avoids discriminatory practices, valuable information can be used to fairly evaluate the candidate.

Appendix

Interviewing Checklist

Dos and don'ts to avoid privacy invasion or discrimination claims:

Dos

■ DO ask questions that are job related or necessary for determining the applicant's qualifications for employment.

■ DO question applicants in a consistent and uniform manner, regardless of race, sex, national origin, age, or handicap or other protected-class categories.

■ DO state attendance requirements, and ask whether the applicant can meet them.

■ DO solicit information about previous work attendance records in the interview, on the application form, or in reference checks, but don't ask questions that refer to illness or disability.

■ DO ask questions about the applicant's ability to perform job-related functions.

■ DO ask whether the applicant knows of any reason that he or she cannot perform the essential functions of the job (since the applicant may not be able to perform essential job functions for reasons unrelated to a disability).

■ DO ask questions regarding the applicant's ability to perform all job functions, not just those that are essential to the job. However, remember that the applicant cannot be screened out because of his or her inability to perform marginal or nonessential job functions.

■ DO describe or demonstrate a job function and ask all applicants whether they can perform the functions with or without reasonable accommodation.

■ DO evaluate applicants on job-related criteria, in accord with the actual requirements for successful performance of the job.

■ DO accord reasonable accommodations for qualified disabled applicants. Consider whatever minor adjustments or accommodations may be made to enable the handicapped to perform the job successfully.

■ DO make reasonable accommodations to the religious observance obligations of employees.

- DO select the best-qualified individual for the job. Equal opportunity laws do not require that you select unqualified workers.

Don'ts

- DO NOT ask any questions of a female applicant that would not be asked of a male applicant (e.g., inquiries pertaining to child care, marital status, birth control methods, or hindrances to travel or working weekends).

- DO NOT ask questions of one race that would not be asked of another (e.g., questioning the applicant's ability to work in a location with members of another racial group).

- DO NOT establish a negative tone to the interview in an effort to discourage any applicant from seeking the position.

- DO NOT give undue emphasis to the hazardous or tedious aspects of a job, especially if such occurs on an infrequent basis.

- DO NOT inform an applicant that the position is "reserved" or must be filled by a female or minority group applicant due to equal opportunity or affirmative action obligations or regulations. A possible exception to this suggestion may occur when a court or regulatory agency has made a finding of discrimination and directs remedial action in the form of specific hiring goals.

- DO NOT impose additional "desirable" qualifications in excess of actual requirements of your job opening.

- DO NOT ask the birthplace of the applicant. Since birthplace may indicate a person of foreign origin, it is better to avoid this question than to risk a discrimination charge on this basis.

- DO NOT ask questions that tend to identify the age of the applicant, where age is not a valid or necessary factor to successful job performance.

- DO NOT ask the applicant's religious affiliation.

- DO NOT ask the citizenship of the applicant. Ask whether the person is a citizen or is legally authorized for full-time permanent employment in the United States.

- DO NOT ask about the applicant's type of military discharge or general military service. You may ask about job-related experience in the Armed Forces of the United States of America.

- DO NOT ask whether the applicant has ever been arrested. You may ask if the applicant has ever been convicted of an offense related to work or job duties.

- DO NOT ask questions about the general physical or mental condition of the applicant.

- DO NOT ask about any physical characteristics such as scars, burns, or missing limbs.

- DO NOT ask whether the applicant has ever received counseling or seen a psychiatrist.

- DO NOT ask whether the applicant has had a drug or alcohol problem.

- DO NOT ask about the applicant's workers' compensation history.

- DO NOT ask how a disability occurred or whether the disability is indicative of an underlying impairment.

- DO NOT ask whether the applicant will need leave for treatment.

- If the applicant volunteers information about a medical condition such as cancer, DO NOT ask about the progress of the illness or whether it is in remission.

- DO NOT ask whether the applicant's family members have had a history of illness.

- DO NOT ask whether the applicant has any disability or medical condition that will prevent him or her from performing the job.

- DO NOT devise additional testing requirements as part of a preemployment screening procedure unless such testing is job related and properly validated.

Copyright 1991 Hubbartt & Associates. Reprinted with permission.

Management Guidelines

Preemployment Inquiries

- Define job duties and essential functions of each job in the organization. Written job descriptions are useful for this.

- Carefully define job-related criteria or qualifications based on the job duties.

- Focus preemployment inquiries on the applicant's skills, experience, training, and education.

- Review application forms and eliminate inquiries that focus on illegal issues.

- Train supervisors and managers on proper interviewing techniques and how to avoid improper or illegal inquires.

- Avoid inquiries that focus on age, race, sex, religion, national origin, color, and other protected-class issues.

- Avoid inquiries that are not job related.

Reference Checking

- Include reference checking as part of your employee selection process, particularly where employees have contact with the public.

- Require all job candidates to complete a detailed employment application. The application should include an applicant certification that all employment, educational, or other information provided on the application and during the interview process is accurate and truthful and that the applicant authorizes former employers to provide information about his or her employment and releases the employer from liability for providing truthful information.

- Include on the application a statement that falsification or omission of significant information is grounds for denial or withdrawal of a job offer or discharge of employment.

- If the applicant is currently employed, check prior references and make the job offer contingent upon verification of a favorable reference from the current job after the applicant has separated from the current position.

- Contact all references provided. Verify employment information provided on the application; make a note of discrepancies for further discussion in a subsequent interview or for denial of employment.

- Try to reach the candidate's direct supervisors. Probe for information on job performance issues, attendance, and work habits. Seek facts, and avoid subjective opinions.

- If the former employer is reluctant to provide reference information, provide a copy of the applicant's signed release authorizing release of information for employment references.

- Request that the applicant show original copies of degrees, certificates, and licenses.

- Protect confidentiality of all application and reference-checking information.

- Use a second or subsequent interview to probe for further details or clarify any discrepancies uncovered in the reference-checking process.

- Be consistent in checking references for all candidates.

Background Checks

- Identify a business purpose or specific business necessity for the background check.

- Identify specific job requirements or issues to be verified through the background check.

- Provide a statement on the employment application that employment is subject to a background check.

- Provide a statement on the employment application that falsification or omission of material facts on the application or during the interview process is grounds to deny employment, withdraw a job offer, or justify termination.

- Avoid inquiries that may be in violation of the law. Without compelling justification, likely sources of violations could include inquiries on arrest records, workers' compensation records, and convictions if the conviction is not job related.

- Apply the same background checks to all candidates or all candidates in a particular job class.
- Protect confidentiality of information obtained in a background check.
- Avoid unauthorized release of information obtained in a background check.

Use of Arrest and Conviction Records

- Check state laws for restrictions on use of arrest and conviction records in employment decisions.
- Define a clear business necessity for considering arrest or conviction records in employment decisions.
- Avoid use of arrest records unless there is a compelling interest for such checks, such as screening child care workers for child abuse arrests or convictions.
- Determine job-relatedness when using conviction records as a basis to screen candidates. Before using conviction records to screen candidates, determine the degree to which a conviction is related to the ability to perform a job.
- Include a statement on the employment application that a conviction record will not necessarily be a bar to employment.
- When evaluating convictions, consider nature of convictions, relationship to job duties, number of convictions, time since conviction, and any rehabilitation.

Use of Credit Reports

- Specify a clear business necessity and purpose for obtaining and considering credit reports on an individual.
- Check the provisions of the FCRA to assure compliance when setting up any credit check procedures.
- Identify specific job-related issues or responsibilities as justification for making a credit check part of the employee selection procedure.
- Include a clear notice in your employment application if a credit check is part of the applicant screening process.
- Keep any credit reports obtained confidential, and avoid any unauthorized release of the information.
- Conduct credit checks on a uniform and consistent basis, checking all candidates for a particular job or class of jobs.
- Observe proper notification procedures if employment is denied in whole or in part because of the credit report.

Work Document Requirements

▪ Check the *Handbook for Employers*, INS Publication M-274, for procedural guidelines on complying with this law.

▪ Designate an individual as responsible for checking documents, preparing the I-9 form, and maintaining I-9 files.

▪ Maintain I-9 records in a file separate from employee personnel files.

▪ It is permissible to refuse employment to individuals who fail to provide appropriate documents specified under the law.

▪ Do not refuse to hire or otherwise discriminate against individuals who appear to be foreign born.

▪ Recognize that I-9 forms are subject to inspection by INS agents and Labor Department inspectors.

▪ Protect confidentiality of records.

Employment of Relatives

▪ Check state or local laws on nepotism practice or marital discrimination.

▪ Consider whether your policy will encourage or discourage the employment of relatives.

▪ Recognize that policies that encourage employment of relatives could be viewed as a discriminatory employment practice if your workforce is predominantly one race or ethnic group.

▪ Recognize that policies that discourage or prohibit employment of relatives may result in a marital status discrimination claim in states or other jurisdictions where marital status is a protected class under equal employment opportunity laws.

▪ For best results in employment decisions, use skills, abilities, experience, and other job-related criteria as the primary basis for the decision.

▪ Common limits to employment of relatives involve preventing direct supervisory relationships or potential conflicts of interest.

▪ Avoid policies that limit or prohibit employment of relatives in organizations that are owned or managed by several family members or where "exceptions" to the policy already exist.

Q & A: Employee Rights Regarding Reference and Background Checks and Other Preemployment Issues

Q   *What rights do employees have when employers conduct reference checks?*

A   Most applications contain a release statement authorizing former employers to provide employment history information. When the applicant signs the release, checking employment references is a lawful practice provided that information sought is job related, that similar information is obtained on all candidates, and that the inquiry does not probe into truly private or non–job-related information.

Q   *Are there any limits to information that an employer can obtain in a background check?*

A   Background checks resemble employment reference checks but focus on driving records, criminal convictions, workers' compensation records, court records, or educational records. With the exception of educational records, these public records are available on request from the appropriate government agency. For this reason, an employer's request for this information is not likely to be a privacy invasion. But an employer's improper use of such information may violate antibias laws or other laws. For example, an employee has a lawful right to file a workers' compensation claim, and an employer's refusal to hire an employee because of a past workers' compensation claim violates the law. Although educational records are not public, most schools will verify an individual's past attendance or enrollment at the school and identify type of degree obtained. But the school will not release detailed grade information without the employee's consent.

Q   *Employers often ask all kinds of questions during employment interviews. Are there any areas that are too private or inappropriate?*

A   Preemployment inquiries that focus on issues relating to race, sex, religion, national origin, color, and disability are prohibited by state or federal antibias laws. Laws in some states may limit an employer's preemployment inquiries on such issues as union membership, prior accidents, or workers' compensation claims, use of smoking materials, marital status, source of income, or sexual orientation.

Q   *Can an arrest or conviction be used to deny employment?*

A   Generally, an employer's consideration of arrest records in an employment decision is a violation of antibias laws. This is because minorities are more likely to be arrested and therefore more likely to be adversely affected by an employment decision based on arrest records. However, conviction records may be considered in an employment decision if there is a reasonable relationship between the nature, recency, and severity of the conviction and job responsibilities.

Q   *Are there any limits on how an employer can use credit check information?*

A   When requesting credit information on an employee, an employer should have a business purpose and comply with the FCRA. If a credit check is part of the preemployment process, the employer should have clear notice on the employment application, advise the applicant if employment is denied because of the results of the credit check, and provide the name and address of the credit agency providing the credit information.

Q   *Why do employers ask to see a driver's license and social security card when an employee*
     starts a new job?
A   Employers are required by the IRCA to view specified employee documents that
     show identity and work authorization. An identity document can be a photo iden-
     tification form. Work authorization is limited to U.S. citizens and to noncitizens
     with an appropriate visa permitting employment. The employer is permitted un-
     der the law to refuse to hire individuals who fail to provide appropriate docu-
     ments.

Q   *Some firms encourage employment of relatives, while others prohibit the hiring of family*
     members. What rights do employees have regarding these nepotism policies?
A   An employer's nepotism policy may violate state antibias laws in one of two ways.
     A policy that encourages employment of relatives could be discriminatory if the
     workforce is predominantly made up of one race or ethnic group. A policy that
     prohibits nepotism could result in marital status discrimination if the policy af-
     fects an individual because he or she has a spouse in the same organization.

5

Truth Serum: Medical, Drug, Psychological, and Skill Testing

Donald Jevic thought he had it sewn up: He would be district sales manager for the Coca Cola office in New Jersey. The application and interview process had gone well, and Territory Development Manager Frank Modia had offered him the job pending the results of a reference check and a preemployment drug test, which Jevic had consented to during the interview.

After signing another statement authorizing the drug test and release of results to Coke, he provided a urine sample to Redi-Med Medical Center. But when a urinalysis and a more sophisticated testing technique showed positive findings indicating presence of drugs in his body, Coke rescinded its employment offer. Jevic maintained that the test was erroneous because he had not smoked marijuana in over a year. To support his position, he voluntarily took another drug test, which reported a negative finding. When Coke refused to reconsider or permit Jevic to retest at its facility, he sued, claiming that the drug test was negligently administered and that the test was an invasion of his privacy.

After acknowledging that the employer has a responsibility to insure that its drug testing procedures are scientifically sound, the court held that the test procedures were the most advanced procedures available and that the second test confirmed the results of the first.

Regarding Jevic's privacy invasion claim, the court acknowledged that while the process of urination is a private act, Jevic's suit did not complain that his privacy was invaded during the procurement of the sample. The court rejected Jevic's privacy invasion claim, noting that

he had signed two consent statements, that he had voluntarily participated in the test, and that there was no law or constitutional provision
in New Jersey that prohibited a private employer from conducting a
drug test.[1]

The intrusive nature of drug testing has resulted in numerous privacy
invasion claims, even in cases like this one, in which a job candidate consents to
take the test. Other kinds of medical and psychological tests, while providing
employers with useful information, have caused great havoc for employers in
the form of privacy invasion claims. A psychological test inquiring about religious beliefs and sexual practices was held unlawful. Medical tests used for
purposes other than those authorized created a legal claim. Tests for AIDS
violate various state laws and the federal disability law. And tests that evaluate
skills unrelated to a job's responsibility violate equal employment opportunity laws.

In a variety of legal forums, employees have claimed that medical, psychological, drug, and skill tests are an invasion of privacy. In this chapter, we
will examine four kinds of tests and provide guidelines on their proper use to
avoid privacy invasion and other legal claims:

- Medical tests and examinations that evaluate an individual's general
  physical health or determine ability to perform the physical requirements of the job
- Drug and alcohol screenings that involve lab work, used to identify impairment due to drugs and alcohol or recent use of illegal drugs
- Psychological tests that measure personality traits, work attitudes, and
  behavioral traits such as temperament, drive, sales orientation, and supervisory personality
- Skill or achievement tests that measure an individual's job knowledge
  and skills, such as tests for typing, keyboarding, or math

Take a Deep Breath:
Employer Use of Physical Exams

After accepting a job offer from a midwestern property management firm, an
accountant was scheduled for a physical exam before actually starting work.

1. *Jevic v Coca Cola Bottling of New York*, 5 IER Cases 765 (1990).

The employer had begun its practice of conducting physical exams for all new hires because most jobs involved travel to meetings, visits to properties, or physical activities of property maintenance. While job offers were contingent on an applicant's successful completion of the physical, the employer recognized its obligation to make a reasonable accommodation for qualified disabled individuals.

The accountant, it turned out, had a medical condition that required immediate surgery but that, once he recovered, would not affect his ability to perform job duties. The employer rescheduled the accountant's start date, permitting employment to begin after recuperation.

A physical exam like this one—administered to applicants *after* a job offer but *before* a starting date—is often the first medical test an employee may encounter during the employment process. A physical exam serves several purposes: it ensures that the candidate is physically able to perform job duties—especially when they are strenuous—and it provides a baseline assessment of the candidate's physical condition that can be used to help evaluate a subsequent workers' compensation claim.

But while a checkup may seem innocuous, the improper use of a physical exam can result in a privacy invasion or discrimination claim. For example, an employee may have a valid privacy invasion claim if an employer:

- Uses a physical exam to investigate aspects of an employee's condition that are not reasonably related to job issues
- Tests a woman for pregnancy without the woman's consent
- Tests for AIDS
- Allows unauthorized release of an employee's medical record

Discrimination may come into play if the employer violates the ADA. This federal law, which prohibits discrimination on the basis of handicap, also prohibits preemployment medical inquiries, such as asking questions regarding health or physical or mental condition during an interview or on a job application. It prohibits preemployment physical exams except after a job offer has been extended. The job offer may be conditioned on the employee's completion of the physical exam, provided that the following conditions are met:

- The medical exam must be given to all candidates in the designated job category(ies).
- Testing only certain kinds of candidates—say, individuals with disabilities—would violate the law.

Sample Policy: Physical Exams

XYZ Company conducts physical exams as part of its screening and hiring process to assure that employees are
physically able to perform job duties. The company will
make a reasonable accommodation for qualified handicapped individuals.

1. All newly hired employees are referred to a designated
    medical facility for a physical exam. The exam should
    be scheduled after the employee has accepted a job
    offer and before actually starting work.

2. The physical exam is paid for by the company. The
    exam will include only the elements needed to deter-
    mine the employee's ability to perform job tasks.

3. The employee shall be expected to sign a release stating
    willingness to participate in the exam and permitting
    release of the exam record to XYZ Company.

4. In the event that the company becomes aware of an
    employee's physical or mental disability, the department
    manager is responsible for considering what reasonable
    accommodation may be made.

5. Physical exam records are confidential. Physical exam
    records are stored separately from the employee's per-
    sonnel file and shall not be used as a basis for
    employment discrimination.

- Medical information must be kept in confidential files, separate from
  other personnel files.
- Information must be kept confidential except that supervisors may be
  informed of an individual's condition to handle work restrictions or accommodations.[2]

2. *Americans with Disabilities Act of 1990, EEOC Technical Assistance Manual* (Chicago:
   CCH, 1992), Sec. 6.4.

Critical Issues in Use of Physical Exams

Preemployment inquiries into a candidate's private medical condition are prohibited under the ADA and many state civil rights laws. This means that an employer should not ask private questions about a person's health or prior illnesses. A physical exam may be permitted if it is done after the candidate has accepted a job offer. Employers generally make a job offer contingent on the candidate's successful completion of the physical exam. When the candidate accepts the job offer, he or she is referred to a medical facility for the physical exam. If a disability is identified, the employer must make a reasonable accommodation for the condition. AIDS is considered a disability under the ADA. AIDS testing is prohibited by law in some states.

Sample Employee Notice:
Physical Exams

Upon accepting a job offer, all new employees are expected to complete a physical exam as a condition of employment. The cost of the exam is paid by the company. Its purpose is to ensure that employees are able to perform job duties. The company will make a reasonable accommodation for qualified disabled workers.

The Drug Testing Controversy

Of the many testing procedures available to employers, drug testing may be the most controversial. Employees often voice very strong opinions about drug tests. A leading employee concern is that mandatory drug tests are a form of oppressive management control. Particularly offensive is a required drug test when the employee has done nothing wrong. Consider the comments of this employee, quoted in the *Chicago Sun-Times:*

> If an employer has no evidence or reason to suspect any wrongdoing (whether it be drugs or anything else), then why should people

who are not guilty have to prove themselves innocent? . . . When an employer has a mandatory drug screening for hiring, one should be alerted instantly that this employer wants absolute control over the behavior and thoughts of its employees. A "shut up and do what you're told" attitude will fail over the long haul.

Another common concern expressed by employees is that management will use the specimens for other tests not authorized by the employee or to reject certain individuals in order to reduce health insurance costs. Said one employee, urging caution:

As a non–drug user, you might expect that I would be in favor of drug testing, and I might be, if it were not for the many other potential uses of drug or urine tests made possible by medical technology today. These tests reveal things about people that they might not want anyone else to know, or may or may not even know themselves, such as pregnancy, high cholesterol or the risk of prostate or breast cancer. This is just a fraction of what can be revealed by a blood test.

It is possible that a not-so-ethical employer could have these tests performed, in addition to the drug tests, to keep medical insurance costs down, to minimize maternity or other medical leaves or for any other excuse not to hire or promote someone. If a company can demand a drug test to become employed, what's to prevent it from doing so to remain employed as well?

Employees sometimes feel that they bear the brunt of testing and that others should be tested as well. As one employee, said, "If I was going to have surgery, I should be able to know that the doctor is drug-free, too. Why limit testing to employees?" Some individuals question the whole testing process, asserting that there are ways to foil the test procedure. Said one individual: "Drug tests are totally worthless. I know plenty of people who use drugs and find ways to cover it up and have even used other people to take the test for them."[3]

Despite the controversy, companies continue to use drug tests because they are an effective tool in identifying drug users in the workplace. A survey by the American Management Association found that 81 percent of major cor-

3. Sue Morem, "Job Drug Tests Raise Opposition, Warnings," *Chicago Sun Times*, Jan. 27, 1997, p. 42.

porations test employees or new hires for illegal drug use, compared to only 22 percent of firms conducting drug testing ten years ago. One-third of all U.S. job seekers are tested for drugs, compared to less than 10 percent when the AMA study began in 1987. Periodic or random testing of employees has increased substantially from 2.5 percent in 1987 to the present rate of 34 percent of surveyed firms.[4]

According to AMA data, the test-positive rate for the half-million job seekers in the survey sample rose slightly to 4 percent in 1995, up from 3.8 percent the year before. The test-positive rate for employees subject to drug tests was 1.9 percent, compared to 2.5 percent test positives in 1993 and 4.2 percent in 1990. The apparent decline is attributed to an increase in the use of random testing rather than a decline in drug use, caution AMA test administrators.[5] Another study released by SmithKline Beecham Clinical Laboratories, which provides drug testing services for employers, revealed that slightly more than 3 percent of U.S. transportation industry workers tested positive for drugs. Of job applicants tested by SmithKline, 4.2 percent tested positive for drugs. In the general workplace, 13.8 percent of applicants and employees tested positive for drugs.[6]

Drug testing occurs at various phases of the employment process:

- *Preemployment drug screens* are required of an individual before he or she is hired. Generally, the firm makes a job offer contingent upon the successful completion of the drug test. A test result showing the presence of drugs in the body is grounds for withdrawing the job offer and denying employment.
- *Incident or cause testing,* conducted as a result of misconduct or disruptive behavior or other cause, is part of management's investigation of the incident. Generally, only the employee or employees involved in the incident are referred to a medical facility for the drug test.
- *Postaccident testing* is scheduled immediately for an individual involved in a workplace accident or an accident occurring while operating a vehicle on the job.
- *Random testing* tests randomly selected employees on a periodic basis.

4. "Drug Testing of Employees, New Hires on the Increase," *Policy & Practice Update,* May 2, 1996, p. 3.
5. Ibid.
6. "Drug Testing of Applicants," in *Personnel Practices/Communications* (Chicago: CCH, 1991), Par. 326.

- *Universal testing* requires all employees to take a scheduled or unscheduled drug test. It is used when management believes that a serious drug problem exists.

Drug testing continues to lead the tug-of-war between employee privacy rights and management rights. Even though employers have found drug testing to be an effective tool in identifying drug users in the workplace, the resulting employment decisions have lead to numerous privacy invasion claims.

- Railway employees claimed that mandatory drug tests following an accident violated their constitutional rights to protection from unreasonable search and seizure.
- Government employees filed a privacy invasion claim over a policy that required employees to provide a urine sample under direct supervision.
- Teamsters alleged that a supervisor's observations were insufficient cause to require a drug test.
- Government workers in non–safety-sensitive positions alleged that a drug testing requirement was an unwarranted intrusion and privacy invasion.
- An oil drilling worker who gave a urine sample during a mandatory physical exam alleged a privacy invasion because the urine was tested for drugs without his knowledge or consent.[7]

Urination Privacy Expected

While employees have raised a variety of legal challenges to drug testing, in many instances the court has upheld drug tests because an employer's interest in ensuring safety outweighs an employee's concerns about privacy.

Government employees receive certain protections, because the U.S. Supreme Court long recognized that "compelled intrusions into the body for blood to be analyzed for alcohol content" are Fourth Amendment searches. However, the courts have granted some latitude to government employers. In one case, the Supreme Court upheld postaccident alcohol and drug testing by the Federal Railroad Administration, noting that a warrant is not needed to make a search (in this case, a drug test) reasonable, but a search must be based on probable cause. Further, the Court noted that urine testing presented realistic privacy questions because an individual's process of urination is "tradition-

7. "Drug/Alcohol Testing," IERM 509:101–122.

ally shielded in privacy." In spite of these issues, the court held that the government's compelling interest to ensure public safety by requiring that rail workers not be impaired outweighs the minimal intrusion on employee privacy rights.[8]

Because the constitutional claims raised against governmental employers generally do not affect private-sector employers, private-sector employers are free to conduct drug testing unless specifically limited by a state law. However, they must use reasonable drug testing practices to avoid a common-law privacy invasion claim.

Generally, private-sector employees have not been successful in making claims against an employer's drug testing procedure when the employer can show that its policy complied with the law. In California, for example, the Privacy Initiative in the California Constitution provides privacy protections for employees in both public and private sectors of that state. The preemployment drug testing procedures of the California-based Times Mirror Corporation withstood a legal challenge by job applicant Wilkensen. The court held that there was no privacy invasion where job applicants had advance notice of the policy, the testing was part of a regular preemployment physical exam conducted by medical personnel, test procedures were minimally intrusive, and safeguards were in place to restrict access to these test results.[9]

Likewise, when a Massachusetts employee named Folmsbee was fired for refusing to participate in an employer-directed drug test, he sued his employer, Tech Tool Grinding & Supply. The Massachusetts court upheld the employer's action because the employee failed to comply with a lawful policy that provided a reasonable interference to employee privacy.[10]

A similar result was obtained in Nebraska, where employee Ritchie challenged his employer, Walker Manufacturing.

> Concerned about drug abuse on its premises, Walker issued a drug policy stating that the company may require a drug test of persons suspected of using drugs or being under the influence of drugs or alcohol while on the job and that a positive test result or refusal to take a test may result in discharge. To detect drug use among its employees, Walker hired a private investigator who identified Ritchie as using or being under the influence of drugs on company time and property.

8. *Skinner v Railway Labor Executives Association,* 489 US 602 (1989).
9. *Wilkensen v Times Mirror,* 4 IER Cases 1579 (1989).
10. *Folmsbee v Tech Tool Grinding & Supply,* 9 IER Cases 789 (1994).

As a result of the investigator's findings, Ritchie was ordered to take a drug test. Ritchie refused and was fired according to company policy. Ritchie sued, claiming that the employer's action was a privacy invasion, in violation of a Nebraska law. Ritchie cited a portion of the law saying that any person that intrudes on a person in his or her place of solitude in a way that is highly offensive to a reasonable person is liable for an invasion of privacy. The court sided with the company, noting that the privacy invasion stated was not interpreted under Nebraska law to include drug tests, that Nebraska law did not prohibit employers from conducting drug tests or firing employees who refuse to take a test, and that Ritchie was identified as a suspected user in line with the company's policy.[11]

However, employers may run afoul of the law if drug testing procedures do not comply with state laws, as Home Depot found out in a Connecticut court.

Jeffrey Doyon, a salesperson in the Southington, Connecticut, Home Depot Store, was moving a pallet of mulch with a forklift when the load shifted and a few bags of mulch fell onto a customer's truck, causing over $200 damage. As required by the Home Depot substance abuse policy, Doyon submitted to a drug test. When it indicated that Doyon had tested positive for marijuana, Doyon was fired.

Doyon sued Home Depot, claiming that the discharge was in violation of a Connecticut statute prohibiting employers from requiring employees to undergo drug testing unless the employer has a reasonable suspicion that the employee is under the influence of drugs or alcohol. In his claim, Doyon argued that mere occurrence of a serious accident does not establish a reasonable suspicion. The court noted that both Doyon and the company acknowledged that the accident occurred but there was no other independent suspicion of drug use by Doyon. The court found in favor of Doyon, saying that the Connecticut legislation was intended to prohibit mandatory postaccident drug testing. The court said that there must be some form of individualized suspicion of drug or alcohol use such as unusual behavior before an employee is required to take a drug test in Connecticut.[12]

11. *Ritchie v Walker Manufacturing*, 7 IER Cases 694 (1992).
12. *Doyon v Home Depot, USA*, 9 IER Cases 1079 (1994).

Sample Policy: Drug Testing

It is the policy of XYZ Company to maintain a drug-free workplace.

1. The human resources manager is responsible for development and implementation of workplace practices and controls as summarized by this policy.

2. Each employee is responsible for reporting in a fit condition to work. Employees must not attempt to work while under the influence of alcoholic beverages or illegal drugs. Also, each employee shall acknowledge receipt of the company policy.

3. The manager is responsible for orienting his or her newly hired employees about the company's drug policy, providing a copy of the drug policy, and obtaining the employee's signed receipt. The human resources manager shall periodically provide drug-free workplace employee awareness messages such as bulletin board postings, payroll stuffers, etc.

4. To promote safety and minimize the likelihood of drug abuse problems, job applicants who are considered for hire are required to successfully complete a drug screen test prior to starting work. The drug screen test is conducted with a postoffer physical exam. A job offer shall be extended to the candidate, conditioned on successful completion of the physical exam and drug screen.

5. Refusal to submit to the test or any "positive" test finding is grounds to withdraw a job offer or refuse to offer employment to the individual at the discretion of management. The requirements for participation in the physical exam and preemployment drug test also include individuals who were separated and rehired.

Sample Policy: Drug Testing

6. In the event that management becomes aware of an individual's physical or mental disability, the manager or supervisor is responsible for considering what reasonable accommodation may be made for the individual.

7. Any illegal manufacture, distribution, dispensing, possession, or use of illegal drugs on company time or premises is strictly prohibited and is grounds for discharge.

8. Any unauthorized possession, manufacture, distribution, dispensing, or other use of alcoholic beverages on company time or premises is strictly prohibited and is grounds for discharge. Alcoholic beverages may be served at company business or social functions as authorized by a company officer. In such instances, employees should use common sense and demonstrate moderation.

9. Any employee reporting to work under the influence of drugs, alcohol, or in an otherwise unfit condition to work may be subject to suspension without pay, referral for testing, or discharge, or other action as deemed appropriate by management.

10. Each manager is responsible for enforcing company rules and policies through use of corrective discipline up to and including discharge if necessary.

11. In the event of an altercation, accident, near-miss accident, driving under the influence (DUI) on company time or business, or other incident, a supervisor, upon conferring with a second-level manager and/or company president, may direct an employee to a designated medical facility for a drug screen as part of the investigation of the incident. Behavioral problems such as slurred speech, alcohol on breath, poor gait or

Sample Policy: Drug Testing

lack of coordination, or other irrational/inappropriate behavior, as judged by the supervisor, also are examples of reasonable grounds for a drug test.

12. Management may elect to schedule random drug testing if deemed necessary. When random drug testing is scheduled, designated individuals may be directed to participate in tests, or all employees may be directed to participate in the tests.

13. The following testing guidelines are provided:
    a) A supervisor shall drive the employee to the facility and coordinate any return transportation.
    b) The employee shall sign a consent form and receive regular pay for time lost from work, up to eight hours for the day.
    c) If the test result is negative (showing no drugs in the body), the employee shall return to work but may be subject to appropriate corrective discipline based upon management's investigation of the incident. In the event of a positive test result showing the presence of drugs, a second confirmation test shall be conducted.
    d) In the event of a confirmed positive test, the employee shall be referred for a chemical dependency evaluation and treatment if warranted.
    e) In the event that the chemical dependency evaluation counselor recommends inpatient or outpatient drug or alcohol rehabilitation treatment, the employee is expected to immediately begin such treatment. The employee shall be placed on a medical leave of absence as appropriate, and arrangements shall be made for any health insurance benefits as applicable.

Sample Policy: Drug Testing

f) If the employee refuses to submit to the drug test or refuses to cooperate in referral or recommended treatment, or in cases of subsequent incidents, the employee shall be subject to corrective discipline, which may include discharge.

14. In the event that an employee receives a positive test result, and management at its discretion elects to permit the individual's continued employment, the individual shall be subject to subsequent scheduled and/or random retesting as directed by management.

15. If an employee voluntarily seeks help regarding a drug or alcohol problem, he or she shall be referred to the human resources manager on a confidential basis. The human resources manager shall then refer the employee to an appropriate counseling or medical facility for assistance. In such cases, the employee may be placed on a medical leave of absence. Any medical costs arising from treatment may be filed under the group insurance plan as applicable.

16. An employee shall not be subject to corrective discipline for requesting medical treatment of drug or alcohol abuse if the request is the first such request or the second.

17. In the event of a question or complaint arising under this policy, the employee should speak first to his or her manager. If the matter cannot be resolved by the supervisor or manager, it may be referred to the human resources manager. If the matter is still unresolved, it may be referred to the company president for a final determination. All matters under this policy shall be treated as confidential.

Sample Form: Drug Testing: Preemployment Screening

PREEMPLOYMENT DRUG SCREEN
CONSENT FORM

To: _____
     Job Applicant

From: XYZ Company
Successful completion of a preemployment drug screen is a condition of employment at our company. You have been scheduled for a drug screen as shown below:

Test Appointment _____
Facility Name   _____
Address   _____
                   _____

Please check the appropriate box and sign in the space below to indicate your consent for the exam.

_____

CERTIFICATION

_____ I consent to the preemployment drug screen and authorize release of test results to XYZ Company. I understand that this test is solely for the benefit of XYZ Company to evaluate suitability for employment. I release XYZ Company and its employees, officers, and directors from any liability arising from participation in this test. Further, I understand that a positive test result showing the presence of drugs in the body is grounds for the company to withdraw or refuse to make an offer of employment.

_____ I do not consent to a preemployment drug screen. I understand that my refusal to participate in the exam is grounds for the company to withdraw or refuse to make an offer of employment.

_____   _____
Job Applicant   Date

Sample Form: Drug Testing: Accident Investigation

CONSENT FORM

To: _____ _____
      Employee   Date

From: XYZ Company

It is our goal to provide a productive, safe, and healthful workplace for all employees. As a result of the following altercation, accident, near-miss accident, DUI, or other incident:

_____

_____

Management has elected to refer you for a drug/alcohol screen test as part of its investigation.

CERTIFICATION

_____ I consent to the drug/alcohol screen and will cooperate by providing samples/specimens as directed and authorize release of test results to XYZ Company. I release XYZ Company and its employees, officers, and directors from any liability arising from participation in this test. I understand that a confirmed positive test result will result in a chemical dependency evaluation, and I will cooperate with the results of that evaluation.

_____ I do not consent to the drug/alcohol screen. I understand that my refusal is grounds for corrective disciplinary action, which may include discharge.

_____ _____
Employee   Date

Sample Employee Notice:
Policy Statement: Drug-Free Workplace

XYZ Company is committed to maintaining a drug-free work-place. Our policy is defined in the interest of good business practices. It is our goal to provide a productive, safe, and healthful working environment for employees.

Under the XYZ Company drug policy, any unlawful manufacture, distribution, dispensing, possession, or use of drugs or other controlled substances on company time, prem ises, customer premises, or while operating a vehicle on the job is strictly prohibited. In addition, any unauthorized possession or use of alcoholic beverages on the job as defined above is a violation of this policy. On occasions when alcoholic beverages are served at company business or social events, employees are reminded to use common sense and moderation. Our policy includes the use of a drug test to screen job applicants who are considered for hire. To promote safety for our employees and customers, it is our intention not to hire individuals when a positive test result shows the presence of drugs in the body.

The use or abuse of alcoholic beverages, drugs, or controlled substances while on the job is a leading cause of workplace injuries. Do not attempt to work or operate a vehicle while under the influence of drugs or alcoholic beverages. In the event an employee encounters work or personal problems related to use of alcoholic beverages, drugs, or other controlled substances, he or she is encouraged to seek appropriate medical care or counseling.

The human resources manager has information on substance abuse treatment programs. Information or referral will be provided on a confidential basis if requested by the employee. The company has group insurance benefits that currently provide insurance coverage for certain medical services related to drug or alcohol dependency treatment.

The company may use drug or alcohol testing as part of its investigation of an altercation, accident, near-miss accident,

Sample Employee Notice:
Policy Statement: Drug-Free Workplace

employee's irrational/inappropriate behavior, on-the-job driving under the influence (DUI), or other incident, or on a random basis.

You are expected to cooperate with any required drug/alcohol testing. Also, if testing shows the presence of drugs or alcohol in the body, you are expected to cooperate with any recommended treatment program. An employee's failure or refusal to submit to drug/alcohol testing or failure to cooperate in recommended treatment, or repeated instances of drug/alcohol abuse are grounds for corrective action, which may include discharge.

Under our drug policy each employee is responsible:

- To comply with the policy as a condition of employment
- To cooperate with and satisfactorily complete any medical treatment or testing program for drug/alcohol abuse if deemed appropriate
- To comply with the above policy requirements or be subject to corrective discipline, which may include discharge

_____   _____

Human Resources Manager   Date

_____

CERTIFICATION

I have received the XYZ Company drug policy and I agree to comply with this policy.

_____   _____

Employee   Date

The Doyon case interprets Connecticut law. Courts in other jurisdictions, applying other laws, may reach different conclusions. The central message is this: Check the law in your state when defining drug testing procedures.

Critical Issues in Drug Testing

Intrusive drug or alcohol searches conducted by the government are considered to be Fourth Amendment searches. But drug or alcohol testing conducted with reasonable cause does not require a warrant. In the balance between employee privacy rights and business needs, an employer can generally justify drug testing by safety or other similar reasons. Employers conducting drug testing should implement procedures that minimize the intrusiveness of testing, allow as much privacy and dignity as possible, and provide prior notice to applicants or employees. Conduct only those tests needed to determine the presence of drug use, use proper testing procedures, and protect confidentiality of records.

Discharge of an employee for refusing to comply with a reasonable procedure will generally withstand a legal challenge. Drug testing is not limited or prohibited by the ADA. While the ADA provides specific limits to use of physical exams, it exempts drug testing from those limits, permitting employers to conduct preemployment drug tests and to reject candidates whose tests show the presence of drugs.

What Makes Him Tick? How Employers Use Psychological Testing

Workplace problems such as theft, drug or alcohol abuse, and violent behavior represent a major threat to productive, profitable business operations. These behavioral problems are often not detected during the traditional employee selection procedures, which are not designed to determine whether a candidate has a drinking problem, is prone to theft, or is an emotional "time bomb" capable of violent behavior. Because the typical supervisor, manager, or human resources specialist lacks sufficient training to deal effectively with these complex issues, some firms have turned to psychological testing to improve their hiring practices.

Psychological testing includes a variety of procedures that are intended to predict a certain aspect of an individual's behavior. Psychological tests have been developed to measure leadership potential, teamwork, assertiveness, honesty, integrity, attitudes toward theft, and other behavioral characteristics. Psychological tests can be used to screen in desired behavior traits or to screen out undesirable ones. By using these tests, employers hope to avoid hiring problem employees and to select individuals with the characteristics needed for success in a particular job.

Miami-based Burger King Corp., for example, developed a psychological test to address problems created by employee turnover. During the late 1980s, the fast food giant was recruiting plenty of workers and investing considerable resources in training them to meet the company's high customer service standards, only to have many recently hired employees leave to accept entry-level jobs at other companies.

With the help of industrial psychologists, Burger King implemented a psychological test battery to aid employee selection by predicting such behavior characteristics as commitment to tenure, work values, customer relations, and safety. The paper-and-pencil test of 100 multiple choice questions could be completed by job candidates in thirty to forty-five minutes. Under a controlled study of test results in a target area, Burger King determined that the average monthly turnover rate in the experimental group decreased from 21.7 percent to 11.6 percent while turnover actually increased in the control group where the new procedures were not used. Burger King estimated its savings between $2 million and $3 million in turnover costs alone.[13]

While the Burger King test was used to identify and avoid hiring candidates with certain behavior traits, Minneapolis-based food distributor Monarch/Minnesota used the Sales Professional Assessment Inventory (SPAI) to identify sales representatives capable of helping the firm to meet its aggressive sales growth goal. Developed by London House of Rosemont, Illinois, the SPAI included about 200 multiple choice questions and took about an hour to complete. The test was intended to identify candidates possessing traits needed for success in sales, including energy level, sales skills, sales interest, and sales experience.

Monarch/Minnesota documented the effectiveness of the test by administering it to fifty-one of its current sales reps and then monitoring performance results. It found that sales reps receiving higher test scores subsequently received higher performance ratings from superiors and achieved average sales of over $1 million compared to sales records averaging $680,000 for those testing lower.[14]

---

13. Scott L. Martin and Loren P. Lehnen, "Select the Right Employee through Testing," *Personnel Journal*, June 1992, p. 47.
14. Ibid., 49.

Psychological tests probe into a variety of issues and attitudes when screening in desirable traits or screening out unwanted behavioral characteristics. However, it is best to focus the inquiry on job-related issues. When a firm uses a psychological test to inquire about personal matters or probe into issues that are not reasonably job related, there is a potential for privacy invasion or other legal claim. Dayton Hudson Corp. learned this lesson the hard way when it used a psychological test to fill store security officer (SSO) positions in its Target stores in California.

> The SSOs observe, apprehend, and arrest suspected shoplifters. They are not armed but use handcuffs and may have occasion to use force against a suspect in self-defense. Dayton Hudson administered a test called Psychscreen as a condition of employment. The test consists of 704 true-false questions, and SSO applicants were instructed to answer every question. The test was scored by a consulting psychologist firm with a rating and report on each candidate provided to Dayton Hudson.
> SSO applicants Sibi Soroka, Susan Urry, and William d'Arcangelo were upset by the test and felt that the test was an invasion of their privacy. Among the questions that they objected to were the following:
>> "I feel that there is only one true religion."
>> "A minister can cure disease by praying and putting his hand on your head."
>> "I go to church almost every week."
>> "I believe there is a God."
>> "I have never been in trouble because of my sex behavior."
>> "My sex life is satisfactory."
>> "I am very strongly attracted by members of my own sex."
>> "I have never indulged in any unusual sex practices."
>
> Soroka and the others ultimately filed a class-action suit against Dayton Hudson alleging that the test violated their privacy rights and fair employment practices protected by the California Constitution and state laws. The court held that the employer's psychological test violated privacy rights guaranteed by the California Constitution when it screened applicants with questions relating to religious beliefs and sexual orientation. Further, the religious beliefs questions violated the California Fair Employment and Housing Act, and the sexual orientation questions violated the California labor code.[15]

15. *Soroka v Dayton Hudson*, 6 IER Cases 1491 (1991).

Privacy concerns have also been expressed about tests designed to determine the integrity of the applicant by measuring attitudes toward theft and the likelihood of theft-type behavior. Used to screen job candidates for jobs in retail, warehouse, or other jobs where theft is a concern, "honesty" tests generally have true-false, yes-no, or multiple choice questions. Honesty tests were examined by the U.S. Office of Technology Assessment (OTA), which estimated that even though five to six thousand businesses use honesty testing to aid in selecting employees, there is no conclusive evidence that the tests accurately predict behavior. Another study conducted by the American Psychological Association encourages use of the tests for preemployment screening.[16]

While there are no federal laws regulating use of honesty tests, the Supreme Court ruled in the Duke Power case (discussed later in this chapter) that test and selection criteria must be related to the job. Further, the EEOC Uniform Guidelines for Employee Selection Procedures, which regulate employment tests, state that tests must be validated if they result in an adverse impact to protected-class individuals.

The increased threat of workplace violence also prompts employers to find new ways to head off potential tragedies. According to a survey by SHRM, nearly half of 1,016 human resources professionals surveyed have had at least one violent incident or threat since 1994. Over half of the incidents involved threats or attacks by one employee against coworkers or supervisors, rather than from an outside nonemployee source. The survey data reflects a 25 percent increase over a similar survey conducted by SHRM in 1993.[17] As a result, some violence prevention experts suggest using psychological tests to identify violence-prone employees.

But testing current employees opens up privacy questions and possible ADA violations. The EEOC recognizes psychological tests as medical tests. This means that there must be a business necessity for the test, a job-related purpose, and an obligation to make a reasonable accommodation if a disability is identified.[18]

Critical Issues in Use of Psychological Testing

The effectiveness of psychological tests has been questioned by some and enthusiastically supported by others. To minimize likelihood of legal claims, it is

16. "Pen and Pencil Integrity Tests," in *Personnel Practices/Communications* (Chicago: CCH, 1991), Par. 306A.
17. *Employee Relations Weekly* (BNA) 14 (July 1, 1996): 74.
18. "Psychological Testing Urged as Defense," *Employee Relations Weekly* (BNA) 14 (Nov. 11, 1996): 1207.

Sample Policy: Psychological Testing

XYZ Company conducts psychological testing to aid in evaluating job candidates prior to hire or placement into designated jobs.

1. Psychological testing is used to aid in evaluation of job candidates subject to a high degree of stress on the job. Candidates for the following jobs will be subject to psychological testing: security, field sales, customer service, collections, and executive management.

2. Psychological testing is considered to be a medical test and shall be administered after the candidate has accepted a job offer.

3. In the event that the psychological test identifies a medical disability, the hiring manager shall consider what reasonable accommodation may be made.

4. Issues addressed in any psychological test shall be limited to job-related issues needed to evaluate the individual's ability to perform essential job functions.

5. The same test(s) shall be administered to all selected candidates for the respective jobs.

6. Test records are medical records and shall be maintained in a medical file separate from the employee's personnel file.

7. All test results are confidential. Results may be viewed only by a manager evaluating the information on a job candidate.

8. Candidates shall be advised that selection to the specified positions will result in psychological testing as part of the selection process.

Sample Employee Notice:
Psychological Testing

XYZ Company takes pride in maintaining a high degree of professionalism in serving our customers. In order to select individuals meeting our high standards of professionalism, candidates for the jobs listed below are subject to psychological testing.

important to show a clear business purpose for the test, limit its inquiry into those areas that are related to job performance, and protect confidentiality of test results. Avoid inquiries that probe into private aspects of employees' lives. If psychological testing is used, it is best to work with an industrial psychologist experienced in development, administration, and interpretation of employment tests.

But Can He Type? A Look at Skill Testing

At the Dan River Station of Duke Power Company in Eden, North Carolina, where high school dropout Willie Griggs was a laborer, jobs were grouped into five categories: operations, maintenance, laboratory and test, coal handling, and labor. Duke Power required new employees and candidates for promotion to higher level jobs to have a high school education and to have satisfactory scores on the E. F. Wonderlick Personnel Test (an intelligence test) and the Bennet Mechanical Comprehension test (a mechanical aptitude test).

Griggs was one of fourteen black employees at Duke Power, all of them in lower paid laboring jobs. Because none of them had a high school education, the effect of the company's policy was to deny promotion and opportunity to Griggs and other black workers. Griggs and his fellow laborers filed suit against Duke Power claiming that the requirements for promotion had a discriminatory effect against blacks. In its defense, the company claimed that the education requirement was applied equally to candidates of all races and that it was not intended to discriminate against a particular race.

In this case, which ultimately reached the U.S. Supreme Court, the court held in favor of Griggs and his fellow workers. The court noted that neither the high school education requirement nor the intelligence test nor the mechanical aptitude test were shown to be a measure of job performance. Further, even though the test requirements did not intentionally exclude blacks, there was a discriminatory effect because a greater proportion of blacks did not have a high school education.[19]

When a test screens out proportionately more protected-class individuals than the general working group, and it is not shown to be a direct measure of the job, the test is discriminatory and in violation of the 1964 Civil Rights Act. The Court summarized its point in this fashion, "Nothing in the [Civil Rights] Act precludes the use of testing or measuring procedures . . . what Congress has commanded is that any tests used must measure the person for the job and not the person in the abstract."

Equal employment opportunity laws prohibit use of employment tests or other selection procedures that discriminate on the basis of race, color, sex, religion, national origin, age, and disability. Antibias laws in certain states define other protected-class categories. The EEOC's Uniform Guidelines on Employee Selection Procedures state that employers may not use tests that intentionally or unintentionally screen out a particular protected-class group unless the test has been validated. According to the EEOC guidelines, a test must relate to some aspect of the job, and it must be a true measure of the skill or ability that is being tested.

Examples of tests that conform to these guidelines are typing tests for typists, keyboard tests for data entry operators, math tests for bookkeepers, or measuring tests for material cutters. Each one measures an individual's ability to perform certain job functions and gives candidates an opportunity to demonstrate that they can actually perform a task proficiently. Each is job related and a valid measure of the skill being tested.

Another way to test candidates and meet these guidelines is to prepare a sample of work activity for the job being tested. The test should use actual work samples; simulated examples may be used if actual work data would create a confidentiality problem. The more closely the sample simulates actual

19. *Griggs v Duke Power,* 3 EPD Cases 8137 (1971).

work activity, the more accurate the test will be as a predictor of the candidate's skill. The skill test can be a paper-and-pencil test, a computer simulation, or other activity where the employee actually demonstrates a particular job skill.

Since a skill test is typically created by the employer, determining a passing score or pass-fail cutoff is also the employer's decision. It is recommended that the passing level or failing cutoff be similar to the work level of employees currently on the job. Take care to administer the test consistently using the same cutoff or pass-fail criteria for all candidates. Keep a test sample with the individual's application or in a test file.

Employment tests must not adversely affect individuals because of race, age, sex, religion, or other categories protected by antibias laws. A height requirement, for example, could adversely affect Hispanics, Asians, or women. But if the employer can show that the test relates to job requirements and fairly measures what the test intends to measure, then the test may be permitted as a valid test.

Critical Issues in Use of Skill Testing

Follow these procedures when administering employment tests to avoid incurring legal liability:

1. Make sure the test is directly related to skills used on the job. The best way to do this is to adapt actual work activities into a sample work test for the prospective employee. This will comply with the court requirements that test and selection criteria be job related.
2. Apply the test uniformly to all job candidates for a particular job. Do not give the test selectively to some candidates and not to others. This will help to avoid a discrimination claim.
3. Use a consistent approach for scoring, grading, or evaluating test results. To reduce the likelihood of a discrimination claim, do not set different levels for passing the test.
4. Protect confidentiality of test results and other application information.
5. Consider what reasonable accommodation in the testing process may be needed if testing a disabled individual.

In general, use of skill testing in employee selection is unlikely to result in a privacy invasion claim. However, take care to protect confidentiality of the individual's application and test results. Any inadvertent or deliberate release of information about an individual's background or test results could result in a privacy invasion claim.

Sample Policy: Skill Testing

XYZ Company conducts skill testing to aid in evaluating job candidates prior to hiring or placement into designated jobs.

1. A department manager may request use of a skill test as an aid in selection of job candidates. Any use of skill testing may be done only after conferring with and receiving approval from the human resources manager.

2. Skill tests must be developed based on actual tasks and skills performed on the job by incumbents.

3. The human resources manager and the department manager shall determine a passing or acceptable score on the test. As a general guide, the passing score should reflect a work level comparable to that of current employees performing satisfactorily.

4. In the event that a handicapped applicant is to be tested, the human resources manager shall consider alternative test measures that reasonably accommodate the candidate and provide a fair measure of individual skills.

5. The same tests shall be administered to all candidates for the designated job(s). Currently, the following tests are administered.

Accounting clerk: Math test, keyboard test
Secretary: Typing/keyboard test
Warehouse worker: Math test, number matching test

6. Tests shall be taken when the candidate prepares a job application prior to the job interview.

7. Test records shall be maintained with the individual's job application. All tests are confidential and must not be disclosed to anyone except managers evaluating a candidate's skills and experience for a job opening.

Sample Policy: Skill Testing

8. The human resources manager is responsible for evaluating test results annually to ensure that there is no adverse effect screening out minorities or females in greater proportions than other candidates.

Sample Employee Notice: Skill Testing

XYZ Company uses skill tests to aid in selecting the best qualified candidate for open positions. Skill tests are currently administered to candidates for the following positions:

Accounting clerk: Math test, keyboard test
Secretary: Typing/keyboard test
Warehouse worker: Math test, number matching test

The company will, of course, make a reasonable accommodation when necessary to evaluate skills of candidates with a disability. For further information or to request accommodation, contact the human resources department.

Summary

Employment tests play an important role in the employment process. Tests are used to aid in employee selection, to evaluate qualifications for employment, and to determine fitness for duty. Some tests, however, are invasive by nature and viewed by employees as an invasion of privacy. Particularly troubling to employees are drug tests, alcohol tests, medical exams, and psychological tests.

Testing procedures are subject to a variety of legal requirements. Certain laws limit use of medical exams and drug tests. Considerable litigation has focused on employer use of drug testing. But when an employer has defined a clear business purpose for testing, complies with applicable laws, uses the least invasive testing method available, and advises employees of the testing process, such testing has generally been permissible.

Appendix

Management Guidelines

Physical Exams

- Define the job groups or category(ies) of applicants that will be subject to physical exams.
- Make the job offer contingent upon successful completion of the physical exam.
- Schedule the exam after the candidate accepts the job, but before the start of work.
- If the physical exam identifies a physical or mental condition that limits the employee's ability to perform essential job functions, consider what reasonable accommodation may be made.
- Identify a business purpose to justify conducting the physical exam.
- Obtain from the employee a consent form granting disclosure of information to the employer.
- Require the physical exam for all individuals hired for a particular job or jobs.
- Limit the focus of the physical exam to medical issues that are reasonably related to job performance.
- Protect confidentiality of health and physical exam records.
- Store health and physical exam records separate from other personnel files.
- Check state laws for limits on who will pay for preemployment exams (certain states require employers to pay for preemployment exams).
- Do not use physical exams or other lab tests to check for AIDS. AIDS is considered a disability and a protected-class category under the ADA. Further, AIDS testing by employers is prohibited by various state laws.

Drug Testing

- Carefully evaluate and define jobs or job classes subject to drug testing.
- Identify whether testing will be done for preemployment screening, cause or incident testing, postaccident testing, or universal or random testing.

- Check local, state, and federal laws related to drug testing procedures or limits.
- Identify a specific purpose and business justification for testing.
- Consider alternative testing procedures and use the least intrusive procedures available.
- Consider and take steps to provide a reasonable degree of privacy and dignity in the testing process.
- Carefully evaluate testing labs or procedures to ensure use of proper testing procedures and chain of custody of specimens.
- Use of a medical review officer is recommended to evaluate positive test results and verify other factors that may contribute to a false positive.
- Use of a second confirmation test is recommended. Currently, the EMIT (enzyme multiplied immunoassay technique) is the recommended preliminary test; positive test results should be confirmed by the more sophisticated GC/MS test (gas chromatography/mass spectrometry technique).
- Define written testing guidelines to aid supervisors in consistently making employment decisions relating to identifying or referring individuals for drug testing.
- Train supervisors, managers, and human resources personnel to recognize and respond to employees who are under the influence of drugs.
- Provide advance notice to applicants and employees that drug testing will occur, the consequences of refusing to take the test, and consequences of a positive test result.
- Consider use of employee assistance plans or other referral for assessment and treatment in the event of positive test results.
- Negotiate with the union regarding drug testing of employees if there is a collective bargaining agreement with a union.

Psychological Testing

- Identify a specific business necessity and purpose for psychological testing.
- Check for state laws that may regulate, limit, or prohibit use of psychological testing.
- Recognize that psychological tests are considered medical exams by the EEOC. Therefore, if the tests are administered during the employee selection process, the tests must be administered after the job has been offered.
- Apply testing uniformly to all candidates for a specific job or job category.
- Identify specific job-related requirements that the test is intended to measure.
- Provide notice to candidates (or employees) that a psychological test will be used in the employee selection process.
- Protect confidentiality of test results.

- Avoid questions or inquiries into personal or other issues that are not reasonably related to job performance.

Skill Testing

- Check state and local laws relating to employment testing.
- Check the EEOC Uniform Guidelines on Employee Selection Procedures to avoid defining tests that violate the guidelines.
- Define skill tests based on actual tasks used on the job.
- Avoid using tests that adversely screen out members of a particular race, sex, or other protected-class category unless there is a clear business necessity for the test.
- Make sure that the test is job related.
- Define a uniform scoring process or cutoff, preferably measuring a skill level comparable to the expected work level on the job.
- Protect confidentiality of test results.

Q & A: Employee Rights Regarding Testing

Q *Can an employer use physical exams to screen out workers with injuries or illness?*

A The ADA prohibits firms from using preemployment medical inquiries or other inquiries focusing on an individual's medical condition or disability. Under the law, an employer may schedule a physical exam *after* the individual has accepted a job offer. The physical must be job related and be given to all individuals hired for the job, and the employer must make a reasonable accommodation for any physical or mental disability.

Q *Is drug testing a privacy invasion? Can an employer require employees to submit to drug tests?*

A Generally, an employer *can* require employees to submit to a drug test unless limited by law or labor agreement. Drug tests conducted by a government employer are considered Fourth Amendment searches, but a government employer that bases a drug test on reasonable cause does not require a search warrant according to the courts. Drug testing of transportation employees in safety-sensitive positions is required by law on a preemployment, postaccident, and periodic or random basis. Some state laws define limits or procedures that must be followed for drug testing. In the balance between individual privacy rights and business needs, employer safety concerns override individual privacy rights as long as the employer follows reasonable testing procedures.

Q *Psychological tests ask a variety of probing personal questions; what rights does an individual have when directed by an employer to take a psychological test?*

A   One firm's use of a psychological test that included questions about religious beliefs and sexual practices was found by the courts to be a privacy invasion. Where a test is related to job performance and does not probe into private aspects of the subject's life, and results are kept confidential, psychological tests have been found lawful and even helpful in certain employment decisions.

Q   *Many firms use tests when hiring or for other employment decisions; what rights do employees have regarding employment tests?*

A   Employer use of tests to aid in employment decisions does not create a privacy invasion. Testing is subject to antibias regulations. This means that any testing must be job related. An employment test that screens out a greater proportion of minorities or females may be discriminatory unless the employer can show that the test is a valid measure of successful job performance.

6

What's That You're Wearing?
Enforcing Dress Codes and
Controlling Conduct

Ann Hopkins was on the fast track to partnership in the Washington, D.C., office of Price Waterhouse, where she was responsible for helping win and carry out management consulting contracts with government agencies. Recognized for a string of outstanding accomplishments, including securing a multimillion dollar contract with the U.S. State Department, she received favorable client ratings and was regarded as a competent project leader who worked long hours.

When the partnership admissions committee began its deliberations on Hopkins's candidacy for partner, the firm's partners followed Price Waterhouse personnel policies and provided written comments on Hopkins's performance to the committee. While many comments were positive, several partners criticized Hopkins's interpersonal skills, suggesting that she was overbearing and abrasive. Comments implied that she was "macho," that she overcompensated for being a woman, used foul language, and should take a charm school course. Partners advised her to walk more femininely, talk more femininely, dress more femininely, wear makeup, have her hair styled, and wear jewelry.

Negative ratings, denial of partnership, and subsequent conflicts led Hopkins to resign and sue Price Waterhouse for sex discrimination in violation of Title VII of the Civil Rights Act of 1964, alleging that she was denied promotion due to sexual stereotypes and then forced to quit. The court agreed that Hopkins was the victim of discrimination because Price Waterhouse's ratings amounted to sexual stereotyping, which encouraged aggressive behavior by men but discouraged it among women.[1]

Most people consider what they wear, how they look, and what they talk about on the job private affairs, not company business. Yet employer policies on these matters often clash with employee sentiments. This chapter looks at these sensitive areas and determines "how much is too much" when it comes to controlling employee dress and conduct on the job.

Show a Little Thigh: The Ticklish Issue of Employer Dress and Grooming Standards

Dress and grooming standards are a key area in the tug-of-war between employer policies and an employee's personal life. Because garments, hairstyles, and jewelry express personality and taste—and may also reflect religious beliefs, national origin, or ethnic heritage—it's no wonder individuals are skeptical of efforts to enforce dress and grooming standards on the job.

Although workplace attire is gradually becoming more casual, most employers still expect employees to meet certain standards of dress and grooming. According to business publisher CCH, nearly a third (31 percent) of 366 companies surveyed say they have written dress codes. Nearly two-thirds of the surveyed firms reported using unwritten or informal dress policy guidelines. Only 10 percent of survey respondents reported that they had no dress policy guidelines.[2]

Employer-set dress and grooming standards have been challenged by employees and the government on grounds of discrimination rather than privacy invasion. Where the employer's dress or grooming standard adversely affects an employee because of a category protected by an antibias law, the employer is in violation of the law. Differing dress code standards for men and women, for example, run afoul of the law and may result in a sex discrimination complaint. Among standards found to be unlawful:

- Northwest Airlines's no-eyeglasses policy for women
- A cocktail lounge's requirement that a cocktail waitress wear "something low-cut and slinky" when she preferred wearing pantsuits

1. *Hopkins v Price Waterhouse*, 55 EPD Cases 40413 (1990).
2. "Dress/Grooming Codes: The Trend among Companies," in *Personnel Practices/Communications* (Chicago: CCH, 1991), Par. 2358.

- A retailer's requirement that female clerks wear smocks while males were permitted to wear business suits

The EEOC, the federal agency charged with enforcing the federal antibias law, has considered many cases concerning dress codes and grooming standards. Among its rulings:

- Male hair length does not fall within the protection of antibias rules because hair length, unlike race or sex, is not an immutable characteristic.
- Males-only neck tie rules were held to be lawful.
- Different hair length rules for men and women must be justified by business need.
- Limits on beards and mustaches have been justified for health and safety reasons.
- Limits on facial hair of police officers did not deprive the officers of their rights under the Constitution.
- Limits on hair or dress styles cannot be imposed against members of a race or religion unless there is a valid business need.[3]

Grooming standards that are directed toward race-linked physical characteristics violate that law. Greyhound Bus Lines' no-beard policy had a disparate impact against blacks because more blacks suffer a skin condition due to shaving.[4] Blue Cross Mutual Hospital Insurance's policy against the Afro hairstyle was found to be illegal.[5]

When an employer implements dress and grooming standards and applies them uniformly among both men and women, the policy most likely will withstand a legal challenge. Consider the case of Christine Craft, a television anchorwoman removed from her position because her dress and appearance were too unattractive.

Craft's employer, Metromedia, Inc., of Kansas City, had criticized Craft for her clothing and makeup. The station gave her a copy of the book *Women's Dress for Success* and assigned a clothing consultant to help her select outfits for on-air appearances.

3. Ibid.
4. *EEOC v Greyhound Lines,* 24 FEP Cases 7 (3d Cir 1980).
5. *Jenkins v Blue Cross Mutual Hospital Insurance,* 13 FEP Cases 52 (7th Cir 1976).

Although Craft claimed discrimination, the court found that Metromedia had instructed male on-air personalities on various appearance issues such as losing weight, getting a hairpiece, properly tying neckties, and avoiding certain garments. As a result, concluded the court, Metromedia had consistently sought to enforce a conservative dress code and did not stereotype Craft because of her gender.[6]

Health and safety issues also offer a strong justification for defining dress code limits. A manufacturing company was not required to accommodate an employee's belief that women should wear skirts since accommodation would have caused an undue hardship. The employer's rule prohibiting skirts and dresses was justified for safety reasons.[7] Likewise, in a case involving a construction site requirement that employees wear hard hats, the U.S. Supreme Court held that the First Amendment does not relieve anyone, on religious grounds, from the obligation of complying with a neutral generally applicable law. The Court acknowledged that the OSHA's hard hat rule is applicable under this theory.[8]

Business Justification: A Key Element of Dress and Grooming Standards

To minimize the likelihood of a legal challenge to its dress code, an employer *must* have a clear business justification for its standard. Equal employment opportunity laws generally permit the establishment of dress and grooming standards where the employer defines a business necessity. Most discrimination claims are based on different dress codes based on sex, or prohibitions on dress or appearance issues unique to ethnic heritage, race, or religion. The EEOC recognizes that different grooming standards may be permissible for each sex as long as the standards are reasonable and appropriate for the sex.[9]

Employers generally define dress guidelines for one of two reasons: public image or safety. Common examples of justifiable business necessity include the following:

6. Alfred G. Feliu, *Primer on Individual Rights* (Washington, DC: BNA, 1993), 219.
7. Ibid.
8. *Smith v Department of Human Resources, Employment Division,* 53 EPD Cases 39826 (1990).
9. "Dress and Appearance," in *Labor Law Course* (Chicago: CCH, 1987), Par. 5538.

Sample Policy: Safety Dress and Appearance

XYZ Company has developed a safety dress policy guideline for employees assigned to production and warehouse work. These dress guidelines prevent painful injuries by ensuring that employees are dressed properly for the work environment. Employees working in production and warehouse areas must wear:

- Safety glasses
- Sturdy leather work shoes with socks
- Long pants
- Shirt or blouse with long or short sleeves
- Hard hat when working in areas exposed to falling objects
- Personal protective equipment as specified by their supervisor

Employees in these areas are not allowed to wear:

- Athletic, open-toed, or high-heeled shoes
- Loose or dangling garments
- Rings or dangling jewelry

Disregard for the safety dress policy guideline will result in corrective discipline or discharge.

Sample Policy:
Dress and Appearance

An important part of XYZ Company's services is presenting a professional image to the customer. XYZ employees who deal with the public are expected to dress in a clean and neat manner, upholding XYZ's high standards of professional conduct, appearance, and dress.

   1. The department manager is responsible for communicating dress and appearance guidelines to employees.
   2. The following dress guidelines are provided:

Hair should be trimmed and neatly combed.

Men are expected to wear traditional business dress including slacks with belt or suspenders, dress shirt, tie, socks, and dress shoes.

Women are expected to wear traditional business dress such as business suit or dress slacks, blouse or sweater, or dress; stockings; and dress shoes.

Jewelry is permitted as long as it is not excessive.

   3. The department manager is responsible for enforcing the dress guidelines. An employee may be sent home without pay to change if work garments are inappropriate.
   4. XYZ will make a reasonable accommodation to these guidelines for an employee's religious beliefs.

**Sample Employee Notice:
Dress and Appearance**

At XYZ Company, we strive to maintain a relaxed yet professional atmosphere. Our facilities are frequently visited by valued customers and prominent suppliers, so it is important for employees to dress in a neat and clean manner that is appropriate for a business environment. Remember that the company's reputation, as well as yours, is judged in part by your personal conduct and appearance. Employees are expected to dress in a clean and neat manner, appropriate for their respective job responsibilities and a business environment.

Dress attire such as slacks, suit, and tie for men, or dresses, suits, skirts, or slacks for women are deemed appropriate. Casual garments such as denims, halters, sweatshirts, thongs, or sandals are not permitted.

Identification of individuals as employees of the firm. Century 21 real estate agents wear distinctive gold sport coats; UPS workers are recognizable in their brown trucks and brown uniforms.

Identification of department, work function, responsibility, or authority. Many hospitals use garment styles and colors to distinguish between medical, nursing, lab, housekeeping, and maintenance personnel.

Safety and accident prevention. Government safety regulations require that most employees in manufacturing and warehousing jobs exposed to hazards wear personal protective equipment such as hard hats, gloves, glasses or goggles, safety shoes, or other protective items.

Public image. Firms that deal extensively with the public often have detailed dress guidelines or even provide uniforms to ensure that employees convey a consistent appearance to the public. For example, airline employees wear uniforms that bear colors and style unique to that airline, making the employees walking billboards that promote the employer's services.

Prevention of distractions. Many employers define dress code rules such as "no 'short shorts,' no tank tops, no bare midriff," because such garments can be distracting to other workers.[10]

Critical Issues in Dress and Grooming Standards

Because employees react strongly when told to dress in a particular fashion, employers need to exercise considerable care when defining dress and grooming standards. Be sure to clearly identify a business necessity for establishing the dress code policy, such as safety, public image, or security reasons. Dress or grooming standards that single out a race, sex, religion, or other protected class violate civil rights laws. Carefully evaluate your policy to ensure that it has no discriminatory effect. Also, take care to communicate the reason and purpose of the dress or appearance requirement to employees.

Wanna Buy Some Cookies?
Controlling Solicitation and Distribution

Can an employee sell Girl Scout cookies, raffle tickets, or cosmetics, housewares, or other products to fellow employees?

Should employees be able to "spread the word" about their religious organization and urge others to participate?

Shall a union seeking to organize an employer's workforce be able to gain access to employees at the workplace and enlist employee activists to solicit other employees about union membership?

Is it an invasion of a worker's privacy when the employer creates a policy limiting topics of discussion on the job or prohibiting discussion of religion on the job?

Like personal appearance, personal, off-work activities that spill into the workplace are a source of contention between employers and employees. Although such nonwork selling and proselytizing can be a disruption to em-

---

10. William S. Hubbartt, *Personnel Policy Handbook: How to Develop a Manual That Works* (New York: McGraw-Hill, 1993), 396.

ployee productivity on the job, employer control of employee solicitation or distribution of literature in the workplace can result in legal claims.

On one hand, the employer has a legitimate business need to manage and control activities on the job during working time and in working areas. On the other hand, certain employee activities on the job are protected under the law. Employee solicitation and distribution activities have resulted in litigation under federal labor relations laws and equal employment opportunity laws rather than as privacy invasion claims.

Employer no-solicitation policies are often formed to counter union-organizing activity. Relations between employers and unions are regulated by the National Labor Relations Act (NLRA) and a series of related laws. The employer is generally able to prohibit union activity on company time and to exclude nonemployee union organizers from company property.[11]

In one case that went all the way to the U.S. Supreme Court, Babcock and Wilcox Company was allowed to prohibit nonemployee union organizers from distributing literature on company property if an alternative means of communication was available and the employer did not discriminate by allowing distribution by other nonemployees. But the Court also held that the no-solicitation rule may not be applied to organizers who are employees. Said the Court, "No restrictions may be placed on the employees' right to discuss self-organization among themselves, unless the employer can demonstrate that a restriction is necessary to maintain production or discipline."[12]

While the employer is free to regulate employee activities during working time and in working areas, employer rules that limit solicitation during breaks, lunch, or other nonworking times have been held to be an unfair labor practice. In part, the NLRA permits employees to organize and bargain collectively, as long as such activities occur in nonworking time and nonworking areas.

It is important to control all forms of solicitation and distribution in order to avoid an unfair labor practice charge. An employer who tolerates other types of employee solicitation during working time and singles out union-organizing activity for prohibition is committing an unfair labor practice.

Employer regulation of an employee's religious solicitation must be handled with care to avoid a claim of religious discrimination under equal employment opportunity laws. An employee at one midwestern manufacturer, for example, distributed religious literature to coworkers, contacted other workers

11. *Labor Law Course* (Chicago: CCH, 1987), Par. 1582.
12. *NLRB v Babcock and Wilcox*, 28 Labor Cases 69209 (Chicago: CCH, 1956).

Sample Policy: Solicitation and Distribution

In order to avoid disruption to operations, XYZ Company
has established the following rules related to solicitation and
distribution of literature on company property.

1. Nonemployees may not solicit or distribute literature on
   company property at any time for any purpose.

2. Employees may not solicit or distribute literature during
   working time for any purpose.

3. Employees may not distribute literature at any time in
   public areas or in working areas. Working time includes
   the working time of both the employee doing the soliciting and distributing and the employee to whom the
   soliciting or distributing is being directed. Working time
   does not include break periods, meal periods, or any
   other specified periods during the work day when
   employees are properly not engaged in performing their
   work tasks.

This policy applies to non–job-related contacts between an
employee and other employee(s), nonemployees, vendors,
customers, prospects, sales representatives, or any other
solicitation on behalf of any social, fraternal, religious, or
other organization or non–job-related activity. Employees
engaged in such activity are not properly performing
assigned job tasks and are distracting others from their job
tasks. Such behavior will be subject to corrective action.

at home to invite them to religious retreats, and displayed religious literature throughout the office. When company management directed him to stop his religious displays and contacts, the employee claimed that he was being discriminated against because of his religious belief.

In responding to this situation, the employer had to balance the employee's right to be free from religious discrimination with other employees' rights to be free from the harassment of unwanted solicitation. In the end, the company developed a carefully worded policy that prohibited solicitation and distribution on working time and in working areas and a prohibition against harassment of others.

Critical Issues in Controlling Solicitation and Distribution

Employers don't generally try to regulate employee private or personal conversations on the job. However, when employee conversations disrupt work activity, constitute fund raising, or solicit for nonwork activities such as union membership, the employer has a business interest in preventing or controlling the discussion. Employee legal claims for solicitation and distribution issues are generally presented under labor relations and antibias laws rather than as privacy invasion claims.

When taking action to control solicitation and distribution, avoid singling out union activity or religious appeals. Rather, take care to define a policy that broadly covers all solicitation or distribution. It is permissible to prohibit all nonemployee solicitation and to limit employee solicitation to nonworking times and nonworking areas. Be sure to uniformly apply the policy.

Summary

When personal appearance and personal activities clash with company procedures and employee productivity, litigation may result. By identifying a business justification for dress code policies—such as safety or business image—and developing such policies in a way that does not create a discriminatory practice, the employer can create a lawful dress code. An employer also has a reasonable justification for controlling non–work-related solicitation and distribution by employees when they occur in working areas during working time. But care should be taken to avoid defining policies that discriminate against gender, race, religion, unions, or other protected categories.

Appendix

Management Guidelines

Dress Code Policy

- Define a clear business purpose for your dress or appearance policy.
- Allow for a reasonable accommodation for religious beliefs of employees.
- If work garments or uniforms are required, define what job(s) or categories of employees are covered and apply the policy uniformly to both sexes.
- Communicate the purpose of the policy to employees.
- Define safety-related dress requirements and enforce them with disciplinary action if necessary.
- Define policy guidelines for what should be worn on the job, recognizing that different dress requirements may be suitable for different jobs.
- Define dress or appearance standards detailing prohibited garments or practices.
- Avoid defining dress requirements merely to respond to customer preferences.

Controlling Solicitation and Distribution

- Recognize that management has a reasonable right to manage and control activities that occur during working time and in working areas.
- Avoid the tendency to single out specific groups or activities when limiting solicitation or distribution.
- Define solicitation and distribution rules broadly covering all non–work-related activity.
- Distinguish between casual conversation among employees and assertive or unwanted solicitation directed toward others.
- Recognize that nonwork time includes breaks, lunch periods, before work, and after work and that generally employees are allowed under law to conduct solicitations during these times and places.
- Retail organizations may prohibit an employee's personal solicitation in selling and in public areas.
- Nonemployee solicitors generally may be prohibited from company property.
- Publish and distribute your policy to all employees; enforce the policy uniformly for all employees.

Q & A: Employee Rights Regarding Dress Codes and On-the-Job Conduct

Q   *Can an employer specify a dress or grooming code or prohibit employees from wearing certain garments?*

A   An employer can define reasonable dress or grooming standards related to job performance or safety. Improper dress or grooming standards may violate state or federal equal employment opportunity laws. Dress or grooming rules applied differently for men and women constitute sex discrimination. Rules against dress or grooming practices unique to a particular race or religion violate the law. Customer preferences are not adequate justification for a discriminatory dress or appearance code. Worker safety or other business reasons are a reasonable basis for a job-related dress or appearance standard.

Q   *Can an employer prohibit an employee from soliciting membership in an organization or selling Girl Scout cookies and other fundraising merchandise to coworkers at work?*

A   Management has a reasonable right to control activities that occur during working time and in working areas. An employer can prohibit solicitation or distribution of literature during work time and in work or public areas. However, under federal labor relations law, an employee may engage in solicitation or distribution for union organizing in nonworking areas and in nonworking times. Nonworking times include lunch and break periods, before and after work, and other times when employees are not performing work tasks.

7

Living in a Glass House: A Look at Privacy in the Electronic Workplace

The electronic workplace: It's a whole new ball game. Although the players and the goal are the same as always, the pace of the game has quickened, and the rules have changed.

In the new high-tech workplace, computers have replaced calculators and drawing boards. Employees use computers to prepare documents quickly and efficiently. Facsimile machines transmit documents across the country in minutes. National or international meetings are conducted via video teleconferencing. And E-mail has sent those tattered interoffice mail envelopes to their eternal rest.

As E-mail, the Internet, and paging systems have revolutionized communications, they have created new areas of controversy over individual privacy in the workplace.

Sending Secrets on a Postcard: E-Mail Privacy Concerns

More than 20 million people use E-mail in the United States—including 60 percent of employees at Fortune 2000 Companies and 75 percent of respondents to a survey of members of SHRM.[1] As E-mail use continues to grow, the conflict between E-mail use and workplace privacy issues grows as well.

---

1. Jenny McCune, "This Message Is for You," *Beyond Computing* (Northbrook, IL), June 1996, p. 39.

In a typical E-mail system, the employee uses a personal password to log onto the system and access his or her private "mail box" for messages from other individuals or systemwide announcement messages sent by the employer. Typically, the user can read, save, download, print, or erase his or her messages, which are date and time stamped and generally backed up in the system. The user can also send messages to mail boxes of other E-mail users or to a "bulletin board" where they can be read by all system users.

The use of a personal password and mail box can lead employees to expect that E-mail communication between two individuals is as private as mail delivered by the U.S. Postal Service. But many companies who have found themselves in court have quickly discovered the opposite:

- An employee was fired for using profanity in the company's E-mail system.
- E-mail messages were used as evidence in a discrimination case and were critical in securing a $3.3 million verdict against the employer.
- An employee filed a privacy invasion claim after losing his job when his employer intercepted unprofessional E-mail messages.
- A West Coast company quickly settled a wrongful discharge lawsuit after a computer sleuth turned up incriminating messages that the employer thought had been deleted from the company's computer system.
- An employee filed a privacy invasion claim after a coworker accessed personal data about the employee on the company's computer system.

What first appears to be a private medium of conversation is not so private after all, as Microsoft learned when it sought to prevent E-mail messages from being entered as evidence in a sexual discrimination lawsuit. A Microsoft supervisor had sent numerous sexually oriented and derogatory E-mail messages. His messages referred to one coworker as the "Spandex Queen," offered a temporary receptionist money if he could call her "Sweet Georgia Brown," and referred to himself as president of the "Amateur Gynecology Club." Microsoft argued that the messages were private communication and irrelevant to a discrimination claim. The court disagreed and permitted the E-mail messages to be entered as evidence.[2]

As Microsoft's case shows, inappropriate use of E-mail creates serious liability potential for the employer and workplace privacy concerns for employees. All too often, E-mail messages tend to be more personal and more

2. "Technology Raises Legal Questions," *Workplace Visions* (SHRM), May/June 1996.

emotional than the restrained conversations and formal memos and written messages traditionally found in the workplace. Individuals may use the E-mail system to schedule a luncheon, arrange an after-work activity, coordinate commuting arrangements, or arrange a date. They may also use them to "flame" someone—send a message with a high degree of anger or emotion, resulting in vulgarity, sexual references, insults, or other unprofessional messages much like private conversation.

Messages exchanged by two employees of the Pillsbury Company in Pennsylvania landed them in trouble, even though Pillsbury had assured employees that communications in the company E-mail system were privileged and confidential and would not be intercepted or used for discipline or termination.

> Believing that their communications were confidential, Pillsbury employee Michael Smyth and his supervisor exchanged a variety of messages that contained derogatory comments and threats against others. The messages included threats to "kill the backstabbing bastards" in sales management. Another message allegedly referred to the office holiday party as the "Jim Jones Kool Aid affair."
>
> Pillsbury intercepted the messages and, despite prior assurances, terminated Smyth for unprofessional conduct. Smyth sued Pillsbury, claiming wrongful discharge and violation of his common-law privacy rights. In considering the facts of this case, the U.S. District Court in Pennsylvania stated that invasion of privacy claims require an intrusion that is substantial and highly offensive to the ordinary reasonable person. According to the court, Smyth did not have a reasonable expectation of privacy when using an E-mail system that was used by the entire company. Further, said the court, Pillsbury's interception of messages was not a substantial or highly offensive invasion of Smyth's privacy. The court stated that once Smyth voluntarily communicated messages over an E-mail system, any reasonable expectation of privacy was lost. The court further supported the company's action asserting that the company's interest in preventing inappropriate comments or even illegal activity by monitoring or intercepting E-mail messages outweighs an employee's privacy interests.[3]

Since E-mail systems may disseminate data outside the organization, there is a potential for careless or unauthorized release of confidential informa-

3. *Smyth v Pillsbury*, 11 IER Cases 585 (1996).

tion. Further, believing that their messages are confidential, employees may use the company E-mail system for personal work or even for illegal activities. As a result, employers are increasingly interested in monitoring E-mail systems. According to the Winter 1996 issue of *SHRM Legal Report*, 30 percent of firms employing over 1,000 workers engage in some form of electronic monitoring. Twenty-two percent of firms with fewer employees monitored employee E-mail transmissions. Of firms acknowledging that they engaged in electronic monitoring, over 73 percent reported that they searched employee computer files, more than 40 percent examined employee E-mail, and some 15 percent monitored employee voice mail messages. Yet less than one firm in five had a written policy regarding electronic privacy for employees![4]

More recently, an American Management Association survey revealed that nearly two-thirds (63.4 percent) of surveyed firms conduct some form of electronic monitoring or surveillance of employees. Of the 900+ medium-sized and large firms surveyed, 14.9 percent indicated that electronic mail messages were stored and reviewed, and 13.7 percent of firms monitor and review computer files. According to survey administrators, employers believe that what is done on company time and on company premises is the company's business.[5]

As E-mail use continues to grow, its role in litigation will increase also. E-mail has become evidence in court cases, as Microsoft and other companies have found.

> An E-mail message proved to be the proverbial skeleton in the closet for one firm that laid off a woman executive "because of a tough economy"—or so her bosses said. Feeling that she had not been dealt with fairly, the woman filed a lawsuit against her former employer. During the discovery phase of the lawsuit, the woman's attorney hired a computer expert to search the firm's computerized records relating to the case. He soon discovered an E-mail message, long since believed to be deleted by the company management. The message from the woman's supervisor to another manager read, "Get that b—— out of here as fast as you can. I don't care what it takes, just do it." Within hours of its retrieval, the company settled the lawsuit for a reported $250,000.[6]

4. D. Michael Underhill and Thomas A. Linthorst, "E-Mail in the Workplace: How Much Is Private?" *SHRM Legal Report*, Winter 1996, p. 1.
5. "Electronic Monitoring and Surveillance," American Managements Association survey published for AMA corporate members with the cooperation of *Employment Testing: Law & Policy Reporter* (University Publications of America, Bethesda, MD), 1997.
6. Jan Crawford Greenberg, "Lawyers Find Smoking Guns in E-Mail," *Chicago Tribune*, Sept. 24, 1995, p. 1.

Certain E-mail is subject to the ECPA, which expands federal wire tap laws to cover emerging technology. The law prohibits E-mail messages from being intercepted and disclosed to third parties except under the following circumstances:

- When consent is given by one of the parties
- When an employer identifies a specific business purpose for monitoring E-mail messages
- When interception of messages is necessary to provide the E-mail service—in other words, the E-mail service provider may need to check messages from time to time to make sure that the system is working properly and all transmissions are being sent and received properly

There are, however, conflicting legal opinions about whether the ECPA applies to messages sent on an E-mail system that is completely internal to a company. Some authorities suggest that the law applies to E-mail systems provided by public services and that messages on an employer's internal E-mail system are not protected by the law.[7]

Developing an E-Mail Policy

In spite of growing concerns about E-mail, a majority of firms using it have failed to define written policies about its use. Of the organizations surveyed by SHRM in 1996, less than 40 percent had written policies addressing employee privacy concerns, even though all of the firms surveyed reported that in emergencies the employer had needed to access information in an employee's private mail box.[8]

To comply with the law and to minimize potential privacy complaints, an employer using E-mail should develop and communicate a policy on E-mail privacy. An E-mail policy will help prevent abuse or misuse of the E-mail system, clarify privacy expectations, reduce tension about privacy invasion, and help to avert possible legal action. When developing an E-mail policy, it is important that the policy reflect the company's unique culture and manner of

---

7. Kent D. Stuckey, *The Internet and On-Line Law* (New York: Law Journal Seminars Press, 1996), 5-24.
8. Michael F. Cavanaugh, "E-Mail, Workplace Privacy Policies Lag Need, Employer Survey Finds," *HR News*, Feb. 1, 1996, p. 2.

dealing with employees. Among the issues to be considered are whether personal messages will be permitted, the level of privacy provided to system users, and the degree of monitoring to be conducted by the company.

These issues and others were considered when the Children's Television Workshop (CTW), creators of the *Sesame Street* television program, struggled to develop an E-mail policy. Should the policy allow unrestricted E-mail, or should there be protective guidelines? CTW settled on a series of soft E-mail guidelines that would promote open communication, rather than hard rules that might stifle creativity or innovation. CTW guidelines stated that the system should be used primarily for business purposes, that confidential information should not be sent on the network, and that information should be sent only to individuals who need it for the conduct of business.

The policy further directed users to respect the privacy of others, and prohibited privacy-violating snooping practices. Staff members, however, can access any E-mail box if there is a legitimate business need. E-mail messages directed to all staff must first have management approval in a manner similar to paper memo distribution. Also, users are reminded to keep their mail boxes uncluttered by using brief messages and by deleting messages after receipt.

To aid employees in determining what communication is proper and what isn't proper for the E-mail network, CTW developed a communication matrix. The matrix helps an employee use E-mail effectively, avoiding the clutter of meaningless messages that can bury an urgent message.[9] A sample of the matrix is shown in figure 7–1.

Critical Issues in E-Mail Use

An expanded federal wire tap law prohibits E-mail messages from being intercepted and disclosed to third parties except when consent is obtained. To avoid violating this law, experts recommend a sign-on disclaimer that reminds users that E-mail is company property and that defines the level of privacy permitted. The message may say that E-mail is for business communication only, subject to monitoring, and that using the system effectively constitutes consent to monitoring.

It is important to define an E-mail policy that reflects the firm's management style and culture. To avoid a privacy claim, users should be told that E-

9. Richard F. Fedrico and James M. Bowley, "The Great E-Mail Debate," *HR Magazine,* Jan. 1996, p. 69.

Figure 7-1 Communication Matrix

	E-Mail	Memo	Phone	Voice Mail	Employee Meeting	Fax	Video	Interactive PC	Company-Wide Announcement
Confidential									
Not confidential									
Limited distribution									
Wide distribution									
Information only—no outlet for response									
Idea sharing/ brainstorming									
Action/response required									
Approval sought									
Speed									
Simple message									
Complex message									
Personal/emotional message									
Two-way communication									

Copyright 1996 *HR Magazine*, Society for Human Resource Management, Alexandria, VA. Reprinted with permission.

Sample Policy: E-Mail Use

XYZ Company has developed the following policy relating to employee use of the company's electronic mail (E-mail) system.

1. The E-mail system is a form of official company communication. All computer terminals, modems, phone lines, and systems software are company property. Employees are permitted use of the company's property and must comply with company policies and procedures regarding its use.

2. The E-mail system is for business use only. Personal and other nonbusiness communications are not permitted. Likewise, non–job-related solicitation, selling, or dissemination of nonwork information or conduct of noncompany business is prohibited.

3. Offensive or improper messages or racial or sexual or other slurs are prohibited.

4. Employees are responsible for using their assigned access code for their E-mail box. Employees must not access or read E-mail messages directed to others.

5. Use of the access code does not mean that E-mail communications are private. The company may access and monitor E-mail messages. This message appears at log-on.

6. Confidential business information must not be sent through the E-mail system.

7. Employees must observe customary business communications practices as used in company correspondence. E-mail messages are official internal company communications, which may be subject to summons in legal proceedings.

Sample Employee Notice:
E-Mail Use

The XYZ E-mail system is company property, and it is a form of official business communication. Take care to use proper grammar and etiquette in all E-mail messages. Please do not consider E-mail to be private communication and do not use E-mail for confidential communication. To ensure that the system is operating properly, the company may, from time to time, monitor and access E-mail messages. Employees must not access or read communication directed to others.

mail is not private. Also, users should be instructed not to send sexual or other inappropriate messages. Users should be informed that E-mail records can become evidence in legal proceedings.

Always on Call: Paging System Privacy

These days, fast communication and prompt response to customer needs are a competitive edge that distinguish an organization from its competitors. Fast internal communication is critical when a key employee needs to be contacted quickly for information or a decision. When employees are scattered throughout a facility, community, or region, one economical way to maintain close communication is with a paging system.

Paging systems operate through a central paging service in a community or through a private paging system operated by the employer. The employee receives a pager, a small electronic receiving device that may be carried in a purse or pocket or on a belt. To reach an employee with a pager, the employer dials a telephone number assigned to the pager. The pager then receives a wireless telephone signal, which alerts the employee that he or she is being paged.

Early paging systems merely beeped or vibrated, showing the caller's number on a digital display. Newer, more sophisticated paging systems relay names and messages as well as numbers. When messages are communicated between employees on a paging system, employees may have some expectation of privacy.

> Two officers of the Reno, Nevada, police department found themselves in trouble after their messages on the department paging system were intercepted. The system, which transmitted messages to visual display pagers, helped send routine messages to officers without tying up telephones or emergency radio communications. When the system was installed, the police chief alerted users that every message was logged on the network and discriminatory messages or messages criticizing the department's policies were not allowed. In addition to receiving messages from headquarters, officers were able to transmit messages to each other. As officers became familiar with the system, some personal and nonpolice communications were sent through the system. In the course of an investigation, the city intercepted messages between two officers, John Bohach and Jon Catalano.
>
> Bohach and Catalano filed suit seeking to block the investigation and prevent disclosure of the contents of the messages because such actions violated privacy rights. The U.S. District Court found that the police department's paging system was essentially a form of electronic mail. The system's messages were, in effect, E-mail messages stored in a routing computer. Because of the absence of human voice in the communications, the messages were deemed to be electronic communications not subject to federal wire tap statutes. As a result, management's search of messages stored in the paging system did not violate the privacy rights of the police officers.[10]

Critical Issues in Paging System Use

Like other forms of E-mail, paging systems may be subject to the ECPA. This law prohibits interception of electronic messages except where there is a defined business purpose and employee consent. To avoid a privacy violation under this law, the employer should communicate to employees that the system is subject to employer monitoring of messages and that by using the system, an employee consents to such monitoring. Alert users that the system is limited to business communication only, and specify whether personal communication is prohibited.

10. *Bohach v City of Reno*, DC Nev (V-N-96 403 ECR 1996).

Sample Policy: Paging System Use

XYZ Company has developed the following policy relating to employee use of the company's paging system.

1. The paging system is a form of official company communication used to facilitate communications with field employees and to provide brief messages.

2. The paging system and all pager units are company property. Employees are permitted use of the company's property and must comply with company policies and procedures regarding its use.

3. The pager system is for business use only. Use of pagers for personal or other nonbusiness communications is not permitted.

4. The pager system must not be used for any improper or illegal communications, or for any coding or other system of improper communications.

5. Upon receiving a pager message, employees are responsible for calling in the designated number immediately.

6. Employees issued pagers must wear the pager during designated working times, including evenings and weekends.

7. Employees are responsible for calling in within one-half hour of being paged.

8. Pagers must not be lent or given to others.

9. Pagers must be turned in at separation of employment.

**Sample Employee Notice:
Paging System Use**

Certain employees receive pagers to aid in communications with the main office. Paging messages are for business communications only. Employees issued pagers must wear the pager during designated working times, including on-call periods during evenings and weekends as instructed. Employees must call in within one-half hour of being paged. Pagers must not be lent to others. Pagers must be turned in at separation of employment.

Surfin' the Web: Employer Control of Employee Internet Use

"I've used the Internet to research data for job assignments," says a human resources specialist. "I've also used the Internet to check consumer reports data when I was buying a car, comparing auto loan rates, and I used it to research data for my night class."

A procurement specialist at a property management firm scans a computer on-line service daily for shopping centers for sale, using the Internet to make preliminary inquiries to obtain information for evaluating their potential purchase. But at the corporate offices of a major retailer, a computer programmer involved in setting up the company's web site was discharged for inappropriate conduct related to Internet use after he linked a corporate message to an erotic picture.

The Internet can offer businesses great value—or expose them to scandal and legal liability. Used by millions of subscribers, the interactive information superhighway lets companies conduct conferences, market or data research, or commerce. On-line sales of products and services, which exceeded $200 million in 1990, are expected to exceed $3.5 billion by the year 2000, when over 30 million subscribers will be connected by the Internet.[11] But with these exciting new possibilities come new management dilemmas:

11. Kent D. Stuckey, *The Internet and On-Line Law* (New York: Law Journal Seminars Press, 1996).

- Ensuring that productivity is not cut by employees spending hours on Internet research, or using the Internet for personal activities
- Protecting confidentiality of business information
- Preventing employees from violating copyright laws by downloading copyrighted software. An employer could be held liable for copyright violation if an employee copied software and used it on the job.
- Protecting the company computer system from viruses introduced by downloaded software

According to a survey conducted by the Bureau of National Affairs, only 5 percent of the 500 firms surveyed had a written policy regarding Internet use, even though half reported having access to the Internet. While most of the firms use the Internet for research and transmission of E-mail messages, some 41 percent limit E-mail use to only a few designated employees.[12] In another survey conducted for Robert Half International, Inc., over half of executives polled said that time spent accessing the Internet for non–job-related purposes cuts worker productivity. Fifty-five percent of survey participants responded "yes" when asked, "Is employee time spent accessing the Internet for nonbusiness purposes considered a threat to productivity today?" The survey polled 150 executives from the nation's 1,000 largest firms.[13]

Many employers have embraced this new technology with policy guidelines to control employee use of the Internet. One such company is Northern States Power Company (NSP). Key aspects of the NSP Internet policy are summarized below:

> *Use of the Internet.* Use of the Internet by NSP workers is subject to periodic monitoring. Transmittal and receipt of information over the Internet, software downloaded through the Internet, and information accessed on the Internet must be in compliance with NSP's Information Management and Software License and Copyright Compliance policies and Corporate Code of Conduct.

> *Transmittal and receipt of information.* The transmittal and receipt of information, including data and software, must be in accordance with all applicable federal and state laws. NSP confidential and pro-

---

12. "Special Survey Report: Employers on the Internet," *Bulletin to Management* (BNA), Jan. 2, 1997, p. 1.
13. "Executives Say Employee's Net Surfing Cuts Productivity," *Business Ledger* (Oakbrook, IL), Nov. 1996, p. 32.

prietary information must not be transmitted over the Internet without prior approval by a department manager.

Downloaded software. Software downloaded through the Internet must be used and purchased according to the United States Copyright Law and NSP's purchasing practices. The purchase of downloaded software must be documented and the documentation retained as defined in the Managing Software License and Copyright Compliance process.

Information accessed. Information accessed on the Internet must be for NSP-related business activities and be consistent with the NSP Corporate Code of Conduct.

Monitoring. Supervisors must monitor use of the Internet by NSP workers under their supervision. Supervisors, in consultation with NSP's Human Resources and I/T areas, are responsible for determining the appropriate disciplinary action for any worker under their supervision who does not comply with this standard.

Auditing. NSP computers will be audited for software downloaded through the Internet as defined in the Software License and Copyright Compliance Management standard.[14]

Another example is the K-mart Internet policy:

K-mart Internet users WILL:

- Remember that electronic mail sent from K-mart travels on K-mart's electronic stationery and, as such, is the same as if it were sent on hard copy K-mart letterhead.
- Assume that all electronic mail can and will be read by systems administrators.
- Take all required precautions against importation of computer viruses. Remember that you represent the company at all times.

K-mart users WILL NOT:

- Take action that causes interference to the network or work of others.

14. "Networking: Internet Raises Questions about Employee Usage," *HR News*, August 1996, p. 7.

Sample Policy: Internet Use

XYZ Company authorizes controlled access to the Internet as defined in the following procedures:

1. The MIS manager is responsible for planning and implementing Internet use guidelines, developing and maintaining an Internet home page, and advising other managers on Internet use that aids in achieving company objectives.

2. Designated computer terminals for Internet use are located in marketing, administration, and service areas. Each department is responsible for assigning one Internet specialist. The Internet specialist is the primary contact who performs Internet searches and assists others with Internet use.

3. Alternative Internet users shall receive training on Internet search and retrieval procedures. Upon receiving training, these users may access the system.

4. All Internet searches, transmission, and data retrieval shall be business related. Personal use or access to the Internet is not permitted on company time or equipment.

5. Confidential information must not be transmitted over the Internet.

6. Internet users must recognize that the Internet is an open communication link and that there should be no expectation of privacy in communications. Use of company computers to access the Internet constitutes consent to company monitoring of Internet use, transmissions, and retrieved data.

7. Internet users must not send or receive any form of harassment or derogatory statements, and no sexually oriented information, material, or images may be sent, displayed, or received.

Sample Policy: Internet Use

8. All data, information, and software downloaded through the Internet are subject to copyright licenses and laws.

9. All software downloaded through the Internet must be virus checked.

**Sample Employee Notice:
Internet Use**

XYZ Company maintains a home page on the Internet. Certain employees are authorized to access the Internet from designated computer terminals. Internet use is for business purposes only. Do not send or receive confidential information over the Internet. Do not send, receive, or display any improper information or sexually oriented information. Please recognize that Internet communications are not private and that use of computer terminals is subject to monitoring by management.

- Post items on the Internet that do not reflect the policies of K-mart.
- Operate a business through the K-mart Internet link.
- Send mail or other communications, files, or programs containing offensive or harassing statements, including comments based on race, national origin, sex, sexual orientation, age, disability, religion, or political beliefs.
- Send or receive sexually oriented messages or images.[15]

15. "Highlights from K-mart's Appropriate Conduct for Internet Users Policy," *Human Resources Management Newsletter* (CCH), May 8, 1996, p. 78.

Critical Issues in Internet Use

Like other E-mail systems, Internet use is subject to limitations defined in the ECPA. Interception of messages is prohibited unless one of the parties consents. Accordingly, the employer granting access to the Internet can require that access to the Internet on company computers implies consent to monitoring. To avoid time-wasting searches, it is recommended that Internet access be limited to business purposes conducted by designated and trained individuals. A policy prohibiting the copying or use of personal software on company computers would help to protect against copyright infringement.

Summary

New, interactive systems like E-mail, paging, and the Internet have revolutionized the way we communicate and created new workplace privacy questions. Employees using E-mail and pager systems may believe that their communication is private and confidential. But stored and deleted messages from these systems have been retrieved and used as evidence in legal proceedings. Further, employers have monitored or intercepted messages and then taken action detrimental to the senders or receivers when messages have been deemed improper.

These incidents have resulted in employee terminations and legal action against employees. The courts generally have allowed employers the prerogative to monitor their internal E-mail systems. And unless the ECPA is directly violated, employee privacy invasion claims have not been successful. To promote positive employee relations, employers need to define an E-mail policy that reflects the firm's culture while clarifying proper use of electronic communications systems.

Appendix

Management Guidelines

E-Mail Policy

- Check federal and state law for any requirements or restrictions relating to E-mail use.
- Develop a written policy to clarify E-mail use and advise employees of E-mail procedures, etiquette, confidentiality, and privacy concerns.

- Tailor the E-mail policy to reflect your firm's culture.
- Advise employees not to use the E-mail system to send confidential messages.
- Identify the E-mail system as the employer's property.
- Specify whether E-mail should be used for business purposes only or whether personal messages will be permitted.
- Specify that the employer may access and review E-mail messages at any time.
- Specify that the E-mail system may not be used for any form of non–business-related solicitation or distribution of information.
- Specify that the sending of any offensive or improper messages or racial, sexual, or other slurs is prohibited.
- Alert users to respect the privacy of others on the E-mail system and to refrain from retrieving or reading E-mail that is directed to others.
- Consider installing an on-screen message highlighting the policy that appears when users log on to the system.
- Communicate E-mail policy in your firm's personnel policy manual or employee handbook.
- Provide training to employees and supervisory personnel on proper use of the E-mail system.
- Obtain a signed receipt from all employees using the system stating that they understand system procedures and recognize that E-mail communications are not private.
- State that E-mail messages, even if erased, may be subsequently retrieved.
- State that the E-mail system may not be used for illegal or unethical purposes or to record any information that may violate the law or create a legal liability for the company.
- State that E-mail records may be used in legal proceedings.

Paging Systems

- Check state and federal laws for restrictions or requirements on use of paging systems.
- Define written policy guidelines to employees stating whether use of the system is for business purposes only or if personal communications are permitted.
- Identify the degree to which the paging system may be subject to management monitoring.
- Obtain a signed statement from employees indicating that they understand paging procedures and that they understand that using the system implies consent to such management procedures as monitoring of the paging system.
- If the paging system permits the transmission of messages, alert users that inappropriate, illegal, personal, sexual, or discriminatory messages are prohibited.
- Identify time limit guidelines for response to pages.
- Obtain a signed receipt for the pager unit, acknowledging that it must be turned in at separation of employment.

Internet Use

- Define a written policy for communication to employees.
- Identify which employees and/or job functions may have access to the Internet while on the job.
- Identify which computers or workstations may be used for Internet access.
- Specify that Internet use will be subject to monitoring by company management.
- Identify that any data or software downloaded through the Internet is subject to copyright laws and/or software licensing restrictions.
- Specify that Internet use while on the job and/or with company facilities must be solely for business purposes and not for personal research or use.
- Advise employees that confidential company information must not be transmitted over the Internet.
- Require that downloaded software be subject to a virus check.
- Specify that no sexually oriented information, material, or images may be sent, displayed, or received through the Internet.
- Specify that no form of harassment or derogatory statements may be made while on the Internet, including any messages relating to race, color, age, national origin, sex, disability, or other prohibited-class category.
- Identify Internet specialists who can perform Internet data searches and can assist other employees.
- Train and instruct employees on how to use the Internet efficiently to avoid time-wasting searches by trial and error.
- Identify enforcement or disciplinary procedures in the event of a policy violation.

Q & A: Employee Rights Regarding E-Mail, the Internet, and Paging Systems

Q   *Isn't E-mail just as private as mail delivered by the U.S. Postal Service?*

A   No. Employees using E-mail systems do not have the same degree of privacy as afforded by the Postal Service. The ECPA prohibits a public E-mail provider from interception and disclosure of E-mail messages to third parties. The law allows monitoring when one party gives consent and allows a system provider to monitor messages where necessary to provide service such as checking to ensure the system is working properly. The courts have generally allowed employers to monitor and intercept E-mail messages on their private intranet or internal E-mail systems when the monitoring is done for a reasonable business purpose. As a result, use of E-mail has been compared to sending messages on a postcard through the mails. Recognize that your E-mail message may be accessed and read by others, so avoid sending personal or private information that you would not want others to see.

Q   *Do employees have any privacy rights when using paging or messaging systems?*
A   Paging and messaging systems used by the public are subject to ECPA protections. As with internal E-mail systems, employer monitoring of communications is generally permissible, provided the employer has a reasonable business purpose and notifies employees that monitoring will take place.

Q   *Do employees have privacy rights when using the Internet?*
A   Employees using the Internet receive certain protections afforded by the ECPA because Internet access is through an electronic communications provider. This means that the Internet access provider is prohibited from interception and disclosure of electronic messages to third parties. The law allows the Internet access provider to monitor when one party gives consent, and the provider can monitor messages to ensure adequate service. As with other E-mail systems, Internet communications should not be considered private. An employer would have a reasonable justification to monitor activities of an employee accessing the Internet on a company computer on company time.

8

Personal, Private, and Confidential: An Employer's Access to and Release of Workplace Information

When Resnik was separated from his job at Blue Cross and Blue Shield of Missouri, his separation agreement stated that Blue Cross would limit reference information to name, job title, and dates of employment. Resnik sought other work, listing Blue Cross on job applications as his last employer. At one firm, Resnik's interview went well and the recruiter mentioned that references would be checked. However, when Resnik failed to be hired, he filed a suit against Blue Cross claiming that his former employer disregarded its own policy on providing references when his former supervisor had an extended telephone conversation with the prospective employer about Resnik's job performance.

In its examination of Resnik's claim, the court noted that the prospective employer's policy was to make job reference inquiries after making a tentative hiring decision, that the prospective employer had a forty-five-minute reference discussion with Resnik's supervisor at Blue Cross, and that subsequent to the reference discussion, a final job offer was not extended. The Missouri Court of Appeals held that Blue Cross breached its employment agreement with Resnik.[1]

Employers routinely collect and maintain information about their employees. Employment information on employees may include pay, pay increases,

---

1. *Resnik v Blue Cross and Blue Shield of Missouri*, 11 IER Cases 124 (1995).

job assignments, performance ratings, and disciplinary warnings. Personal information may include address, telephone number, age, dependents, and educational details. In addition, employee health records may include details about physical exams, medical claims for current illnesses or health conditions, drug and alcohol abuse treatment records, and other health topics.

When employees provide this personal information to an employer, they assume that the employer will keep the information confidential. If the information is carelessly released, the employee may have a claim for privacy invasion or defamation. Unfortunately, many employers do nothing to protect sensitive personal data, according to "Privacy in the Workplace," a survey of 300 of the Fortune 500 firms conducted by Professor David F. Linowes of the University of Illinois. Of the 84 respondents, representing practices affecting 3.2 million employees:

- Three out of ten have no formal policy on releasing personnel records information in response to government inquiries.
- Seventy percent disclose personal information to creditors.
- Nearly 50 percent provide employee information to landlords.
- Thirty-five percent use medical records in making employment decisions—a potential violation of the ADA.[2]

As more business, personnel, and health records are computerized, it will be more difficult for employers to maintain confidentiality of these records. In this chapter, we will examine the issues of responding to employment verifications, proper handling of personnel records, careful use of employee health and medical records, and protecting confidentiality of computerized data.

I'm Calling to Check a Reference On . . . : How Employers Handle Employment Verification

Employers frequently are asked to provide employment verification on current and former employees. Employment verification requests on current employees generally come from creditors, landlords, or financial institutions. Employment or reference verification requests are made on former employees. Careless

2. "Workplace Privacy: More Must Be Done to Protect Employees," *Employment Guide* (BNA) 11, no. 10 (May 6, 1996): 55.

or improper handling of employment verifications opens the employer up to costly legal claims.

An employer providing an employment reference is permitted under common law to provide truthful and factual information and to receive a basic protection from liability of a defamation claim. But when the employer is reckless or malicious with information provided, an employee may have a valid defamation or privacy claim. For example, a supervisor's disregard for policy proved costly for one university, which was held liable for defamation.

> When the university's corporate relations director applied for similar work at another school, the prospective employer was told by the individual's former supervisor that she "did not follow up on assignments," even though the employee had received exemplary performance ratings throughout her employment. The reference was also provided without her permission, a direct violation of the procedures defined in the university employee handbook. The corporate relations director sued for defamation.
>
> Upon examining the issues, the court noted that the employee's former and prospective jobs were similar, that the former supervisor's comment clearly imputed an inability to do the job contrary to documented performance ratings, and that the comments were made in disregard of the policy prohibiting disclosure of employment references without the employee's permission. Because of the matter in which the reference was provided, contrary to the employer's policy and disregarding the performance ratings, the court held that the university was liable for defamation.[3]

In another situation, an employer was sued for *failing* to provide adequate details in an employment reference.

> After being fired from his job at Allstate Insurance Company for allegedly carrying a gun in his briefcase, Paul Calden was hired and subsequently fired by Fireman's Fund Insurance Company. After he was let go, Calden returned to the Fireman's Fund offices and shot three employees before killing himself. Relatives of one victim filed a lawsuit against Allstate for negligent referral. The lawsuit alleged that although Allstate knew about Calden's potential for violence, they provided him

3. *Anderson v Vanden Dorpel*, 9 IER Cases 1820 (1994).

with a letter of reference stating that his termination was not due to performance.[4]

As these examples demonstrate, employers providing employment verifications and references are caught in a real dilemma. Release information about former employees, and risk a privacy invasion or defamation lawsuit; release only minimal information, verifying job dates, and you may be subject to a negligent referral claim. You're damned if you do and damned if you don't! The specter of lawsuits has caused many human resources specialists to limit employment verifications to "name, rank, and serial number"; that is, name, dates of employment, job title, and salary. This situation makes it hard for companies like Fireman's Fund to find out whether a job applicant may have a loose screw. Recognizing the employer's dilemma, many states have passed reference-checking immunity laws designed to provide for the employer immunity from employee lawsuits for providing employment references (see chapter 4). These laws allow employees to provide truthful information without fear of reprisal. Generally, these state statutes:

- Define covered employers and/or covered employees
- Assume that the references are truthful and are provided in good faith
- Permit the employer to provide job performance information
- Permit the employer to provide information on job dates, job title, job duties, and pay data
- Give a qualified immunity for providing information in good faith, provided the information does not violate the individual's civil rights
- Prohibit the disclosure of "confidential" information
- Do not require the employee's consent to release information[5]

Some states prohibit blacklisting, a practice in which an employer deliberately communicates a message to other employers not to hire an individual. However, blacklisting laws do permit an employer to disclose truthful information concerning the employee's work abilities or the reason for discharge.

Another type of law relating to employment verification is a service letter statute. Generally, the service letter statute requires the employer to provide a truthful statement or letter upon request by the employee about the individu-

---

4. Bill Leonard, "Reference Checking Laws: Now What?" *HR Magazine*, Dec. 1995, p. 57.
5. Donna C. Meindentsma, "Implications of the New Job Reference Immunity Statutes," *SHRM Legal Report*, Fall 1996.

States and Territories with Laws Dealing with Blacklisting

Alabama	Kansas	North Carolina
Arizona	Louisiana	North Dakota
Arkansas	Maine	Oklahoma
California	Minnesota	Oregon
Colorado	Mississippi	Puerto Rico
Connecticut	Montana	Texas
Florida	Nevada	Utah
Idaho	New Hampshire	Virginia
Indiana	New Mexico	Washington
Iowa	New York	Wisconsin

al's employment and/or reason for separation. These laws generally do not grant immunity to the employer providing the employment information.

Even in states that do not have reference-checking immunity laws, courts applying common-law concepts will often hold that an employer has a "qualified privilege" to communicate personnel decisions to others. A qualified privilege means that the employer is protected from liability for defamation as long as the personnel decision and its communication are not careless, wanton, or based on ill will. Generally, an employer will receive qualified privilege liability protection if:

- Information is provided in good faith
- Factual information is provided without "embroidering"
- Information is provided only to those who have a need to know[6]

An examination of cases where employers were found liable relating to employment references reveals several common faults. Employers generally got into trouble when they failed to check the facts or failed to communicate the facts. Table 8-1 shows common reference-checking inquiries and two kinds of responses: a recommended reply and a reply that could create a liability.

6. "Privacy and Defamation," *HR Services Policy & Practices* (Warren Gorham & Lamont, Boston) 141 (1995): 1903.

Table 8-1   Responding to Employment Verification Questions

Typical Employment Verification Question	Response to Avoid	Suggested Response
I'm Dawn Jones from ABC Company. We're checking references on John Smith.	Smith? That lazy louse! Couldn't pay me to take him back.	Yes, John Smith used to work here. I have an employment reference release from him. What would you like to know?
Smith's application says that he worked at your firm as a machine operator from 1992 until January 1997.	Worked? That's a laugh. He hardly worked at all. I fired him in December.	Our records show that Smith worked on a fabricating machine from July 1992 until December 1996.
What was his salary?	I think he got ten or eleven an hour; wasn't worth it, though.	I can only confirm details that he may have put on his application.
It says here he was laid off.	Like I said, I fired him. Drunk on the job, and we think he was into theft. Inventory was missing.	My record shows that Smith was separated for misconduct.
Tell me more about why he was let go.	Like I said, let go for theft. I think he was into drugs.	To provide further details, I would need a written inquiry from you. You can fax me at . . .

Critical Issues in Employment Verification

The trend in litigation relating to employment verification seems to place employers between a rock and a hard place: negative references may result in defamation lawsuits, but failure to provide negative references on individuals who subsequently cause injury to others may result in negligent referral lawsuits. It is important to verify or provide only factual information that is documented in an individual's personnel file. Be sure to document an accurate

Sample Policy: Employment Verification

It is the policy of XYZ Company to provide employment verification information in a manner that protects privacy of
personnel records.

1. All personnel records are confidential. Personnel records
   are stored in locked files, under the direction of the
   human resources manager.

2. All requests and inquiries relating to employment verifications of current employees and reference checks of
   former employees shall be referred to the human
   resources manager.

3. Verification that an individual is currently (or was formerly) employed by XYZ Company can be provided in
   response to a telephone inquiry. To receive additional
   information, the requesting organization must mail or
   fax its inquiry with the employee's signed release for providing information.

4. Employment verification will be released only upon the
   employee's signed authorization.

5. At separation of employment, the manager shall obtain
   the employee's signed release for providing employment
   references.

6. Information provided in employment verifications and
   references shall be limited to factual information that is
   contained in the employee's personnel record.

7. Avoid releasing confidential or private information. Confer with the human resources manager if there is a
   question about how to handle a sensitive issue or
   inquiry.

8. Access to personnel records shall be granted in response
   to a properly documented summons, subpoena, or government audit.

> **Sample Employee Notice:**
> **Employment Verification**
>
> XYZ Company recognizes its responsibility to protect the privacy of personnel records. Information in personnel records is used strictly for business purposes relating to pay, benefits, and employment. Your written authorization is needed if you wish the company to provide employment verification to financial creditors, and for reference upon separation of employment.

reason for separation. Avoid communicating incorrect information regarding employment or reason for separation.

State laws in some areas provide reference-checking immunity, prohibit blacklisting, or require issuance of a service letter upon request. Generally, court decisions applying common law tend to grant the employer a limited degree of immunity for good-faith references. However, until employers see some degree of protection from the law, references are likely to be limited to "name, rank, and serial number."

Protecting Privacy of Personnel Records

A personnel file consists of the records an employer maintains about an individual's employment. It can include employment application, resume, salary history, tax exemptions, home address and telephone, pay level and pay increases, performance appraisals, disciplinary warnings, educational level or training, and reason for separation of employment. In addition, many files contain medical records, drug or alcohol test data, insurance plan claims, or other medical information.

Whether this information is stored on a computer or in files, the employer has a responsibility to protect its confidentiality and to avoid releasing it to unauthorized persons. When information is inappropriately released, an employee may have a privacy invasion claim.

Ellenwood, an employee of Exxon Shipping Company, worked aboard the ship *Wilmington*. Returning to work after a period of absence, Ellenwood learned that his supervisor told fellow employees about his treatment for alcoholism when he off-handedly responded to an inquiry about why Ellenwood was gone. Understandably upset, Ellenwood alleged in a lawsuit that Exxon publicly disclosed to shipmates the fact that he had undergone treatment for alcoholism. Ellenwood contended that the release of this information from his personnel records was an invasion of his privacy.

The federal district court judge hearing the case applied Texas law. To recover, Ellenwood was required by Texas law to show that:

1. Publicity was given to matters of his private life
2. The publication of these matters would be highly offensive to a reasonable person of ordinary sensibilities
3. The matter publicized is not of legitimate public concern

The court held that publicity requires communication to more than a small group of shipboard coworkers or supervisors. For this reason, said the court, Ellenwood's claim did not meet the Texas requirement of publicity for a claim of public disclosure of private facts.[7]

In this case, the federal court judge applied Texas law on privacy issues using the criteria identified. As a general guideline, however, an employer should not release information on an employee's medical condition to fellow workers. An individual victimized by such a release may be able to bring a claim under the ADA. The ADA gives protection to individuals who are *regarded as being disabled*. If Ellenwood had been treated differently because of the information release, he may have had a claim under the ADA.

An employer may be liable for a privacy invasion if "confidential" information about an employee is disclosed to others, released to fellow employees, or obtained by management and used for an inappropriate purpose. However, the courts allow the employer some latitude in the use or disclosure of personnel records when there is a clear business purpose. For example, information about an employee's disability or medical condition may be released to the individual's supervisor to facilitate work restrictions or accommodations. Further, the courts will weigh the employee's expectation of privacy with the employer's business purpose for use or disclosure of the data.

7. *Ellenwood v Exxon Shipping*, 6 IER Cases 1628 (1991).

For an invasion of privacy claim to succeed, private facts must be widely disseminated. Courts have allowed disclosure of private facts to appropriate management personnel and to an employee's former wife. Disclosure of a personnel director's termination agreement to fellow staff members was held lawful.[8]

Courts have also allowed disclosure of private facts during union-organizing drives. The court held that there was no privacy invasion when the NLRB released employee names and addresses to a union seeking to organize workers.[9] Likewise, the publication, during a union election, of a credit sheet showing wages and deductions was held to be lawful even though it was published and distributed without employees' permission.[10]

While the Privacy Act defines privacy requirements for personnel records maintained by federal government agencies, no broad federal law deals with personnel records maintained by firms in the private sector. Thirty-two states have laws that regulate access to personnel files. Typically, these laws define that class of employees or employers that is subject to the law. The Illinois law, for example, covers firms with more than five employees; the Nevada law covers employees with sixty days of service or more. The laws generally allow an employee to view information in his or her personnel file and to copy information in the file. But not all records are open to employees. Records that some laws do not require to be disclosed include information or records being gathered for a criminal investigation, letters of reference, management planning, and testing information. Some laws permit the employee to insert corrected information or alternative information.

In areas where there is no state law on personnel records access, employee access is a matter of employer discretion and policy. The employer may define a policy that permits employee access. But if the employer decides to prohibit an employee from seeing or gaining access to information in his or her personnel file, the employee's only recourse would be to file suit on an employment matter and obtain access through the legal discovery process.

Critical Issues in Use of Personnel Records

While there are no statutes or federal laws that specifically require employers to maintain personnel records, other laws do require the maintenance of vari-

8. Alfred G. Feliu, *Primer on Individual Rights* (Washington, DC: BNA, 1993), 214.
9. *NLRB v British Auto Parts*, 71 LRRM 2057.
10. *Wheeler v Sorenson Mfg.*, 65 LRRM 2408.

Sample Policy: Personnel Records

It is the policy of XYZ Company to maintain personnel records as needed to administer payroll and benefits for employees.

1. All personnel records are confidential. Personnel records are stored in locked files, under the direction of the human resources manager.

2. Supervisors or managers may be granted access to personnel records for employees under their direction.

3. An employee may request to view information in his or her personnel file. Supervised access may be granted in the presence of the human resources manager.

4. Separate files shall be maintained for medical records and employment eligibility forms.

5. The personnel file shall include application or resume, pay information, job description, performance ratings, disciplinary warnings, and personnel action forms.

6. All requests and inquiries relating to employment verifications of current employees and reference checks of former employees shall be referred to the human resources manager.

7. Verification that an individual is currently (or was formerly) employed by XYZ Company can be provided in response to a telephone inquiry. For release of additional information, the requesting organization must mail or fax its inquiry with the employee's signed release for providing information.

8. Employment verification will be released only upon the employee's signed authorization.

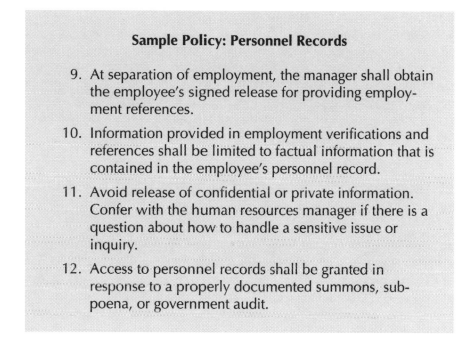

Sample Policy: Personnel Records

9. At separation of employment, the manager shall obtain the employee's signed release for providing employment references.

10. Information provided in employment verifications and references shall be limited to factual information that is contained in the employee's personnel record.

11. Avoid release of confidential or private information. Confer with the human resources manager if there is a question about how to handle a sensitive issue or inquiry.

12. Access to personnel records shall be granted in response to a properly documented summons, subpoena, or government audit.

Sample Employee Notice: Personnel Records

The company keeps personnel records to administer pay and benefits. Be sure to keep your supervisor informed if there are changes to name, address, phone, marital status, exemptions, dependents, beneficiary, etc.

ous records that generally end up in an employee's personnel file. Wage hour law, for example, requires the employer to maintain a record of pay rates and hours worked. Further, human resources professionals advise that employment decisions, performance ratings, misconduct warnings, and the like be documented and kept in the individual's personnel file. The key issues in avoiding liability are to keep only those records needed for managing personnel, to limit access to personnel records only to persons with a job-related need to know, and to avoid unauthorized release of private information.

Between Me and My Doctor: Keeping Employee Medical Records Confidential

Many employers obtain and keep medical information on employees, including preemployment physical exams and drug or alcohol screens, doctors' excuses for absences, physicians' certifications regarding disabilities, leaves of absence, workers' compensation claims, and group health insurance claims. For the most part, employees cooperate with these kinds of medical requirements, but employees also expect that their employer will protect the confidentiality of the medical information. Legal claims and privacy invasion claims occur when the employer carelessly handles employee medical information. While Ellenwood failed to win his claim against Exxon Shipping Company, other courts have found that inappropriate release of confidential medical information to coworkers can result in a privacy invasion claim.

> When Motorola employee Miller went on a medical leave to have a mastectomy, a supervisor disclosed details of Miller's operation to members of her work team. Miller sued Motorola, alleging a privacy invasion because the employer had disclosed a private fact to a group of coworkers. Applying Illinois law, the appeals court judge held that where the employee had a special relationship with coworkers, making the disclosure particularly embarrassing, the publicity requirement was satisfied and a privacy invasion occurred.[11]

In the Ellenwood and Miller cases, the courts reached different decisions because they applied different laws. One court applied Texas law, the other Illinois law. In fact, Ellenwood's lawyer cited the Miller case in his legal argu-

11. *Miller v Motorola*, 5 IER Cases 885 (1990).

ment, but it was not supported by laws in Texas. California law provides an even greater degree of protection for the individual, as E. I. DuPont de Nemours discovered.

> Pettis was employed by E. I. DuPont de Nemours for twenty-two years. When Pettis requested a disability leave for what he said was work-related stress, DuPont directed Pettis to submit to a medical examination as required by the firm's short-term disability leave policy. A doctor under contract with DuPont verified the employee's stress-related condition and agreed that he needed time off but recommended that Pettis also submit to a psychiatric evaluation. The doctor who conducted the psychiatric evaluation reported that the stress might be related to alcohol abuse. As a result of the medical report, DuPont tried to enroll Pettis into an alcohol treatment program. Pettis refused and was fired by DuPont.
>
> Pettis sued DuPont and the doctor, alleging that both company and doctor violated the California Confidentiality of Medical Information Act and the California Constitution. The court found that, under the California law, health care providers are not to disclose medical information without written patient authorization. The court concluded that the employee was not an alcoholic and that he did not authorize the doctor to disclose full details of discussions with him. As a result, the court held that the psychiatrist's disclosure to the employer of details about the patient was unlawful.[12]

On occasion, an employer may request medical or other information for a legitimate business purpose. An employee's refusal to cooperate with an employer's reasonable policy or refusal to provide information can affect the outcome of a privacy claim, as Carmella Mares learned.

> Carmella Mares worked for Con Agra Poultry Company in Colorado. When the company implemented its drug testing policy, it directed each employee to complete a "Prescription Drugs and Over the Counter Medication Form." Mares refused to complete the form and refused to submit to a drug test. When she declined to reconsider her refusal, she was terminated. Mares sued Con Agra, alleging wrongful

12. "Psychiatrist's Disclosure to Employer of Details about Patient Held Unlawful," *Legal Developments Newsletter* (BNA) 14 (Sept. 23, 1996): 1024.

discharge and invasion of privacy and seeking compensatory and punitive damages.

In defending its case, Con Agra pointed out that the medical information was needed to assure accuracy of drug test results and to provide the employee an opportunity to explain any positive test result. The company noted that the information was kept confidential. Further, the company asserted that since Mares refused to complete the form and did not provide the information, there was no invasion of privacy. Ultimately, the court agreed with Con Agra, dismissing Mares's claim. Mares failed to state a claim of invasion of privacy because the mere completion of the medical information form would not be objectionable to a reasonable person.[13]

The preceding three cases demonstrate that an employer must exercise care in handling medical information about employees. Employee medical information is subject to certain state and federal laws. Generally, medical records are included in the broad definition of personnel records. It is important to check the wording of the law in your state to see whether employee medical records are subject to the requirements of that law.

OSHA has defined a standard or regulation relating to access to medical records. Referred to as the Access to Employee Exposure and Medical Records Standard, it requires employers to permit employees or their representatives, such as a doctor, lawyer, or union representative, to inspect their personal medical records pertaining to exposure to hazardous workplace substances. Other general health or medical records are not covered by this rule.[14]

OSHA also requires employers to maintain a log of occupational injuries and illnesses and to keep a supplemental record of illnesses and injuries. The OSHA Hazard Communication Standard requires the employer to keep a record of employee exposure to toxic substances for the period of employment plus thirty years.

The ADA, which prohibits discrimination on the basis of physical or mental disability, includes several provisions regarding employee medical records. These provisions stipulate that:

- An employer must maintain employee medical information separate from other personnel records.

13. *Mares v Con Agra Poultry,* 7 IER Cases 997 (1992).
14. OSHA Medical Records Standard, 29 CFR 1910.120 (f).

- Any medical information that is maintained must be related to job requirements only.
- Any medical information must not be used in a way that discriminates on the basis of physical or mental disability.[15]

The recently passed HIPAA imposes penalties for unauthorized release of personally identifiable health information. Under this law, an employer is prohibited from:

- Using or causing to be used a unique code or classification system to identify employee health conditions for the purpose of limiting insurance coverage of persons with preexisting conditions
- Obtaining individually identifiable health information relating to an individual
- Disclosing individually identifiable health information relating to an individual

A knowing violation is subject to a one-year prison sentence, $50,000 fine, or both. A knowing violation with intent to sell such information is subject to up to ten years in prison, a $250,000 fine, or both.[16]

To reduce health insurance costs, a growing number of employers are becoming self-insured. A self-insured firm receives health benefits claims information and pays health benefits directly to employees rather than paying for such services through an insurance company. This direct relationship gives the firm access to private medical information that the employee probably does not want disclosed to others or to be used as a basis for an employment decision. Yet in some instances, the information may be very pertinent to an employee's performance on the job. Consider these examples:

- A heavy equipment operator with a past history of substance abuse has now kicked the habit and is performing satisfactorily. Part of his substance abuse treatment included the use of a particular prescribed drug. Your health claims administrator notes that he has stopped submitting claims for this drug. Is this a safety or health hazard? Should management be notified?

- A project manager is now turning in prescription drug charges for health benefits reimbursement. The reimbursement documents show that the

15. *Americans With Disabilities Act of 1990, EEOC Technical Assistance Manual* (Chicago: CCH, 1992), Sec. 6.5.
16. "Law Enhances Portability of Health Benefits," *HR News*, Oct. 1996, p. 4.

drug purchased is lithium, a strong antidepressant. Should the claims administrator report this information to others? Will consideration of this information in an employment decision violate this employee's privacy rights?

Before considering medical information in an employment decision, a claims manager should carefully weigh the factors to justify the action. Further, the claims manager should:

- Make sure that there is a clear business need for the disclosure.
- Check that such use of medical information is not prohibited by law.
- Be sure that the information is verifiable.
- Know whether medical information can be released only with the employee's consent or if nonconsensual release is permitted.
- Know whether company policy permits such a disclosure.
- Have safeguards in place to prevent further unauthorized disclosure.[17]

After considering these issues, the claims administrator may confidentially communicate information to an individual's manager solely for the purpose of addressing safety or performance concerns.

A good example of a justified medical records review procedure is the policy pursued by Children's Hospital of Akron, Ohio, for individuals who return to work following substance abuse rehabilitation. Employees sign a reentry contract acknowledging that their records and performance will be closely monitored, and then a designated individual reviews their attendance, sick days, and benefits records. The employee's history of prior substance abuse justifies the need for closer monitoring of personnel and medical records, and the reentry contract lowers expectations of privacy to help minimize the likelihood of privacy invasion claims.[18]

Critical Issues in Use of Employee Medical Records

Employers accumulate employee medical information as a result of physical exams, drug or alcohol tests, and health plan administration. As computerized records and employer self-insurance plans become more common, medical records privacy concerns are increasing. Because medical information is particu-

---

17. Bill Leonard, "Tough Decision to Use Confidential Information," *HR Magazine,* July 1993, p. 73.
18. Ibid., 74.

Sample Policy: Employee Medical Records

It is the policy of XYZ Company to protect the privacy of medical records obtained in the course of employment and benefits administration.

1. All medical records are confidential. Medical records are stored in locked files, separate from other personnel records, under the direction of the human resources manager.

2. Medical records are acquired for business purposes only, relating to administration of employment and benefits such as preemployment physical exam and drug test, physical exam and/or drug test, medical certifications for absence or medical leaves of absence, workers' compensation claims, health insurance claims, or other similar job-related reasons.

3. Medical records shall not be accessed, used, or considered in a manner that discriminates against an applicant or employee because of physical or mental disability.

4. Medical information on an employee may be shared with a supervisor or manager only for the purpose of considering reasonable accommodation for disability, or when medical information is provided as justification for an absence.

5. Medical records will be released only for insurance claim administration or to a health care professional for evaluating an employee's medical condition for work capability. Any other release is only upon receipt of employee's written authorization.

6. An employee may be granted supervised access to his or her personal medical file only in the presence of the human resources manager.

larly private, a successful privacy invasion claim is highly likely in the event of inadvertent or careless release of medical information. To prevent an unauthorized release of information and privacy claims, employers must establish control procedures limiting access to records and specifying a business purpose for release of medical information.

Passwords, Privacy, and Productivity: Computerized Business Records

Nearly every business organization stores all or part of its business records in computerized record systems. Systems that include private information about employees are vulnerable to legal claims because an employee with system access can view data, produce records or lists, combine data, enter or change information, or cause unauthorized disclosure of information. Careless release or inappropriate use of business records identifying an individual could result in a privacy invasion claim, as Amoco Oil Company learned.

> Amoco employee Thaddeus Pulla, who worked in the credit card department, frequently called in sick. A coworker who covered Pulla's shift checked his Amoco credit card records and found that Pulla had used his credit card at restaurants and bars on some of the days that he had claimed to be sick. When she reported her findings to her supervisor, she was admonished for making an unauthorized search of company records, but the supervisor placed a printout of the information into Pulla's personnel file.
>
> When Pulla learned that the employer had accessed his credit card information, he filed suit against Amoco for invasion of privacy, claiming that he suffered feelings of being watched. A jury found that the employee's search of Pulla's records had violated common-law principles of privacy in Iowa and held Amoco liable for invading Pulla's privacy.[19]

Whether records are manual or computerized, an employer has an obligation to set up reasonable procedures and controls to prevent unauthorized release of private information. Further, the employer has a responsibility to

19. *Pulla v Amoco Oil*, 72 F3d 648 (8th Cir 1995).

take corrective action to deal with unauthorized access or handling of data by an employee.

Many computerized record systems and E-mail systems contain passwords and security codes. An employer's information system policy needs to identify levels of systems access, assign passwords to employees, and instruct employees on proper system etiquette. If an employee disregards system etiquette or procedures, or causes unauthorized system entry or release of data, then strong corrective action would probably minimize or prevent a privacy claim.

Other computer system security safeguards can help prevent unauthorized or casual disclosure. Try to include one or more of these electronic "locks and doors":

Log-in procedures. Devise a series of steps and procedures a user must take to enter a computer network system.

Lock and key. Lock computer terminals, keyboards, and drive bays to prevent unauthorized entry. Lock the office or room in which the computer is located when unattended.

Password. Define password entry codes to control access to certain data or files. Use the password to restrict access to select screens, data, or files and to control who may view, enter, or change data or produce reports. Be sure to change the password periodically.

Screen saver. A screen saver program prevents a casual passerby from viewing confidential on-screen data during brief periods of work inactivity. It is a good idea to position the computer screen away from hallways or open work areas to prevent unauthorized viewing of the screen.[20]

Critical Issues in Business Records Privacy

Business records that do not deal with employment or medical issues are not subject to state or federal laws on personnel or medical records privacy. A common-law privacy invasion claim is the most likely source of a privacy claim relating to inappropriate release of business information if private facts about an individual are disclosed or widely publicized in an outrageous manner. To prevent such an incident, the employer needs to set up administrative and computer systems controls to protect record confidentiality.

20. Sandra O'Connell, "Security for HR Records," *HR Magazine,* Sept. 1994, p. 37.

Sample Policy: Computerized Business Records

It is the policy of XYZ Company to protect the confidentiality
and privacy of business records obtained in the course of
business operations.

1. All business records are confidential. Business records
   are stored in locked files under the direction of the
   respective department managers.

2. All records are acquired for business purposes only, relating to business operations such as product development,
   sales, marketing, accounting, service, and personnel.

3. All computerized records are entered, stored, and
   reported according to procedures defined by the information systems department.

4. Certain computerized records are stored under security
   passwords for use only by designated employees in the
   respective departments. Passwords are issued and
   changed periodically by information systems personnel.

5. Employees are responsible for protecting their assigned
   passwords and for reporting any system security
   breaches immediately to their managers.

6. Business records shall not be accessed by any employee
   except those individuals with responsibility for use of
   such information and who have received a password for
   access to the information.

7. Business information on an employee may be shared
   with a manager only for authorized business purposes.

8. Business records will be released to other employees
   only for carrying out job responsibilities. Any other
   release is only upon receipt of management authorization.

9. Any unauthorized release of business records is grounds
   for corrective discipline, which may include immediate
   dismissal.

Summary

Every organization creates records of its operations and activities. Financial data tracks income, costs, expenses, and profits. Sales data shows which products and services are selling where and to whom. Employment data includes information on personnel, payroll, benefits, and medical claims. Any information that deals with or identifies an employee should be viewed as personal, private, and confidential. Companies work hard to keep product and pricing information from reaching competitors. A similarly concerted effort to protect personnel and medical information from unauthorized release will go a long way toward preventing privacy invasion claims.

Appendix

Management Guidelines

Employment Verification

- Check the law in your state to determine whether there is a reference-checking statute, service letter requirement, blacklisting prohibition, or similar law regulating the employment verification process.
- Define a policy and procedure for handling employment verifications and references.
- Assign responsibility for handling reference-checking inquiries. For consistency, direct all employment verification inquiries to that individual.
- Identify the type of information that will be provided or verified.
- Provide training to managers and supervisors who may be authorized to provide reference information under your policy.
- Limit information to details that are actually documented in an individual's personnel file. Avoid providing subjective opinions.
- Do not release "confidential" information such as health records, drug/alcohol test results, or drug/alcohol treatment records.
- Carefully evaluate all facts regarding reference inquiries on individuals who may have been prone to violence or other criminal behavior. Recognize that withholding factual information on propensity for violence or criminal behavior may pose liability for negligent referral.
- Determine whether references will be provided in response to telephone or written or other documented inquiry.
- Obtain employees' signed release for providing information in reference checks.

Personnel Records

- Check applicable state law relating to personnel records access.
- Define what records will be maintained in the employee file.
- Limit records to information on job-related issues.
- Specify that personnel records are confidential, to be kept in a locked file cabinet or locked desk drawer.
- Limit release of personnel records to supervisors or managers who are in the direct chain of command over the employee or those who may be considering the employee for a pending personnel decision.
- Define whether employees are permitted access (as allowed by applicable law).
- Define guidelines for release of personnel records or information to third parties. (See management guidelines for employment verification.)
- Do not collect confidential, personal, or other non–job-related data.
- Obtain employee authorization before releasing data to creditors, financial institutions, or landlords.
- Define whether employees are permitted to correct records or to insert alternative information into their personnel files.
- Separate medical files from personnel records.

Employee Medical Records

- Identify a specific business purpose if your firm is collecting or maintaining employee medical records.
- Store employee medical records separate from regular personnel files to comply with the ADA.
- Check state and federal laws to ensure that use, storage, and disclosure of medical records complies with the law.
- Define a written policy to guide proper procedures on use, storage, and disclosure of employee medical records.
- Designate an individual(s) as responsible for maintaining medical files and protecting their confidentiality.
- Maintain medical records in confidential locked files or drawers.
- Determine whether employees are permitted access to their own medical records. If so, identify procedures for employee access.
- Identify whether release of medical information will be nonconsensual or only upon employee consent.

- Avoid using medical records or information in personnel decisions unless there is a clear or overriding safety or health justification.

- Identify limits for third-party access to or disclosure of medical records.

Computerized Business Records

- Limit the collection or retention of records that identify individual employees only to data collection for which there is a specific business purpose.

- Evaluate computerized records to determine what jobs or persons should have access to data and files.

- Limit access to data or files based on job responsibility and need to know.

- Define different levels of access to control access to specific screens, data, or files.

- Define different levels of access to control ability to view data, enter or change data, or report data.

- Develop a written computerized records policy to communicate procedural, access, and privacy issues.

- Define privacy responsibilities as part of an employee's job description.

- Assign responsibility for computer system security to a computer systems or other administrative manager.

- Train and instruct employees in proper use of data and need to protect confidentiality.

- Identify and communicate disciplinary procedures for unauthorized use or disclosure of confidential information.

Q & A: Employee Rights Regarding Access to and Release of Workplace Information

Q *What rights does an employee have when an employer releases information in response to an employment verification request?*

A A major concern for a job applicant is that release of a bad employment reference by a former employer will keep him or her from finding other work. If an employer releases or publicizes false information about an individual to others, the individual may have a basis to sue the former employer for defamation. Likewise, if an employer releases truly private information about an individual to others, the individual may have a basis for a privacy invasion claim. However, many states have passed reference-checking immunity laws, and common law in most states recognizes an employer's right to release truthful information to a fellow employer who is checking employment references, provided the applicant has authorized the prior employer to release such information.

Q   *Does an employee have any privacy protections or a right to view information in his or her personnel file?*
A   Personnel and pay records for federal government employees are subject to the Privacy Act, which limits unauthorized disclosure of personnel records or other private information. There is no broadly encompassing law that protects individual privacy or confidentiality of personnel records in the private workplace. Personnel records access laws in some states grant an employee permission to view certain information in his or her personnel file. But in states with no such law, employee access to personnel records or any privacy protections may be allowed solely as defined by employer policy.

Q   *What privacy protections does an employee have regarding medical records held by the employer?*
A   An employer may receive medical information on an employee through physical exams, drug/alcohol tests, medical insurance claims, workers' compensation claims, or requests for medical leaves of absence. Medical information is truly private information, so an employer's careless handling or inappropriate publicizing of medical details could be a privacy invasion depending on state common-law requirements.
    Certain laws limit employer use of medical information. The ADA:

- Prohibits preemployment medical inquiries
- Limits use of physical exams to after a job offer has been accepted
- Prohibits discrimination against an employee because of a physical or medical disability
- Requires that medical records be stored separately from personnel records

The OSHA Access to Employee Exposure and Medical Records Standard requires employers to permit an employee to view his or her medical records. And the recently passed HIPAA prohibits use of a classifying system to identify health conditions, or obtaining or disclosing certain health information.

Q   *What privacy rights does an employee have relating to other business or computerized records held by an employer?*
A   General business records are not subject to laws dealing with medical or personnel records privacy. However, if an employer discloses private information about an employee in an outrageous manner, the individual may have a common-law privacy invasion claim. An employer should take care to ensure that all business records, including any records identifying an individual employee, are handled in a confidential manner and not disclosed to others in an inappropriate manner.

9

Let's Look in Your Drawers: Monitoring Performance and Conducting Searches, Surveillance, and Investigations on the Job

After a customer accused her of taking $20 the customer had left on the counter, K-mart retail checker Bowderwig was ordered to strip to her underwear in the store's public rest room, as a female assistant manager and the complaining customer watched. Following this humiliating incident, Bowderwig sued K-mart for invasion of privacy. An Oregon appeals court held that Bowderwig may have grounds for a legal claim against the store and the customer because of their outrageous conduct based on the humiliating and degrading experience of submitting to a search to satisfy a customer. The court found that this form of search may have exceeded the bounds of social toleration.[1]

Employees don't expect to have their desks or work areas searched by their employer or be subjected to a strip search on the job. On the contrary, employees expect privacy in their personal activities and personal spaces, including their desks, lockers, tool boxes, computer files, or mail boxes in the office E-mail system. When an employer conducts a search of personal property or work areas, employees feel that their privacy rights have been violated. Likewise, when the employer monitors or observes personal or even work ac-

1. "Search and Surveillance," IERM 509:702 (1995).

tivities, employees may have the feeling that Big Brother is watching and invading individual privacy.

Yet investigations, searches, and surveillance are valid tools that employers can use *legally* to combat workplace problems that interfere with business operations. When evidence of drug or alcohol problems, theft, fraud, threat of violence, or other misconduct emerges, the employer will seek to identify the problem. Simple measures like performance monitoring and supervision can help uncover routine problems that can be easily corrected. But when an audit identifies inventory irregularities or hints at theft, or drug trafficking is suspected, or violence is threatened, management is likely to conduct more aggressive investigation, using investigation interviews, polygraph tests, surveillance of work areas or premises, and searches of work areas or even individuals.

This chapter will look at these investigation techniques and describe their potential for litigation. For each technique, we will examine representative cases that show how the action is regarded by the courts and suggest management guidelines, policy statements, and employee notices that minimize the chance that the technique or action will lead to litigation.

Counting Keystrokes:
Monitoring Employee Performance

Employer monitoring of employee performance has long been an essential management responsibility. The courts recognize that the nature of the employer-employee relationship entitles an employer to set reasonable standards for quality of employee performance. Further, the employer is entitled to require employees to meet those standards.[2]

To ensure that employees meet acceptable levels of performance, many firms use a process called performance management—ongoing communication and feedback about job responsibilities and performance—or the traditional, annual performance appraisal. According to a Labor Department–sponsored survey of 495 large U.S. businesses in a variety of industries, over 80 percent of large firms conduct performance appraisals.[3] In another survey of 109 smaller firms, 84 percent of managers reported belief in a pay-for-performance philosophy, but only 34 percent of those companies had perfor-

---

2. *Manikko v Harrah's Reno,* DNev 630 F Supp 191.
3. Columbia University Graduate School of Business, Survey of Human Resources Policies and Practices (Washington, DC: U.S. Department of Labor, 1989), 56.

mance appraisal procedures in place.[4] While these two surveys should not be viewed as a comprehensive picture of performance monitoring practices, they do demonstrate sizable management support for employee performance monitoring and widespread use of performance appraisals as a tool in that process.

According to author Michael Levy, American business has always monitored its workers. Early in the twentieth century, mechanical keystroke counters called cyclometers were used to measure speedy typists. Employers have observed employees on their jobs, checked the quality of work output, tracked attendance, and monitored other job performance issues in order to conduct performance appraisals. But today's high-technology systems give employers new ways to monitor performance. Levy cites a 1987 report of the OTA that indicated that:

- Six million office workers are evaluated using computer-generated statistics.
- Twenty-six million workers have their work tracked electronically.
- Ten million workers have their work evaluated and pay levels determined by statistical data collected through monitoring.
- In the New York area, 40 percent of companies use some form of electronic monitoring.[5]

Levy cites three concerns about computerized monitoring of workers:

1. *Privacy.* Computerized monitoring is intrusive.
2. *Fairness.* It does not allow for work style differences, and workers may question the fairness of work standards.
3. *Quality of work life.* Continual monitoring induces stress and greatly increases pressure on workers.

For example, Levy notes that flight reservation sales agents for one airline were required to handle 275 incoming calls daily, achieve a 90 percent booking ratio, limit calls to less than 215 seconds, and not spend more than 12 minutes away from the computer to use the bathroom. These data were used for performance evaluation and disciplinary action if the employee failed to meet standards—making monitoring a source of pressure and stress!

4. William S. Hubbartt, *Performance Appraisal Manual for Managers and Supervisors* (Chicago: CCH, 1992), 10.
5. Michael Levy, "Electronic Monitoring in the Workplace, Power through the Panopticon," http:// . . . s.umich.edu/impact/students/mike/mike_paper.html.

Sample Policy: Performance Monitoring

To assure a high level of quality and productivity in order entry operations, XYZ Company monitors all orders entered into the company's computerized order system.

1. The department supervisor is responsible for conducting performance monitoring on an ongoing basis as defined by this policy.

2. All customer orders entered into the computerized order entry system are subject to the following: (a) computerized audit of entries, (b) price check comparing part numbers with price, and (c) error list.

3. The department supervisor is responsible for advising employees that performance monitoring is occurring.

4. The first ninety days of employment are monitored solely for the purpose of establishing the employee's individual performance level.

5. Each employee shall receive a weekly performance report with error and audit lists. The employee is responsible for posting error corrections.

6. The supervisor is responsible for evaluating employee performance, defining a performance goal for each employee, and discussing goals with the employee.

7. In the event that an employee's performance level falls significantly below goal levels, the department supervisor is responsible for conducting a performance discussion with the employee. Serious and repeated performance problems are grounds for discharge.

8. The supervisor is responsible for recognizing employees for exceptional levels of performance.

> **Sample Employee Notice:**
> **Performance Monitoring**
>
> At XYZ Company, we are committed to maintaining our rep-
> utation for providing prompt, accurate handling of customer
> orders. To ensure that customer orders are handled properly,
> you will receive a weekly order audit report showing com-
> puter comparison of your entries. In addition, your
> supervisor monitors and checks order entry transactions and
> provides corrective instructions as needed. Your computer-
> ized audit reports are one factor that influences performance
> ratings as well as pay adjustments.

An employer can easily move from checking employee work results to
monitoring employee behavior and activities on the job. But an employer's misuse of performance monitoring, communications, and computer systems to
monitor employee behavior can result in allegations of privacy invasion.

Critical Issues in Performance Monitoring

Employers who use traditional supervisory techniques of observing workers
or check or audit work results are not creating a privacy invasion. But when
performance monitoring becomes more aggressive, employees will feel pressure from the monitoring process.

Making performance standards reasonably attainable will alleviate some
of the pressure. Informing employees that their performance is being monitored will minimize privacy expectation and reduce the likelihood of a privacy
invasion claim. But when employee conduct or performance is monitored in
areas that are normally viewed as private, a successful privacy invasion claim
is possible.

We're Listening: Trends in Telephone Monitoring

Employer monitoring of employees' telephone conversations is a fairly widespread practice, particularly in the telephone and telemarketing industries. But

it does not have to be viewed as a negative practice. At California-based Toyota Motor Sales, where employees in the customer relations department handle 1,000 to 1,200 calls a day, monitoring ensures consistent, high-quality performance.

On their first day on the job, customer relations representatives are asked to sign a consent form and told that all incoming calls that they receive may be monitored by Toyota management. Employees are not told exactly when the monitoring will occur. After listening into the employee's telephone conversations with customers, the manager completes a performance scorecard and conducts a feedback session with the employee. Information from the monitoring process is also included in the employee's performance appraisal.[6]

Toyota employees do not find the telephone monitoring intrusive. Says one employee, "I've never had anything but positive experiences." Adds another employee, "It is not a Big Brother kind of thing. . . . We have to be consistent. . . . It's quality control." Another Toyota employee adds, "The majority of the people in the department want to be monitored more often. . . . They value the feedback."[7]

Employers conducting telephone monitoring are subject to Title III of the Omnibus Crime Control and Safe Streets Act of 1968. Commonly referred to as the federal wire tap law, it prohibits intentional interception of a wire or electronic communication, including a company telephone call, and intentional disclosure of the communication. Under one portion of the law, telephone communications may be monitored if one of the parties consents to the monitoring. Also, the law permits an employer to use an extension telephone to monitor business calls as long as employees are aware that the monitoring is occurring.

However, many employers are unaware that surreptitious listening to an employee's phone conversation creates a serious legal liability. Eavesdropping on personal calls or monitoring or recording employee conversations without notifying caller or employee violates the wire tap law and can lead to privacy invasion claims. An "I'll listen in whenever I feel like it" attitude is bound to get an employer in trouble.

> Sibbie Deal worked as a retail clerk in the White Oak Package Store, a liquor store near Camden, Arkansas, owned by Newell and Juanita Spears. When the store was burglarized and approximately $16,000 was stolen, the Spears believed that Deal may have been involved.

6. Jennifer J. Laabs, "Surveillance: Tool or Trap?" *Personnel Journal*, June 1992, p. 100.
7. Ibid.

The store and the Spears' mobile home adjacent to the store shared a single telephone line. Hoping to catch Deal in an admission of the burglary, the Spears attached a recording device to the extension phone in their mobile home to record Deal's phone conversations as she worked in the store.

Over twenty-two hours of Deal's phone conversations were recorded and listened to by Newell Spears, including personal conversations. Spears did not tell Deal that her conversations were being recorded. The recordings revealed that Deal, a married woman, was having an extramarital affair with Calvin Lucas, a married man. Often, their telephone calls were sexually provocative. Spears's recording did not reveal any evidence related to burglary, but it did show that Deal sold Lucas a keg of beer at cost, in violation of store policy. Upon learning about the beer sale, Spears played a few seconds of the incriminating tape and fired Deal for violating the store policy.

Deal and Lucas filed suit against the liquor store claiming that the recording was electronic monitoring, creating a privacy invasion and violating the federal wire tap law. The court found that the liquor store owners violated the law and awarded $10,000 damages to Deal and Lucas. The court held in favor of the employee because the employers used a recording device, failed to distinguish between personal and business calls, and did not obtain consent or provide notice of monitoring.[8]

Employer telephone monitoring that complies with the law will generally withstand a court challenge:

A Colorado newspaper agency installed telephone monitoring equipment and informed employees in writing that departments that dealt with the public would be monitored for quality-control purposes and to protect employees from obscene calls. A privacy invasion lawsuit was filed. The court noted that monitoring was not done surreptitiously, and it was allowable under the law.[9]

Likewise, Southwestern Bell Telephone Company's monitoring of employee phone calls was upheld by the court in response to an employee's privacy invasion lawsuit.

8. *Deal v Spears*, 8 IER 105 (1992).
9. *James v Newspaper Agency*, 591 F2d 579 (10th Cir 1979).

Sample Policy: Telephone Monitoring

In order to assure a high level of quality control in customer service operations, XYZ Company conducts periodic and random monitoring of telephone calls, as outlined in the following procedures:

1. Telephone monitoring shall be done on business calls only. Monitoring shall stop as soon as it is determined that a telephone call is of a personal nature.

2. The manager shall conduct monitoring at the manager's extension, on a random and periodic basis.

3. For all outgoing telephone calls, employees are instructed to advise callers that XYZ telephone calls may be monitored to ensure quality control and a high level of customer service.

4. For all incoming calls, a recorded message shall advise callers that XYZ telephone calls may be monitored to ensure quality control and a high level of customer service.

5. Employees shall be advised not to make or receive personal calls on company telephone lines during company time.

6. Designated nonmonitored telephones are available for employee use for personal calls during nonworking times such as breaks, lunch periods, and before or after work.

7. The manager is responsible for recording which employee was monitored, when the monitoring occurred, and for appraising the employee's telephone manner and level of service provided.

**Sample Employee Notice:
Telephone Monitoring**

When answering XYZ telephones, answer by saying, "XYZ
Company. This telephone call may be monitored to assure
quality control. (Your name) speaking. May I help you?"
Remember to be pleasant and professional but avoid excessive or unnecessary discussion.

In order to maintain a high degree of professionalism in
customer service [or other specified business purpose], XYZ
Company monitors incoming customer telephone calls. Telephone monitoring will be done on a random basis by your
manager listening in on an extension telephone. Monitored
telephone calls are used to measure the quality of our customer services and for training purposes. After a phone call
has been monitored, you will be advised by your manager
about your telephone techniques and suggestions.

The employee, Simmons, complained that personal calls were monitored in violation of the law. The company monitored business calls
for quality control purposes. A separate nonmonitored telephone was
available for personal calls. The court held that the phone company's
actions were lawful, and that Simmons had been warned about excessive personal calls on monitored lines.[10]

When telephones are monitored secretly or without proper notice, or if
monitoring focuses on personal calls, a violation is likely. A manufacturing
firm was found to be in violation of the wire tap law when it used a voice
logger device to secretly record a security officer's telephone conversations.[11]
In another case, an employer who advised employees that calls were subject
to monitoring still went too far because it monitored personal calls as well as

10. *Simmons v Southwestern Bell*, 611 F2d 342 (10th Cir 1978).
11. *Sanders v Robert Bosch*, 10 IER Cases 1 (1994).

sales calls, even though the employee's consent form had specifically authorized sales call monitoring.[12]

Critical Issues in Telephone Monitoring

All monitoring of employee telephone calls is subject to the federal wire tap
law. Some states may have similar prohibitions against telephone monitoring.
When setting up security policies, performance monitoring procedures, or conducting investigations, it is important to make sure that company telephone
procedures are not in violation of the law. A section of the wire tap law permits
an employer, upon giving notice to one participant, to monitor phone calls for
business purposes by listening in on an extension telephone. An employee's
personal calls, however, should not be monitored, or monitoring should stop
when the employer determines that the call is personal. It is best to communicate telephone policy guidelines to employees and provide an unmonitored
phone for personal calls.

Under the Interrogation Spotlight:
A Look at Conducting Internal Investigations

When an employer becomes aware of a theft, sexual harassment claim, drug
problem, or other similar problem, it may wish to conduct some form of investigation. Conducted by security personnel, a loss control manager, a human
resources specialist, or another manager, a thorough investigation will get to
the heart of the issue and help determine appropriate corrective action. But
costly liabilities are possible if an employer makes an employment decision
without investigating, for example, discharging an employee because of an
unconfirmed rumor.

   After learning during a telephone conversation that employee Babb had
supposedly "mooned" another employee, supervisor Minder informed Babb's
supervisor of Babb's behavior and urged him to fire Babb. Based on Minder's
representations, Babb was fired for "mooning another employee and offering
sexual favors to another." Babb then sued, claiming defamation. In its defense,
the employer claimed qualified privilege, meaning that its actions were not
careless or in bad faith. However, the court noted that Minder acted on an
unconfirmed rumor without asking Babb to verify the incident, contacting the

---

12. *Watkins v L. M. Berry*, 704 F2d 577 (CA 11 1983).

witness, or conducting any other investigation. As a result, the employer's lack of an investigation resulted in liability to the firm.[13]

As this case illustrates, an improper investigation or an employment decision made without any investigation can create a serious liability. If an issue is not witnessed firsthand by a manager, then the matter must be investigated. An investigation can be as simple as an interview of witnesses and the individuals who are the focus of the investigation or may consist of a number of investigatory techniques, including workplace searches, surveillance, telephone monitoring, records checking, drug/alcohol testing, polygraph testing, and use of private investigating firms.

Properly done, an investigation can yield valuable information. However, an improper investigation or investigatory techniques that are coercive, threatening, or intrusive upon private aspects of the employee's life can lead to a privacy invasion claim.

> Variety Wholesalers, Inc., which operates a Super 10 Discount Store in Alabama, had received complaints through a company hotline about store manager Nipper's conduct. In addition, company management was investigating a $30,000 inventory loss. The company's loss prevention manager Allen conducted an investigation by interviewing the manager and other employees at the store.
>
> Allen interviewed employees individually at a table in a back room with the door open. Interviewees were free to come and go. No force or threat was used to restrain employees being interviewed. When Allen interviewed Nipper, he got her to admit that she had taken prescription drugs that made her sleepy on the job, that she had carried a handgun at work, and that her boyfriend often visited her at the store. These actions violated company rules against possession of a weapon on company property and prohibitions against receiving personal visitors while on the job. Shortly after the interview, Nipper was fired for inability to perform her job.
>
> Nipper sued her former employer alleging that the employer's conduct in the investigation was outrageous and constituted defamation and an invasion of privacy. In support of her suit, Nipper claimed that the investigator stated a belief that she was "doing drugs," that he cursed during the interview, and that he threatened her with dismissal if she talked about the interview with anyone.

13. *Babb v Minder*, 806 F2d 749 (7th Cir 1986).

In considering her suit, the court held that the employer's conduct
was not so outrageous in character and so extreme in degree as to go
beyond bounds of decency. It felt that the company's investigation was
within reasonable limits, that information obtained in the investigation
was obtained in private, and that the investigator cursed only to the
extent necessary to investigate the loss.[14]

If an investigation involves illegal conduct, the firm is encouraged to work
with local law enforcement authorities. An employer's use of local police for a
locker search for illegal drugs, for example, resulted in a conviction of an employee for cocaine possession.[15] However, when cooperating with local authorities in a criminal investigation, the search warrant issue becomes significant.
When police officers conduct a search, the search is likely to be subject to the
Fourth Amendment search warrant requirement.

Critical Issues in Conducting Internal Investigations

While an effective investigation is an essential tool in finding out the facts
about certain job problems, an improper investigation can result in even greater
liabilities. Because company investigations may wind up in court, it is important to keep a factual, objective tone in all actions and documents. Avoid
making threats, using intimidation, or restricting the employee's exit.

Investigations should be conducted solely in response to a specific business purpose. Limit inquiries to issues reasonably related to the investigation.
Internal investigations often turn up information that, if released to the public,
could be embarrassing to employees or the company. Since employment decisions may result in litigation, it is important to recognize that records gener-
ated during an investigation could end up as a matter of public record in a
court decision.

Attorney Rebecca Spar, writing in *HR Magazine*, suggests that there are
certain things an employer can do to protect the confidentiality of records
turned up during an investigation. Spar suggests that if the employer contacts
legal counsel when conducting an investigation, the employer may be able to
take advantage of certain forms of confidentiality privilege in the attorney-
client relationship.[16]

14. *Nipper v Variety Wholesalers,* 9 IER Cases 274 (1994).
15. *Faulkner v Maryland,* 4 IER Cases 1441 (1989).
16. Rebecca K. Spar, "Keeping Internal Investigations Confidential," *HR Magazine,* Jan.
    1996, p. 33.

Sample Policy: Internal Investigations

It is the policy of XYZ Company to conduct internal investigations as needed to protect the safety, security, and well being of company employees, facilities, property, and products.

1. The loss control manager is responsible for conducting the investigation. The investigation shall be recorded on the XYZ Company Investigation Report Form. In preparing the report, the following issues shall be considered:

   a) Observe the scene of the incident under investigation.
   b) Obtain statements from the affected employee and any witnesses.
   c) Ask questions to determine sequence of events prior to, during, and following the incident.
   d) Determine whether correct policies or procedures were followed.
   e) Answer all questions on the Investigation Report Form.

2. The results of the investigation shall be referred to the vice president for appropriate action.

3. Contact legal counsel and/or law enforcement authorities if the investigation is likely to result in litigation and/or criminal prosecution.

4. Protect confidentiality of all investigation records and avoid disclosure of information to unauthorized persons.

According to Spar, confidential information may be deemed subject to attorney-client privilege if it is revealed during an investigation conducted under the direction of an attorney and submitted back to the attorney. Attorney-client privilege means that the information a client tells his or her lawyer is private and cannot be disclosed to other parties in a legal proceeding. Another protection, referred to as "work product doctrine," means that records prepared by an attorney cannot be used against the client. Third, an employer's records related to self-criticism, policy evaluations, or opinions referred to as critical self-analysis, may not be used against the employer in a legal proceeding.[17]

Wired for Truth: Polygraph Exams and Investigations

A polygraph exam is a stress analysis exam that is intended to determine the truthfulness of an oral statement. Referred to as a lie detector test, the exam uses a device that monitors a subject's pulse rate and skin while the examiner asks a series of questions. The device measures the subject's involuntary reactions to questions. By its nature, with the employee wired to a machine, the polygraph is an intrusive and intimidating test.

Employers use the polygraph during investigations of theft or other economic loss of property or funds. If an employer's routine inventory, audit, or other check-and-balance procedures identify a shortage of inventory, products, or funds, the employer may direct employees who had access to the property to participate in a polygraph exam. The polygraph exam may turn up additional information, an indication of guilt, or an admission of theft.

Because of past abuses in which employers used polygraph exams to probe private matters of employees, some states have passed laws limiting use of the polygraph. Twenty-seven states define certain limits or prohibitions on use of the polygraph. Massachusetts and Maryland require employers to provide notice to employees about polygraph exam rights. Other states define areas of inquiry that may not be subject to a polygraph exam. Among the topics limited from inquiry in polygraph exams in some states are sexual practices, sexual preferences, religious beliefs, political opinions, union matters, and racial matters.[18]

17. Ibid., 34.
18. "The Lie Detector," in *Personnel Practices/Communications* (Chicago: CCH, 1991), Par. 324.

States That Restrict or Prohibit Use of Polygraph Exams

Alabama	Kansas	Oregon
Alaska	Maryland	Pennsylvania
California	Michigan	Rhode Island
Connecticut	Minnesota	Texas
Delaware	Montana	Vermont
District of Columbia	Nebraska	Virginia
Hawaii	Nevada	Washington
Idaho	New Jersey	West Virginia
Iowa	New Mexico	Wisconsin

Employer use of lie detectors or polygraph exams has been curtailed by the Employee Polygraph Protection Act of 1988. Prior to its passage, some employers used lie detector tests in preemployment screening as well as for investigations. The law prohibits most private employers from using lie detector tests for screening job applicants or routine testing of current employees. The law permits an employer to ask an employee to submit to a polygraph exam in the investigation of a workplace theft or other economic loss to the employer if:

- The employee had access to the property under investigation
- There was a reasonable suspicion that the employee was involved
- The employer provides written notice to the employee

The law permits fines up to $10,000 for violations and authorizes civil suits by the Labor Department as well as litigation by employees or applicants.[19]

An employer that fails to meet the procedural requirements of the law is subject to enforcement action.

When Rapid Robert's, Inc., suffered inventory losses, management began an investigation. The company identified a reasonable suspicion of certain employees, noting their anticompany attitude, ownership of possessions that typically could not be afforded based on the employee's wage level, unsupervised working conditions, frequent visits by

19. Employee Polygraph Protection Act of 1988, 29 USCA Chap. 22.

Sample Policy: Polygraph Exams

It is the policy of XYZ Company to use polygraph exams only in the investigation of loss of property or funds as summarized below.

1. In the event of a workplace theft or other economic loss to the company, XYZ Company may direct use of polygraph exams as part of its investigation.

2. Use of polygraph exams shall be according to the following procedures:
   a) There must be a specific actual theft or economic loss being investigated.
   b) Only employees who had access to the work area, merchandise, or item may be requested to take a polygraph exam.
   c) There must be a reasonable suspicion regarding the employee(s) to be tested.
   d) The company must provide written notice to the employee, forty-eight hours in advance, identifying the specific incident under investigation.

3. Polygraph exams must not be used in preemployment screening.

4. An employee may not be disciplined or discharged solely on the basis of the polygraph exam results.

5. In the event an employee refuses to participate in a polygraph exam when requested, such refusal shall be considered insubordination and grounds for discharge.

6. All polygraph exam records are confidential and are stored in security records.

Sample Employee Notice:
Polygraph Testing

In the event of a workplace theft or other economic loss, the company may use polygraph exams as part of its investigation. An employee's refusal to cooperate with an investigation including use of a polygraph exam, if so requested, is grounds for discharge.

friends, possessions of keys and security code, prior admissions of theft and drug use, and the company's inventory loss despite exceptionally accurate cash accounting methods. On the basis of these suspicions, the company ordered employees who had access to the inventory to take polygraph exams. The firm threatened to fire and then suspended employees who refused to take the test.

In its investigation of the case, the Labor Department determined that the company had not given notice to employees forty-eight hours in advance and that it failed to identify a specific incident being investigated. These procedural failures constituted a violation of the act. Rapid Robert's was subject to a $1,000 fine for each violation of the employee notice requirement, a $500 fine for violation of the notice content requirement, and a $1,500 fine for making unlawful threats to force compliance with the test.[20]

Critical Issues in Use of Polygraph Exams

Federal law now prohibits use of preemployment polygraph exams and provides detailed restrictions on their use in investigation of losses. Various state laws restrict use or specify notice requirements. Failure to strictly comply with procedural requirements can result in costly fines and litigation. Take care to protect confidentiality of test results. Avoid releasing information on employment decisions that may result in a false-light privacy invasion.

20. *In re Rapid Robert's*, 7 IER Cases 946 (1992).

He's Faking It! Investigating
Workers' Compensation Fraud

Employees in every state are covered by some form of workers' compensation, which provides medical insurance for the employee in the event of job-related injury and disability insurance in case of temporary or permanent disability arising from employment.

Occasionally, employees make fraudulent claims in order to receive disability benefits. For example, an employee may report a non–work-related illness or injury as a job-related occurrence because the workers' compensation plan provides better coverage than the employee's group health plan.

When an employee reports an illness or accident, the employer typically conducts an accident investigation. The accident investigation seeks to identify the environmental conditions and acts that led up to the accident or illness. If the employer suspects that the employee is falsifying any aspect of the claim, the employer may investigate the matter more thoroughly by hiring a private investigator to observe the employee's activities at home or in public. Generally, investigators use photographs or video camera film to document the employee's activities and physical abilities and "catch" him or her performing tasks the employee claims he or she cannot do because of the job injury. The data and photos or videos are reported back to the client company for use in denying the claim. Since the workers' compensation investigation involves following and observing the employee at home or elsewhere, these kinds of investigations may be vulnerable to the employee's claim of privacy invasion.

> In a Michigan case, for example, the employer hired a private investigator to tail an employee on disability leave because the firm suspected the employee was a malingerer. The employee, Saldana, had filed a workers' compensation claim for injuries to his elbow and arm sustained from a fall from a bicycle occurring in the course of employment on company property.
>
> Suspecting that the injuries may have been exaggerated or falsified, the employer, Kelsey-Hayes Company, hired a private investigator. The investigator visually observed the employee in his home from a parked car in the street and from the sidewalk in front of the employee's home. The investigator also viewed the disabled employee through the windows of his home using a magnifying telephoto camera. In addition, the investigator followed the disabled employee as he visited doctors' offices. The investigator also visited the employee's

Sample Policy: Workers' Compensation/Accident Investigation

It is the policy of XYZ Company to investigate all accidents in order to determine accident cause and to take appropriate steps to prevent a recurrence.

1. The supervisor is responsible for conducting an accident investigation following any job-related illness, injury, or accident.

2. The accident report shall be prepared on the Supervisor's Accident Investigation Report Form. In preparing the accident report, the supervisor should:

   a) Observe the scene of the accident to identify any conditions that may have contributed to or caused the accident.
   b) Obtain statements from the injured employee and/or witness.
   c) Ask questions to determine the sequence of events prior to, during, and following the accident.
   d) Determine whether correct procedures were followed.
   e) Answer all questions on the accident report form.

3. The accident report shall be submitted to the human resources manager by the next business day.

4. The human resources manager shall review the accident report within three days of occurrence. The employee and/or supervisor may be called in for clarification of information when necessary. Management shall then initiate appropriate corrective action as necessary to prevent a recurrence of a similar accident.

> ### Sample Policy: Workers' Compensation/Accident Investigation
>
> 5. The human resources manager shall then determine whether the accident is reportable and for workers' compensation and/or OSHA reporting. The accident report is then routed to the office administrator for preparation of reports if any and for filing.
>
> 6. In the event that management suspects workers' compensation fraud, the human resources manager may retain a private investigator to conduct an investigation including surveillance of the individual as needed.

house posing as a process server for the purpose of looking around the house. Further, a company manager sent a letter to the employee's doctor seeking information about the employee's health condition and ability to work.

Saldana sued his employer for intrusion upon seclusion, a form of privacy invasion under common law. While acknowledging that some of the investigator's methods may have been objectionable to a reasonable person, the court held that the employer's surveillance of the employee at his home involved matters that the employer had a legitimate right to investigate.[21] In this case, the employer won its case in spite of the objectionable surveillance techniques of its investigator because, in weighing the evidence, the judge apparently gave more weight to the employer's need to investigate fraud than the employee's privacy rights.

It is important to remember that each case is tried on the unique facts of that case and the standard of law in the state. See the Bethlehem Steel surveillance case in this chapter, where the court held that certain actions of the investigator were lawful while other actions were a privacy invasion.

21. *Saldana v Kelsey-Hayes,* 4 IER Cases 1107 (1989).

**Sample Employee Notice:
Workers' Compensation/Accident Investigation**

It is the policy of XYZ Company to conduct an investigation in the event of a job-related accident or illness. Each employee is expected to report any accident or illness occurring on the job to his or her immediate supervisor. The supervisor is responsible for conducting an investigation by completing the XYZ accident report form. The report shall be submitted to the human resources manager by the end of the next workday. In the event that there is cause to suspect fraud or falsification by an employee in providing information for an accident report, the company may conduct an investigation. In the event that the investigation determines that fraud or falsification of information occurred, the employee shall be subject to discharge, and the company may elect to impose criminal charges if warranted.

Critical Issues in Workers' Compensation Investigations

Because a workers' compensation investigation inevitably involves observing employees in their personal lives, it is best to have a clearly defined business purpose for the investigation. While this type of investigation may prompt privacy invasion claims, the courts try to balance the employee's privacy right with the employer's right to investigate a business matter and recognize that the employer may be trying to catch an employee's illegal behavior. In the Saldana case, for example, the court said that the employee's privacy protection is not absolute, and there is, in effect, a minimal expectation of privacy if the employee has engaged in illegal activity.

Nosy or Necessary? A Look at Workplace Searches

Searching employees or their possessions holds real potential for privacy invasion if the employer fails to carefully justify the search or to carry out the search in a proper manner. Even though the U.S. Supreme Court in the *O'Connor* case (see chapter 3) stated that employees have a privacy expectation in their desks and offices, the court gave employers wide latitude to search offices, desks, and files of employees. The *O'Connor* Court ruled that a state hospital was not required to obtain a search warrant or to have "probable cause" to justify its search. The Court felt that these requirements would be unduly burdensome, unwieldy, and unreasonable for a supervisor who needs to gain access to an employee's office or desk on a job-related matter.

Some searches are casual and impromptu, as when a supervisor needs to check an employee's desk or office to find a document, report, key, or other item. One midwestern company requires employees to turn in desk and file keys during vacations so that work documents can be located if necessary. The key policy was implemented after management was unable to obtain a critical report for an important customer meeting. The report was in the locked desk of an employee who was on a two-week vacation.

Often employer searches are conducted for reasons related to security, theft control, or drug activity occurring at the workplace. In these cases, an employer may set up a security checkpoint at a premises entrance or conduct a search of desks or lockers.

To minimize the likelihood of a privacy invasion claim, the employer should identify a business purpose for the search, define a search policy, and notify employees about the search policy. The courts generally will look favorably on employer searches that are conducted reasonably and justified by safety, security, or drug control purposes, as the following cases demonstrate.

> When Williams was on leave from his job with the Philadelphia Housing Authority, his supervisor had occasion to enter Williams's office and remove a computer disk from his desk. In a legal claim that resulted, the court held that the housing authority supervisor was exercising discretion to maintain efficiency and productivity in the workplace. Prior to his leave, Williams had been instructed to clear the office of his personal items. Court records showed that the supervisor's search was initiated solely for work-related material and that the supervisor's review of the employee's personal files in her search for official documents was reasonable.[22]

22. *Williams v Philadelphia Housing Authority*, 8 IER Cases 1121 (1993).

Security was the motivation for searching Ronald Koepplin, a haul truck driver for Zortman Mining, when he was fired after making phone calls to supervisors who were investigating sexual harassment charges against him. During the investigation, a Zortman supervisor reported receiving a phone call from Koepplin in which the employee told the supervisor that "he had best get packed for his little trip to hell." This statement by Koepplin was perceived by the company to be a threat. Anticipating potential disruption by Koepplin, the employer arranged to have a deputy sheriff on hand for the discharge discussion. The sheriff's deputy elected to frisk and search the employee at the start of the meeting.

Koepplin sued Zortman Mining, alleging that the frisk and search was an invasion of privacy. In considering the case, a Montana superior court held that Koepplin had no claim for invasion of privacy because the search lasted less than two minutes and the decision to frisk the employee was made independently by the sheriff without the employer's participation.[23] The search of Koepplin was indeed justified by his threat against management.

Drug-Related Searches

Because drug abuse issues create significant safety concerns, the courts tend to give employers some latitude in searches for drugs.

U.S. Steel Corporation considered drug activity at its Gary works to be so pervasive that an antidrug hotline was established to encourage employees to anonymously report any drug activity occurring at the plant. When anonymous calls did reveal drug use in the workplace, the firm obtained the assistance of Drug Enforcement Agency officers with drug-detecting dogs and local police officers. Police officers merely observed, and the search was witnessed by a union representative. Employee Melton sued the steel giant, alleging that the search was a warrantless search in violation of Fourth Amendment rights. The federal district court noted that published company policies prohibited storage or use of drugs on company premises. Further, the union president testified that employee lockers had been subject to searches in

23. Ibid.

the past. As a result, the court held that these were lawful searches, conducted by a private sector employer, observed by police, and organized solely to enforce a legitimate safety policy.[24]

In *Faulkner v Maryland,* the employer had reason to believe that drugs and alcohol were being used at work in violation of company policies. The employer's undercover security firm had confirmed drug use and distribution by second-shift employees. Further, company policies gave the employer the right to conduct a general locker search. The police were called in to supervise. Cocaine was found in the locker of an employee who first denied that the locker was his. The search resulted in criminal charges and ultimate conviction of the individual. The employee sued, claiming that the warrantless search violated his constitutional rights. A Maryland appeals court held that the employee had minimal expectation of privacy in his locker, especially since he initially denied that the locker was his. The court held that the employer's search was proper for the following reasons:

- The employer owned the locker.
- The lockers were used to store company and personal property.
- The employer had a reasonable basis for the search because the drug activity had been confirmed by undercover investigators.
- Drug use and possession violated company policy.
- Company rules clearly stated the employer's right to search lockers.
- The police were called in at the request of the employer.[25]

Expectation of Privacy

If the employer's policies or practices permit the employee to have an expectation of privacy, the employer's search may run afoul of the law. Trotti, an employee of K-mart in Texas, filed an invasion of privacy claim after K-mart entered her locker, for which she had provided the lock. Applying Texas law, the court held that since Trotti had supplied the lock with the knowledge of her employer, she had a reasonable expectation of privacy with respect to the items stored in the locker.[26]

24. *Melton v United States Steel,* 8 IER Cases 687 (1993).
25. *Faulkner v Maryland,* 4 IER Cases 1441 (1989).
26. *K-mart v Trotti,* 677 SW2d 682 (Tex App 1984).

Further, if an employer fails to provide notice of searches or if the search practices are coercive, it is highly likely that the search will be viewed as a privacy invasion.

Employer searches of an employee's personal property or vehicle appear to be subject to a greater degree of scrutiny by the courts.

> An appeals court in Illinois, for example, held that a railroad may have violated employees' Fourth Amendment rights when it conducted searches of employee vehicles as they sought to exit the railroad parking lot. The employer's search procedures were questioned when the case went to court. Even though the employer had posted signs on the parking lot gates stating that vehicles entering or exiting the lot were subject to search, there appeared to be numerous questions about the individual's implied consent for the search. The search occurred in a fenced parking area. Exit gates were half-closed, and police officers stood in the path of exits. Employees were asked to get out of their cars and to open the trunks, and they were not told that they were free to leave without being searched.
>
> In their suit, employees argued that the police presence and blocked exit made the search coercive. The court was not swayed by the employer's argument that implied consent occurred at the same time as the seizure. Further, the court noted that the area had not been subject to prior searches. As a result, the court held that the employer's actions may have violated constitutional rights of the employees.[27]

Employer searches of employee personal property or vehicles may be permissible when the employer has sound justification for the search, follows reasonable guidelines, and notifies employees of the likelihood that personal property or vehicles on company property may be subject to searches. Searches of knapsacks, purses, briefcases, or similar items may be allowed under properly communicated and implemented search practices. Employees and visitors to federal buildings and most courthouses are subject to parcel searches or required to place items on X-ray machines as they walk through metal detectors.

> New York's Bellevue Hospital established a policy of conducting random spot inspections of employees' packages as employees were leav-

---

27. *McGann v Northeast Illinois Regional Commuter Railroad*, 8 IER Cases 1697 (1993).

Sample Policy: Workplace Searches

XYZ Company recognizes its obligation to protect the safety of employees and visitors to our premises. To protect the safety of individuals and to prevent theft, XYZ Company implements this policy for workplace searches.

1. All company property provided for use by employees is subject to search if deemed necessary by management. This includes desks, files, cabinets, lockers, offices, computerized files or disks, computer hard drives or other storage media, and computerized or electronic data.

2. All parcels removed from the premises are subject to search by the security manager.

3. All searches are normally conducted by the security manager or a security staff person. A second manager may witness the search.

4. Searches are conducted only for purposes related to business operations, or safety or security of our operations.

5. When there is grounds to suspect criminal activity or if it is determined that there is a need to search an individual's person, local law enforcement authorities shall be called in to conduct the search.

6. Searches shall be conducted in a nonthreatening and noncoercive manner.

7. An employee's refusal to cooperate with searches shall be subject to corrective discipline, which may include discharge.

**Sample Employee Notice:
Workplace Searches**

In order to promote the safety and security of our premises, XYZ Company reserves the right to gain access to and search company property including but not limited to desks, files, cabinets, lockers, offices, tool boxes, computerized or document records, and data or text files. To avoid loss or theft of valuables or other personal items, it is recommended, however, that you not bring personal items or parcels onto company property.

ing the building. The hospital had established its policy to control pilferage, announced its search policy to employees, used noncoercive search tactics, and permitted employees an opportunity to check parcels to avoid possibility of search. The court noted that, even though Bellevue employee Chenkin had an expectation of privacy in his knapsack and its contents, the hospital's policy was not an unreasonable intrusion into the employee's privacy. These practices, according to the court, rendered the employee's expectation of privacy unreasonable.[28]

Critical Issues in Use of Workplace Searches

Employers conducting workplace searches are most likely to be subject to legal challenges based on common-law claims of privacy invasion. A Fourth Amendment violation may be claimed if the employer is in the public sector. While the courts recognize an employee's privacy expectation with regard to desks and offices, an employer's search of company property is generally considered an appropriate employer prerogative if there is a business justification. A search may violate the law if the employer permits an expectation of privacy. Further, an employee's refusal to permit a search may negate a privacy invasion claim. Searches of employees' personal property and vehicles may be allowed

28. *Chenkin v Bellevue Hospital Center,* 479 F Supp 207 (DC SNY 1979).

where prior notice is given, but such searches are more likely to run afoul of the law when the employer's purpose or methods are unreasonable.

An employer's improper restraint of a employee may result in a claim of false imprisonment. Employer use of police officials may be justified in searches of individuals, particularly if illegal activities such as illegal drug possession or violent action are a likely result. However, use of police officials also reopens the need to consider whether a search warrant is needed. Consult with local law enforcement officials on this matter.

We're Watching You:
Surveillance of Employees and Customers

Employers use visual surveillance, voice monitoring, and electronic or computer surveillance techniques to monitor employee performance, improve security, prevent or catch inventory or cash losses, and detect such improper conduct as possession or use of drugs, alcohol, or weapons. According to the American Civil Liberties Union (ACLU), the number of workers subject to electronic surveillance has grown from 8 million in 1990 to 20 million in 1996.[29]

To protect against theft, violence, or property destruction, many employers use security personnel, closed-circuit televisions, and videotape cameras to conduct visual surveillance of employees as well as customers or visitors to their premises. Security personnel acknowledge that the key benefit of visible security and surveillance systems is their deterrent value.

Visual surveillance in "public areas" is generally lawful. However, a practice of observing employees in areas that are normally not considered public may be unlawful if employees could reasonably expect such areas to be private. Observing employees in rest rooms, locker rooms, and lounges is likely to be viewed as a privacy invasion. Such areas are not considered public, and employees could reasonably expect the area to be private.

For example, a court held that video surveillance of postal workers in their break room was an invasion of privacy under the Hawaii constitution. The employees had a subjective expectation of privacy in the room, which was neither a public place nor subject to public view or hearing. The court held that society would recognize their expectation of privacy as objectively reasonable.[30]

29. "Employee Privacy: An ACLU Campaign," *HRM News* (Chicago), Sept. 9, 1996, p. 3.
30. *State of Hawaii v Bonnell*, 8 IER Cases 1226 (1993).

Surveillance of employees during nonwork time or at home represents a significant potential for privacy invasion claims. In a Michigan case, for example, a company hired a private investigator to tail a suspected malingerer who had filed a workers' compensation claim. As a result of the investigator's actions and a company letter to the employee's doctor regarding his medical status, the employee sued his employer, claiming an invasion of privacy.[31]

The employer's business purpose for conducting surveillance can be a significant factor in justifying the surveillance. General Electric, for example, was allowed to photograph employees over their objections. The company took motion pictures of employees at work. The purpose of the films was to increase employee effectiveness and to promote safe work practices. Applying Kentucky law, the court held that the company could photograph employees as long as there was a legitimate business purpose.[32] Likewise, a government employer did not violate an employee's constitutional right to privacy when it observed the off-duty conduct of two police officers who were dating each other. The court noted that the employer's investigation probing possible violation of department rules against cohabitation was reasonable justification for the surveillance.[33]

A Maryland case helps to distinguish an employer's lawful surveillance from an unlawful invasion of privacy.

Bethlehem Steel hired a private detective to observe the activities of employee Pemberton, a union activist. The detective observed the employee's activities outside his home, at various stores, and along public roads. The detective also discovered that the employee was having an affair and observed him at his girlfriend's house. After tracking the employee to a motel, the detective placed a detection device on the employee's motel room door and monitored the employee's actions from the motel stairwell. Information about the affair was eventually disclosed to the employee's wife. The employee sued, claiming unlawful invasion of privacy.

The court determined that observing the employee from public places was lawful and considered the purpose of the employer's surveillance acceptable. But placing the detection device on the motel

---

31. *Saldona v Kelsey-Hayes*, 4 IER Cases 1107 (1989).
32. *Thomas v General Electric*, (EDKY) 207 F Supp 792.
33. *Shawgo v Spradlin*, 1 IER Cases 114 (1983).

Sample Policy: Surveillance

XYZ Company has experienced recent incidents of work-place disruption due to theft of merchandise. To protect the security of XYZ property and merchandise, XYZ Company implements this policy on workplace surveillance.

1. All surveillance activities shall be carried out solely for business purposes as defined in this policy.
2. Surveillance shall be done by the loss control manager or security manager, or by professional security/surveil-lance services.
3. The security manager is responsible for posting notices advising employees that XYZ premises are subject to sur-veillance.
4. Personnel performing surveillance as authorized by this policy are responsible for conducting surveillance from open and public areas. Surveillance is not permitted in "private areas" such as rest rooms.
5. Surveillance cameras are mounted at the main entrance, parking area, and at the shipping dock. Information and videotapes obtained in the course of surveillance are confidential, and their use is limited to investigatory pur-poses only.

door and monitoring the employee's actions from the motel stairwell were held to be privacy invasion.[34]

Critical Issues in Use of Surveillance

Surveillance that occurs in public or work areas where there is little or no reasonable expectation of privacy is generally allowable. Surveillance of private areas in the workplace such as rest rooms, break rooms, or lounges is

34. Alfred G. Feliu, *Primer on Individual Rights* (Washington DC: BNA, 1993), 213.

Sample Employee Notice:
Surveillance

In order to promote safety and security of our premises and to deter theft, XYZ Company conducts surveillance of company property, work areas, and premises and may conduct other surveillance as necessary.

---

likely to be viewed by the courts as an unreasonable privacy intrusion. An employer announcement that surveillance will occur reduces privacy expectation and minimizes the likelihood of privacy invasion claims.

An employer's surveillance of employee activities occurring off the job represents a greater likelihood of a privacy invasion claim if the employer does not have a justified purpose for the surveillance or if the surveillance intrudes upon a private aspect of the individual's life.

Summary

When monitoring, investigation, search, and surveillance become personal, private, or demeaning, employees may cry foul and claim privacy invasion. If the employer's actions violate the law, or outrageously intrude into a private aspect of an employee's life without good cause, a privacy invasion has occurred. By conducting a probe for a legitimate job-related reason in a manner that recognizes personal dignity and complies with the law, an employer can avoid committing a privacy invasion.

Appendix

Management Guidelines

Performance Monitoring

- Define a business purpose for performance monitoring, such as tracking productivity for an incentive-based pay plan, quality control, or training.

- Communicate to employees that performance is monitored, explaining how and why the monitoring occurs.
- Where productivity or performance standards may be defined, set the standard at a reasonable attainable level for a qualified employee.
- Allow for a fatigue factor when setting a performance guideline.
- Avoid performance monitoring practices that may be highly offensive or create undue pressure.
- Avoid monitoring performance or employee conduct in areas that are viewed as private.

Telephone Monitoring

- Check the federal wire tap law and any state workplace privacy laws to avoid defining a procedure that is in violation of the law.
- Define a clear business purpose for telephone monitoring. Typically, monitoring may occur for performance monitoring, quality assurance, training, investigations, and security or loss control purposes.
- Define procedures that show that calls are monitored in the ordinary course of business.
- Post the telephone monitoring policy or communicate the policy to employees.
- Ask employees subject to telephone monitoring to sign a written consent form.
- Conduct telephone monitoring using an extension telephone.
- Avoid recording phone calls unless all federal wire tap law requirements are met.
- Protect confidentiality of information obtained through telephone monitoring to avoid unwanted release of proprietary or private information.
- Avoid monitoring personal calls. Monitor calls to the extent needed to determine the nature of call, and stop once a call's personal nature is identified.
- Provide unmonitored telephones for personal use.
- Issue warnings to employees who make personal telephone calls from monitored business telephones.

Conducting Investigations

- Define a specific business purpose for the investigation.
- Train managers in proper investigating techniques or limit participation in the investigation process to trained individuals only.
- Avoid using threats or intimidation when conducting investigative interviews.

- Limit the focus of the investigation to job-related issues or conduct.

- Take care to ensure that investigation or interview notes are objective and factual, since such documents may end up as evidence in litigation.

- Avoid investigation techniques that would be embarrassing or humiliating to the individual or otherwise outrageous conduct in the eyes of a reasonable person.

- Have another manager or human resources representative on hand to witness the investigation interviews.

- Have a union steward on hand to witness the investigation interviews of union employees.

- Use broad, nonthreatening questions at start of the investigation interview, then move to increasingly more detailed inquiries.

- Verify improper conduct by obtaining information from two or more sources if possible.

- Limit disclosure of information obtained during the investigation to management personnel with a job-related "need to know."

- Involve legal counsel or law enforcement officers if the investigation is likely to result in litigation or to uncover illegal activity subject to prosecution.

Polygraph Exams

- Check laws in your state to identify polygraph exam limitations.

- Avoid inquiries into subject areas prohibited by any applicable laws.

- Do not use polygraph exams unless your organization is covered by one of the exemptions allowed under the law.

- In general employment, limit use of the polygraph to investigation of theft or other economic loss.

- When conducting testing, identify only individuals who had access to the loss, where there is a reasonable suspicion, and provide required notice to individuals being tested.

- Avoid threatening, disciplining, discharging, or otherwise discriminating against or denying employment to an employee solely on the basis of polygraph test results.

- Request in writing that suspected individuals participate in the test.

- Provide notification details required by law.

- Protect confidentiality of records and information related to any investigation, testing, or subsequent employment decisions.

Workers' Compensation Investigations

- Conduct an accident investigation immediately after an accident occurs.

- Train managers in proper accident investigation techniques.

- Interview the employee and any witnesses to determine events prior to, during, and following the accident.

- Define a clear business purpose for the investigation and for any surveillance.

- Check state and local laws to see whether there are any limitations to surveillance.

- If it is necessary to conduct surveillance of an individual's home or personal activities, conduct surveillance from open or public areas.

- Provide notice to employees if surveillance is conducted from hidden areas.

- Do not conduct surveillance in areas that are viewed as private.

- Discontinue surveillance when the scope of surveillance moves beyond disproving a workers' compensation claim.

Workplace Searches

- Check state laws.

- Define a business purpose for the search.

- Announce the search policy to employees.

- Retain control of locks on desks, files, offices, etc., to prevent an expectation of privacy.

- Use noncoercive search tactics.

- Seek to obtain employee consent to the search.

- Advise employees that bringing personal items onto company premises constitutes consent to search. Personal items that the employee does not want searched should be left at home.

- Conduct searches based on reasonable cause or random selection.

- Conduct searches uniformly with consistent procedures.

- Reserve the right to gain access to and to search company property including desks, files, lockers, etc.

- Involve the union steward in a search of a union employee's items or possessions.

- Involve law enforcement officers if there is any likelihood of encountering illegal contraband or any possibility of violence.

Surveillance

▪ Define a clear business purpose for surveillance: theft control, protection of premises from destruction, limiting access by unauthorized persons, investigation of workers' compensation fraud, or similar concerns.

▪ Check state and local laws to see whether there are any limitations to surveillance.

▪ Conduct surveillance from open or public areas.

▪ Provide notice to employees, customers, or the public if surveillance is conducted from hidden areas.

▪ Do not conduct surveillance in areas that are viewed as private.

▪ Post or display notices to employees that surveillance may be done in the workplace.

▪ Discontinue surveillance when the scope of surveillance moves beyond the business purpose for the surveillance.

Q & A: Employee Rights Regarding Workplace Searches, Surveillance, and Performance Monitoring

Q   *Can an employer electronically monitor work performance?*

A   Generally, an employer can monitor performance and activities of employees while on the job, but the employer should notify employees that performance is being monitored and comply with applicable laws. An electronic communications privacy law limits certain monitoring of electronic or computerized communications; a federal wire tap law limits telephone monitoring. Monitoring should occur in public or work areas and not in areas normally considered private. Monitoring that disregards the law or is an outrageous intrusion into private aspects of an individual's life is likely to be a privacy invasion.

Q   *Can an employer monitor employee telephone calls?*

A   Telephone monitoring is subject to federal wire tap laws. An employer may monitor business calls where there is a defined business purpose for the monitoring, employees are notified of the monitoring, and the monitoring occurs in the usual course of business on an extension telephone. Monitoring personal calls is not permitted, and monitoring should stop when a call is identified as personal.

Q   *Can an employer search desks, lockers, or other workplace areas?*

A   Searches are generally permissible when an employer identifies a business purpose for a search of company property such as desks, lockers, files, or computers, communicates the search requirement to employees, and conducts the search in a reasonable manner. But where an employer permits an expectation of privacy—

say, by allowing employees to supply locks for lockers—the search may be deemed a privacy invasion.

Q   *Can an employer search an individual's or an employee's private property?*
A   An employer's search of employees' private property has been allowed where the employer advised employees of its search policy and conducted the searches consistently in a nonthreatening manner. However, pat-down or strip searches of employees by the employer are generally viewed as privacy invasions. Use of law enforcement authorities is recommended if a personal search is necessary.

Q   *Can an employer conduct surveillance in the workplace?*
A   Visual, video, photographic, or other surveillance of employees (or the public) in work or public areas is generally lawful. The employer should notify employees or the public that an area is under surveillance. But surveillance of areas not considered public, such as rest rooms, is likely to be a privacy invasion. Further, employer surveillance of union-organizing activities is an unfair labor practice.

Q   *Is employer surveillance of employees off the job a privacy invasion?*
A   Employer surveillance of an employee's off-work activities is likely to be judged a privacy invasion if the employer's actions are outrageous or probe into private aspects of an employee's personal life. Surveillance of an employee's off-work activity related to union organizing is an unfair labor practice. However, off-duty surveillance, including surveillance of an employee at home for a legitimate business purpose such as a workers' compensation fraud investigation, has been deemed lawful, provided the surveillance is done from "public" areas.

10

My Time, My Life: A Look at Employer Regulation of Off-Duty Conduct

Sparks flew when Laurel Allen and Samuel Johnson, employees in the sporting goods department of an upstate New York Wal-Mart, began dating. But those sparks quickly became a conflagration when their supervisor learned of their relationship and fired them. When they sued the retailing giant for $2 million apiece, their relationship became front-page news.

According to company representatives, Allen and Johnson were dismissed for disruptive behavior and violation of a company policy prohibiting married employees from dating. Wal-Mart justified its employment decision by pointing out that Allen, although separated from her husband, violated the policy by dating someone other than her own spouse. Further, the company alleged that the behavior of both employees was disruptive, citing excessive breaks together, open displays of affection, and visits to one another while on duty. Allen denied that the couple displayed open affection on the job.

Their lawsuit received a boost when New York Attorney General Robert Abrams filed his own suit against Wal-Mart, claiming the retailing giant violated a New York law that bars employers from firing workers because of participation in legal recreational activities outside of work. In his suit, the attorney general cited a portion of the Wal-Mart Employee Handbook that states that the company "strongly believes and supports the family unit. A dating relationship between a married associate, other than his or her own spouse, is inconsistent with this belief and is . . . prohibited."[1]

In considering this case, the appellate division of the New York Supreme Court noted that the law prohibits adverse employment actions based on an individual's legal recreational activities outside of work hours, away from the employer's premises, and without use of the employer's equipment or other property. After evaluating the facts, the court ruled that the attorney general had no cause of action, that dating is not a recreational activity within the meaning of the law, and that Wal-Mart did not violate state law by firing two employees for violating its nonfraternization policy.[2]

Dating isn't the only area in which employers have developed policies. A variety of off-duty activities have come under the scrutiny of employers, including:

Secondary employment. A retail building materials and hardware chain became concerned about sales clerks performing after-hours home repair jobs for hire because the clerks were soliciting customers for work while on the job.

Conflict of interest. A tool and die shop wanted to prohibit die makers from performing work for competing firms after hours because of the potential for unauthorized disclosure of confidential information and trade secrets and because the second jobs limited their availability for overtime assignments.

Noncriminal misconduct. A bank sought to fire an employee for "bouncing checks" in her personal account because her actions reflected unfavorably on the bank in the community.

Use of lawful products off the job. A delivery company disciplined a delivery driver for drinking in a local bar after hours while wearing the company uniform.

Religious beliefs. Owners of a manufacturing firm issued a warning to one employee because of his repeated after-hours attempts to invite fellow employees to religious services.

Criminal misconduct. A printer discharged an press operator involved in a drunken barroom brawl who spent the next few days in jail.

---

1. "Wal-Mart's Dating Rule Draws Suits," *Chicago Tribune,* July 15, 1993, sec. 1, p. 3.
2. *State of New York v Wal-Mart Stores,* 10 IER Cases 255 (NY Sup Ct App Div 1995).

Smoking. A major electronics firm announced a policy against employee smoking both on and off the job but backed down after employee and public outcry.

The response to actions like these is predictable: "They can't tell me what to do on my own time. They've got me for eight hours a day, forty hours a week. But what I do on my own time is my own business!" When employer actions affect an employee during off-duty time, employees often view the action as a privacy infringement. Generally, an employer has little latitude in regulating off-duty conduct by employees unless there is some relationship between off-duty conduct and job performance or if there is a negative impact on the employer's business. If the job relationship cannot be shown, the employee may have a privacy invasion claim or a discrimination claim under a state or federal law.

Go Directly to Jail, Do Not Pass Go: Employer Response to Criminal Misconduct

Most employees are law-abiding citizens who fill their off-duty hours with family, recreational, or social activities. But some individuals just can't seem to stay out of trouble. Some have difficulty controlling use of alcohol and become involved in traffic accidents or are arrested for driving under the influence. Others may become involved in shoplifting, theft, or "bouncing" checks. Individuals who become drug abusers engage in criminal activity when buying or selling illegal drugs.

Criminal misconduct is a big concern of employers, whether it happens on the job or off. When it occurs on the employer's time or premises, the employer has a clear basis to deal with the matter. Many employee handbooks state that an employee's criminal conduct on the job is grounds for discharge.

Justification for dealing with off-duty criminal conduct may not be as clear. But if there is a reasonable relationship between the conduct and job performance or company well-being, an employer's action in response to off-duty criminal misconduct is less likely to be challenged. For example, an employee's discharge following his arrest for possession of cocaine was held by an arbitrator to be sufficient cause for discharge. In upholding the employer's decision, the arbitrator noted that, due to the highly publicized arrest and the employee's extensive prior criminal record, the employer had a well-grounded fear that the employee might engage in subsequent criminal misconduct. Further, the arbitrator noted that possession of cocaine is "inherently disreputable," and an employer who knowingly employs such individuals risks its reputation.[3]

Other examples in which there is a clear correlation between criminal activity and the employee's job responsibilities include:

- A company driver arrested or convicted of drunk driving
- A bank employee who commits check-writing fraud
- A purchasing agent who accepts kickbacks
- A retail employee who steals cash or merchandise
- A teacher or day care worker charged with child molestation

In each of these cases, corrective action by the employer would certainly appear to be warranted. Likewise, when an employee commits a crime of violence, the employer will have a strong justification to take corrective action to ensure the safety of employees, customers, or the public.

An employer has several options when responding to employee criminal misconduct. An employee may be discharged immediately following arrest if:

- The employee's criminal action occurs on company time or premises
- The crime is violent
- The crime is widely publicized and detrimental to the employer's operations

Because arrest does not necessarily mean guilt, sometimes an employer should use other options for alleged criminal conduct. Transfer, reassignment, demotion, or suspension with or without pay are all actions that may be taken at time of arrest, with discharge delayed until the employee is convicted of the crime. However, an employee in jail because of criminal misconduct is certainly not at work. Discipline or discharge for an unreported or unauthorized absence may be appropriate.

Several laws may affect employment decisions made based on criminal misconduct. State and federal enforcement of antibias laws prohibits discrimination based on arrest records. Discharging an employee because of an arrest could result in such a claim. On the other hand, employers that sell to the federal government are subject to the DFWA, which requires the employer to report to the contracting agency any drug-related criminal conviction occurring

3. *Paperworkers Local 1468 and C & A Wall Coverings*, 90-1 ARB Par. 8110.

in the workplace and permits the employer to refer the employee for medical treatment, discharge the employee, or take another similar action. The DFWA does not require employers to report off-duty drug convictions.

Employers are also concerned when an employee's off-duty activities bring police to the workplace to interview or arrest the employee. An employer who handles such an investigation clumsily faces a number of unsavory consequences:

- Public humiliation of an employee
- Disruption of the workplace
- Potential false-arrest claim by an employee who is inappropriately detained
- Obstruction of justice charges by the police for interfering with the law enforcement process

An employer's inappropriate release of publicity relating to a criminal investigation or arrest could result in a privacy invasion claim.

During a police investigation or arrest, the employer's primary concern should be maintaining the safety of the workforce. A second concern is allowing the police to perform their job in a way that permits the individual being investigated to maintain his or her dignity. It is a good idea to verify the officers' identification, review any arrest or search warrant, and then bring the employee into a private office or conference room to meet with the police.[4]

Critical Issues in Responding to Criminal Misconduct

When criminal misconduct occurs on its premises, an employer has a clear basis for dealing with the matter. If local police conduct a criminal investigation in your workplace, it is best to cooperate in a way that promotes safety of employees, minimizes disruption to work, and protects individual dignity of individuals subject to the investigation. Recognize that any management action taken because of an employee's arrest may be subject to state laws that ban employment decisions based on arrest records. Job action based on off-duty criminal misconduct will be better justified when there is a close relationship between the crime and job duties, the crime is violent, or the criminal conduct adversely affects business operations.

---

4. N. Elizabeth Fried, "When the Police Come Knocking," *HR Magazine,* June 1995, p. 78.

Sample Policy: Criminal Misconduct

It is the policy of XYZ Company to cooperate with law enforcement investigations of criminal misconduct in a manner that protects the safety of XYZ employees and security of company property.

1. The security manager is responsible for managing and coordinating all details relating to law enforcement investigations and/or criminal misconduct involving XYZ employees.

2. In the event that a manager becomes aware of a law enforcement investigation or criminal activity of an XYZ employee, he or she shall report the matter to the security manager.

3. The manager and security manager shall evaluate all facts and issues of the matter to determine an appropriate course of action.

4. When law enforcement officers appear at the company, the security manager shall determine the purpose of the visit, verify identification, and check the nature of warrant or summons.

5. The security manager shall arrange for any investigation interview or arrest action to occur in a private office or conference room.

6. When company management uncovers evidence of criminal misconduct occurring on the premises, law enforcement authorities should be consulted immediately.

7. An employee's failure to report absence or extended absence(s) due to arrest and/or incarceration is sufficient grounds for discharge.

8. An arrest or conviction that adversely affects an individual's ability to perform job duties or reflects negatively on the company in the community is sufficient grounds for discharge.

Need Extra Cash? When Secondary Employment Conflicts with the Regular Job

According to a recent Labor Department study, approximately 18 percent of the workforce is in part-time work and more than 6 percent of workers hold two or more jobs. Many companies have policies that limit or prohibit employees from taking second jobs in order to prevent conflict of interest or working for a competitor. These policies also endeavor to ensure availability for overtime, or on-call job assignments, and enforce secondary employment prohibitions in an employment agreement.

A conflict of interest can occur if an employee is involved in employment, purchasing, or selling decisions where he or she or a member of the immediate family will be directly or indirectly affected or receive some form of gift or income beyond regular compensation because of the decision. An employer has a legitimate interest in preventing conflicts of interest. For example, an employee buying products from a supplier owned by a family member receives—in effect—added income from the purchase; such a transaction is a conflict of interest.

A firm would have a reasonable basis to prevent employees from working for a competitor in order to protect trade secrets or to avoid an unfair loss of business opportunity. Also, an employer who schedules frequent overtime work or who has employees on an on-call status would have a valid reason for controlling secondary employment. If the employee is not available for work as scheduled, the employer would have reasonable grounds for taking corrective action.

Generally, there are no legal requirements prohibiting overtime work of adult workers. An employer may establish a work schedule and enforce employee adherence to that schedule. Federal wage hour laws merely require that the employer provide overtime pay for nonexempt covered workers for all time worked over forty hours in a week. Some state laws limit overtime work by prohibiting work on Sunday or the Sabbath, or on the seventh consecutive workday. Child labor laws define working time limits for youths under eighteen years of age during days that school is in session.

Some states have laws that prohibit discrimination against an employee because he or she is engaged in a lawful activity off the job. Depending on the precise wording of these statutes, and subsequent court interpretation, such laws may affect an employer's policy on secondary employment.

A North Dakota sales representative started a part-time business in which he marketed products and services to selected customers based on sales made in his full-time job. The company learned that the sales representative was soliciting its clients for the part-time business. The sales representative was discharged for owning a business that represented a violation of a company policy prohibiting conflicts of interest. Following his discharge, the employee sued the employer, claiming the firing violated his right to engage in lawful activities during non-work hours. The case ultimately reached the U.S. Court of Appeals. Upon its examination of the facts, the court sided with the employer. According to the court, the state statute exempts certain activities. One exempted activity is that employees cannot use confidential information gained through their employment to further personal interests that may jeopardize the employer's relations with a client. The sales rep's actions violated this policy.[5]

At some firms where moonlighting or secondary employment is a primary concern, employees are required to sign an employment agreement that prohibits secondary employment. When an employee at the time of hire or during the course of employment signs an employment agreement that limits or prohibits secondary employment, he or she is bound to the terms of the employment agreement.

Critical Issues in Responding to Secondary Employment

An employee who accepts employment is expected to be available for the employer's specified work schedule. Unless the employment agreement prohibits secondary employment, the employee is generally free to accept other work.

An employer's ban on secondary employment may violate state law prohibiting discrimination because of lawful off-duty activities. Preventing conflicts of interest or competition are an employer's strongest basis for controlling secondary employment. Also, if an employee's secondary employment affects performance on the main job, the employer can appropriately deal with the performance problem. It is best to communicate any secondary employment limits prior to the start of the employment relationship, such as requirements to be available for overtime work or on-call assignments.

---

5. *Fatland v Quaker State,* 10 IER Cases 1569 (1995).

Sample Policy: Secondary Employment

XYZ Company permits employees to engage in secondary employment subject to the limits defined in this policy.

1. Employees are expected to report to work in a fit condition to work as scheduled.

2. Secondary employment is viewed as a lawful off-duty activity that is permitted by the company and the laws of this state.

3. Secondary employment or other outside activities that affect an individual's performance, result in competition with XYZ, or result in a conflict of interest are not permitted.

4. In the event that an employee evidences performance problems or fails to meet work schedules, the manager is responsible for providing corrective job instructions or disciplinary actions as warranted.

5. In the event that an employee's off-duty activity or secondary employment presents an actual conflict of interest or competition with XYZ Company, the employee is directed to discontinue the job or activity.

6. In order to avoid a conflict of interest or competition, an employee is responsible for disclosing secondary employment or outside activities to XYZ management.

7. Employees are not permitted to take a leave of absence for the purpose of engaging in other full-time work.

Sample Employee Notice: Conflict of Interest[6]

XYZ Company and each employee have a responsibility for maintaining a high standard of ethical and legal conduct in all business transactions or activities. Ethical business conduct applies to any business decisions relating to clients, client personnel, competitors, government agencies, etc. Employees are reminded that it is unethical and illegal to solicit, offer, or accept directly or indirectly, any gift, favor, loan, or other item of significant monetary value in order to influence a business decision or receive any financial enrichment beyond normal compensation provided by XYZ Company. In the event that you are faced with circumstances which may appear to conflict with this policy, you are encouraged to speak with your supervisor. Disregard for this policy is sufficient grounds for discharge.

Sample Employee Notice: Secondary Employment

The company recognizes that employees may engage in secondary employment or other outside activities. You are responsible for disclosing to the company any secondary employment or activity that represents a potential or actual conflict of interest or results in competition with XYZ. Any secondary employment or outside activity that affects job performance, limits or prevents availability for scheduled work, or results in conflict of interest or competition is not permitted. Failure to comply with these guidelines may result in discipline or discharge.

---

6. William S. Hubbartt, *Personnel Policy Handbook: How to Develop a Manual That Works* (New York: McGraw-Hill, 1993), 424.

A Smoldering Issue: Employer Control of Smoking

Ever since the U.S. Surgeon General determined that smoking was a health hazard, concerns about the health affects of smoking have been growing. According to the American Lung Association, smoking adds $23 million every year to direct health care costs in the United States. Further, more than 80 million workdays are lost because of smoking-related illness.[7]

It's no wonder that three out of four employers now prohibit smoking in office areas, according to a 1996 survey of 2,000 firms conducted by Business and Legal Reports, Inc. Over 60 percent of respondents have banned smoking in their plant areas; 21 percent prohibit smoking altogether except in designated areas. Overall, 14 percent of all respondents and 23 percent of manufacturing firms permit smoking in the cafeteria. Seventy-four percent of firms answering the survey reported that they have a written smoking policy.[8]

The smoking issue raises controversy among smokers and nonsmokers alike. Individuals who choose to smoke feel that smoking is their right and should not be infringed upon, such as Arlene Kurtz (see chapter 1), who sued the city of North Miami, claiming a privacy invasion over the city's requirement that job applicants certify that they have been smoke free for a year before seeking city employment. On the other side of the coin, nonsmokers assert that their health is endangered by secondhand smoke—a complaint supported by the U.S. Surgeon General, whose studies show that secondhand smoke does have an adverse health effect on children, individuals with respiratory diseases, and other nonsmokers.

On-the-job clashes over smoking can escalate into disruptive incidents or litigation, as Dyna Pro management learned when its office manager Pechan claimed that she experienced an acute sensitivity to secondhand smoke. In spite of her complaint, management at Dyna Pro permitted coworkers to continue smoking. Further, Pechan was reassigned to perform the menial task of data entry. Pechan then sued. The Illinois court found that Dyna Pro had retaliated against Pechan for her complaint about smoking. The court noted that the employee's reassignment to menial tasks following her complaint to management about smoking in the office was held to be a violation of the Illinois Clean

7. "Smoking," *Business and Legal Reports* (Madison, CT), August 1995, p. S-29.
8. "Smoking Banned in Most Workplaces," *Business and Legal Reports* (Madison, CT), 1996.

Indoor Air Act and that the employer had written in her file that her duties were being reassigned due to "recent events."[9]

Employer regulation of off-the-job smoking creates even greater concerns. Electronics giant Motorola announced a policy prohibiting employee use of smoking materials off the job as well as on company premises but rescinded it after a flurry of media activity and employee reaction. But in another case, Oklahoma City firefighter trainee Grusendorf lost his job when he was caught smoking after agreeing, as a precondition of employment, that he would not smoke cigarettes either on or off duty for one year after hire. Grusendorf sued, claiming that his constitutional rights of liberty and privacy were violated. The court upheld Oklahoma City's decision to discharge Grusendorf. In evaluating the circumstances of this case, the court noted that there is a rational connection between a no-smoking regulation and the health and safety of firefighter trainees.[10]

Some forty-five states now have guidelines on smoking issues for public- and private-sector employers. State laws dealing with smoking have taken two directions: clean indoor air laws and smokers' rights laws. The clean indoor air laws generally restrict use of smoking materials in public places and in private workplaces that are open to the public. The smokers' rights laws generally prohibit employers from discriminating against individuals for use of smoking materials off the job. Depending on the laws in its state, a firm may be subject to either or both types of laws.

States with Smoking-Related Laws

Arizona	Minnesota	Rhode Island
Connecticut	New Hampshire	South Dakota
District of Columbia	New Jersey	Utah
Illinois	New Mexico	Vermont
Indiana	New York	Virginia
Kentucky	Oklahoma	West Virginia
Maine	Oregon	Wyoming

---

9. *Pechan v Dyna Pro*, 8 IER Cases 1793 (IL App Ct 1993).
10. *Grusendorf v Oklahoma City*, 2 IER Cases 51 (CA 10 1987).

Sample Policy: Workplace Smoking

XYZ Company limits the use of smoking materials on company property in order to promote fire safety and promote health and well-being of employees.

1. XYZ offices are designated "smoke-free." This means that employees and visitors are not permitted to use smoking materials in our offices.

2. Smoking is permitted only in a designated area of the XYZ warehouse and outside the building.

3. Smoking is permitted only during nonwork times such as before work, after work, and during lunch and break periods. Smokers are not permitted additional smoke breaks.

4. Smokers must properly dispose of ashes and smoking materials in the containers provided.

5. Each supervisor or manager is responsible for enforcing this policy throughout the XYZ facility.

Critical Issues in Responding to Smoking

The battle over workplace air pitches those who feel that they have a right to smoke against those who complain about the need for clean air and the harmful effects of secondhand smoke. When an employer lets this matter smolder, it can easily erupt into a "flaming feud." To maintain a productive workplace, consider defining a smoking policy and offering stop-smoking assistance. Various laws and regulations provide some guidance. OSHA rules prohibit smoking when working with flammables. Clean air laws prohibit or limit smoking in public facilities or private facilities open to the public. Smokers' rights laws and use of lawful products laws prohibit discrimination against smokers.

**Sample Employee Notice:
Workplace Smoking**

XYZ Company has established some guidelines regarding use of smoking materials in order to promote safety, good health, and prevention of fires. The warehouse and general office areas are designated no-smoking areas. Smoking is permitted in the lunchroom during nonworking time. An employee with a private office may elect to designate that office a smoking or nonsmoking area. Please be considerate of fellow employees and cooperate with these guidelines.

**Sample Employee Notice:
Workplace Smoking**

At XYZ Company, we feel that whether you smoke or not makes a statement about your long-range view on your life. We believe that an individual who is concerned about his or her health is more likely to display those same concerns for well-being and productivity in the daily performance of job duties. For this reason, we have established a no-smoking policy within the building.

Get a Life: Employer Regulation of Employee Dating and Other Nonwork Activities

Whether or not employees date each other is generally not a concern of an employer, unless it results in a sexual harassment claim. In fact, a 1993 survey of members of SHRM found that more than half of the human resources specialists who responded disagreed with employers' policies prohibiting dating between coworkers, between supervisors and employees, and between employees and competitors.[11]

The potential for a sexual harassment claim is the main reason why employers prohibit dating between an employee and a supervisor. As long as men and women work together, there will be instances where sexual attraction occurs. When conduct leads to a sexual harassment claim, the courts try to evaluate the facts of the individual case to determine whether the conduct violates the law. As one appeals court judge noted, the difference between invited, uninvited but welcome, offensive but tolerated, and flatly rejected sexual advances is sometimes difficult to determine.

Sexual harassment is more about power than sex, as the landmark case *Meritor Savings Bank v Vinson* demonstrates.

> Vinson was a bank teller who became assistant manager. In the course of her employment, Vinson began dating and having sexual intercourse with her supervisor. Vinson went along with the relationship for fear of losing her job, although the supervisor had not expressly conditioned her job on sex. According to Vinson, the supervisor compelled her to have sex forty to fifty times, including forcible sex on occasion. He openly made intimidating and sexual remarks in front of others and followed her into the rest room. Vinson ultimately filed a sexual harassment claim.
>
> The bank claimed that Vinson's failure to complain and repeated participation in sex meant that the conduct was consensual and not harassment. The U.S. Supreme Court held that the supervisor's conduct was so severe and pervasive that it altered the conditions of employment, creating a hostile and abusive work environment. Such conduct, said the Court, is sexual harassment.[12]

In another case, a woman's claim of hostile environment was rejected when court records showed that she encouraged offensive sexual conduct. In this case, the complaining employee used vulgar language, shared her own sexual experiences with alleged harassers, and asked coworkers about their sex lives and whether they engaged in extramarital affairs.[13]

---

11. Jonathon A. Segal, "Love—What's Work Got to Do with It?" *HR Magazine*, June 1993, p. 42.
12. *Meritor Savings Bank v Vinson* 477 US 57 (1986).
13. Alfred G. Feliu, *Primer on Individual Rights* (Washington DC: BNA, 1993), 223.

Because of the potential for sexual harassment claims, employers do have a legitimate concern regarding dating relationships between employees, co-workers, and supervisors or subordinates. And, when properly developed, a reasonable policy that is communicated to employees can withstand a common-law privacy invasion claim.

> In Mississippi, Ronald Watkins was discharged by UPS after he began a sexual relationship with a female truck driver assigned to his division. In justifying its termination of Watkins, UPS cited its management policy book, which stated, "Fraternization is discouraged throughout our organization. Fraternization between a supervisor or manager and an employee who is directly or indirectly supervised is not permissible."
>
> After being fired, Watkins sued UPS, claiming wrongful discharge and privacy invasion. In evaluating Watkins's privacy invasion claim, the court reviewed UPS's actions against Mississippi law relating to privacy. While acknowledging that Mississippi has recognized the common-law right to privacy, the court noted that Watkins's claim failed to reach specified standards for privacy invasion, stating that Watkins:
>
> - Failed to show that UPS's actions were based on bad faith and utterly reckless prying
> - Did not allege that UPS snooped in his bedroom or electronically wired his work area for sound
> - Did not show, as another case did, that the employer intentionally opened his private mail and read it without authorization
> - Did not show that his employer engaged in unauthorized and surreptitious wiretapping of his private telephone conversations
> - Failed to submit his claim within a one-year statute of limitations
> - Failed to show that UPS's actions were so extreme, outrageous, or repulsive, but rather that the company's actions were based on a published policy of which Watkins was aware[14]

In response to employer actions to control employee dating, employees have brought legal challenges on several fronts. An employee may have a privacy invasion claim if the employer's action in some way creates an outrageous

---

14. *Watkins v UPS*, 7 IER Cases 1081 (DC So Miss 1992).

intrusion upon a private part of the employee's life. One employee brought a dating-related claim against the employer alleging employment discrimination on the basis of marital status. Employer regulation of dating has also been challenged on the grounds that such policies violate the law in those states where discrimination is prohibited because of lawful off-the-job conduct. This was the essence of Judy Pasch's claim against her employer.

> Judy Pasch had been employed by Crystal Radio, a division of Katz Media Corp. She began dating and then living with Mark Braunstein, a vice president and general manager of the company. Braunstein was fired, and within two days, Pasch was told her job would be eliminated under a company reorganization. She was demoted without a decrease in pay or benefits. However, the company then ran advertisements in the *New York Times* for a replacement and then replaced her with a man who had fewer qualifications. Pasch soon resigned and sued the company, claiming that she was fired for cohabitation. Her claim asserted that her separation was a forced resignation due to intolerable circumstances and for this reason should be considered a discharge in violation of New York's lawful off-duty conduct law.
>
> In permitting Pasch to pursue her claim, the judge stated that the statute's purpose is to prohibit employers from discriminating against their employees simply because the employer does not like the activities an employee engages in after work and that cohabitation that occurs off the employer's premises should be considered a protected activity under the law.[15]

A number of states have passed laws prohibiting discrimination against an individual for participating in lawful activities off the job. Similar to the so-called smokers' rights laws, off-duty conduct laws prevent employers from taking adverse employment action against an employee who engages in lawful conduct off the job. Examples of such conduct may include dating a fellow employee, smoking, consumption of alcoholic beverages, or accepting part-time employment.

One approach to dealing with employee dating, suggests attorney Jonathan A. Segal, is to adopt a rule that prohibits the existence of a supervisor-subordinate relationship between employees who have an intimate relation-

15. "Cohabitation a Protected Activity," *Individual Employment Rights Newsletter* (BNA), Sept. 12, 1995, p. 4.

States with Laws on Lawful Off-Duty Conduct or Use of Lawful Products Off the Job

Colorado	Montana	North Carolina
Illinois	Nevada	North Dakota
Mississippi	New York	Wisconsin
Missouri		

ship. Defining the policy based on relationship intimacy, whether married or unmarried, argues Segal, achieves the same results as a no-spouse policy while avoiding the potential for a marital status discrimination violation.[16]

Regarding the setting of limitations on employee dating of competitors, Segal suggests that a carefully worded written confidentiality agreement helps to protect proprietary information without attempting to interfere with an off-duty consensual relationship. When properly worded, such a policy would make an employee's failure to disclose an actual or potential conflict of interest grounds for discharge.[17]

Critical Issues in Responding to Employee Dating

When an employer sets rules about employee dating or other lawful off-duty conduct, human resources managers (and most employees) strongly disagree with this intrusion into employees' personal lives. Further, state laws prohibiting discrimination for lawful activities off the job may be applied to dating relationships. Any rules on dating should be based on a clear business purpose. Limits on dating between employee and supervisor may be justified by a desire to prevent potential sexual harassment. If a no-dating policy is administered differently for men and women, an employee may prevail in a claim of discrimination based on marital status or sex.

16. Ibid., 38.
17. Ibid., 41.

Sample Policy: Dating and Fraternization

XYZ Company discourages dating or fraternization between a supervisor and subordinate.

1. The company recognizes that social dating and romantic relationships may occur between employees. Such relationships are permissible as long as the relationship does not adversely affect job performance or business operations.

2. Any social dating or romantic relationship that results in job performance problems or disruptive conduct, affects business operations, or reflects poorly on the company will result in corrective action.

3. Any sexually oriented conduct that is unwanted by the recipient or that has the effect of creating a hostile or intimidating environment is considered sexual harassment and is prohibited.

4. Any social dating or romantic relationship between a supervisor and a subordinate is discouraged because such conduct is deemed to be unprofessional.

Sexual Preference, Sexual Orientation, and Other Alternative Lifestyles

- An airline was permitted to consider an employee's alleged transsexuality as a basis for a negative employment decision.
- An employee's claim of harassment based on sexual orientation was rejected by the court.
- An employee's discharge for effeminate appearance by an insurance company was not overturned by the court. Employment action against an individual for being gay was allowed under federal civil rights law.

**Sample Employee Notice:
Dating and Fraternization**

It is the goal of XYZ Company to maintain a work atmosphere where individuals treat each other with respect and professionalism. While we recognize that social dating or romantic relationships may occur between employees, any social or romantic relationship that results in job performance problems or disruptive conduct, affects business operations, or reflects poorly on the company will result in corrective action.

Should an employee's sexual preference or sexual orientation be a matter of concern to the employer? Does it make a difference if an employee is homosexual or lesbian, as long as he or she can do the job? An individual's sexual preference or orientation is certainly a private matter, and inappropriate release of such information could result in a privacy invasion claim. But sexual orientation is not a protected class under federal equal employment opportunity laws, although a growing number of states and some municipalities are recognizing sexual orientation or sexual preference as a protected-class category under state or local equal employment opportunity laws. In areas where sexual orientation or sexual preference are protected, an employee victimized by discrimination may prevail in court, as Shell Oil Company learned.

Collins, an executive at a Shell Oil facility in California, used the office computer to prepare invitations to a nude party at which homosexual activity was planned, including a discussion on safe sex. Management learned of the event and fired Collins because he was a sexually active homosexual. The company based its firing on Collins's use of the computer for a personal activity. Collins claimed he was fired for off-the-job sexual activity, a matter that was personal and of no business to the company. Collins sued for wrongful discharge and the court agreed, awarding a $5.3 million judgment against Shell.[18]

18. Alfred G. Feliu, *Primer on Individual Rights* (Washington DC: BNA, 1993), 230.

Critical Issues in Responding to Employee Sexual Preference

Basing employment decisions on a non–job-related issue such as sexual preference opens the employer to potential liability. Even if sexual preference is not a protected-class category in the employer's jurisdiction, a job-related basis for employment decisions is recommended. Wrongful discharge lawsuits have been more successful when employers deal unfairly in the termination of an individual. Further, inappropriate release of private information could result in a privacy claim.

States That Include Sexual Orientation as a Protected Class under Equal Employment Opportunity Laws[19]

District of Columbia	Minnesota	New York
Hawaii	New Jersey	Pennsylvania
Massachusetts	New Mexico	Wisconsin

Cities and Counties with Ordinances Prohibiting Discrimination Based on Sexual Orientation

Berkeley, CA	West Hollywood, CA	Pittsburgh, PA
Los Angeles, CA	Denver, CO	Austin, TX
Sacramento, CA	District of Columbia	Alexandria, VA
San Francisco, CA	New York, NY	Cook County, IL

19. Ronald M. Green, William A. Carmell, and Jerrold F. Goldberg, *State-by-State Guide to Human Resources Law* (New York: Panel Publishers, 1993), table 1.21.

Sample Policy: Sexual Preference

It is the policy of XYZ Company to make all employment
decisions on a nondiscriminatory basis.

1. All employment decisions must be based on an individual's skills, abilities, and other job-related criteria.

2. Any employment decision that considers an individual's sexual preference or orientation is in violation of this policy.

3. Each supervisor and manager is responsible for carrying out employment decisions in a manner consistent with this policy.

4. In the event of any question or complaint relating to this policy, employees may speak to the human resources manager.

Sample Employee Notice:
Sexual Preference

It is the policy of XYZ Company to afford equal opportunity
for employment. All employment decisions are made without regard to race, color, age, sex, religion, national origin,
ancestry, physical or mental disability that can be reasonably
accommodated, sexual orientation, type of military discharge, source of income, and parental or marital status.

Saints and Sinners: Tips for Employer Accommodation of Religious Beliefs

Religious beliefs and practices sometimes conflict with an employer's employment practices, work schedules, or job responsibilities.

- A high school teacher's religious beliefs required that he refrain from secular work on six holy days, causing conflict with school work schedules and the school district's leave policies.
- An atheist objected to her employer's practice of conducting a brief religious talk and prayer following monthly staff meetings.
- A Jewish employee was subjected to derogatory comments from co-workers and supervisors.
- An airline employee complained that he was unable to perform the Saturday work schedule set by his employer because his religious beliefs prohibited Saturday work.
- A factory employee's religious beliefs requiring the wearing of certain garments created a conflict with the employer's safety dress code policy.

Conflicts between employee religious beliefs and employer work practices generally fall into one of these categories:

Schedules. Conflicts between employer work schedules and employee observation of the Sabbath or other holy days

Assignments. Conflicts between a particular work or task assignment and the employee's religious beliefs

Dress. Conflicts between an employee's religious dress or appearance and the employer's dress or appearance expectations

Harassment. Religious harassment or proselytizing by one worker directed toward another

Constitution. Introducing or permitting religious activities by a public-sector employer that violate the constitutional requirement for separation of church and state.

Conflicts between employers and employees' religious beliefs may result in discrimination claims rather than a privacy invasion claim. Under Title VII of the Civil Rights Act of 1964 and many state antibias laws, employers are prohibited from discriminating in any aspect of employment because of an individual's religious beliefs. This means that an employee should not be treated differently in hiring, promotions, transfers, discipline, benefits, or other terms of employment because of religious beliefs.

An employee does not have to belong to an organized religious sect to have these beliefs protected. An individual's sincere and meaningful moral and ethical beliefs, as well as traditional religious beliefs, receive protection under the law. The employee has an obligation to inform the employer if his or her religious beliefs conflict with a work practice. Upon learning that an employee's religious beliefs conflict with work, the employer is required to make a reasonable accommodation for the employee's religious practice. A leading case on this issue involved Trans World Airlines (TWA).

> TWA employee Hardison could not work on Saturdays because of his religious beliefs. To resolve the issue, TWA scheduled several meetings with Hardison, requested that a union steward search for another worker to change shifts with Hardison, and unsuccessfully sought another job for Hardison. The airline's inability to resolve the matter resulted in a lawsuit. A lower court held that TWA could have considered other alternatives, such as allowing Hardison to work a four-day week while a supervisor or other employee filled in on the fifth day, replacing him for Saturday work even though it would have resulted in overtime work, or arranging a shift trade even though it would have resulted in a seniority system violation. Upon review, the U.S. Supreme Court held that these alternatives created an undue hardship on TWA. The court stated that in making a reasonable accommodation, an employer does not have to violate a seniority system, violate a collective bargaining agreement, or incur more than a minimal expense.[20]

Another significant case that provides guidance on employer obligations to make reasonable accommodations for an employee's religious beliefs involved Ronald Philbrook, a high school teacher in Connecticut.

> A member of the World Wide Church of God, Philbrook was required to refrain from secular work on six holy days a year. Philbrook's employer, the Ansonia Board of Education, provided teachers with three days' annual leave to observe mandatory religious holidays. The leave policies were defined in the labor agreement between the local teacher's union and the Board of Education. Teachers also were permitted

20. *Trans World Airlines v Hardison,* 432 US 63 (1977).

three days of accumulated leave for necessary personal business, which could not be used for religious activities or observance. An annual sick leave benefit was also available.

Initially, Philbrook used the three religious holidays and then took three additional days off without pay. Dissatisfied with this arrangement, Philbrook requested that the school board permit him to use the annual leave days as religious holidays or to permit him to pay the cost of a substitute teacher while he received full pay for the day. The school board refused his request, and he filed suit for religious discrimination.[21]

Philbrook's case ultimately reached the U.S. Supreme Court. The Court held that an employer who makes a reasonable accommodation—not necessarily the employee-requested accommodation— meets the accommodation requirements of the law. According to the Court, the school board's policy of requiring unpaid leave for any holy day observance that exceeded the amount allowed by the collective bargaining agreement was reasonable.[22]

Other court decisions have provided additional guidelines on accommodating religious beliefs by substituting workers, changing job assignments, exchanging hours or work schedules or days off, or implementing flexible work schedules. However, an employer is not required to make an accommodation if the change causes an undue hardship on the business. According to various Supreme Court decisions:

- An employer need not incur overtime costs to replace an employee who will not work on Saturday.
- Complaints by fellow workers filling in for others do not count as an undue hardship.
- An employer is not required to choose an employee-requested accommodation when an alternative reasonable accommodation is available.
- The employer need not violate a seniority system or collective bargaining agreement to accommodate an employee's religious practices.[23]

21. Glen Elsasser, "Court Eases Employers' Obligation to Religions," *Chicago Tribune*, Nov. 18, 1986, p. 3.
22. *Ansonia Board of Education v Philbrook*, 479 US 60 (1986).
23. "Religious Discrimination," *Business and Legal Reports* (Madison, CT), Dec. 1993, p. R-15.

Sample Policy: Religious Accommodation

It is the policy of XYZ Company to make all employment decisions without regard to religion and to make a reasonable accommodation for an employee's religious beliefs.

1. All employment decisions must be made based upon an individual's skills, abilities, and other job-related criteria.

2. Any employment decision that considers an individual's religion is in violation of this policy.

3. In the event that an employee's religious beliefs create a conflict with a company practice, the manager should make a reasonable accommodation, provided that the accommodation does not create an undue hardship upon the company.

4. Nonemployee solicitors are not permitted on company property at any time. In order to prevent work interruptions, employees may not solicit or distribute literature during working time or in working areas.

5. Each supervisor and manager is responsible for carrying out employment decisions in a manner consistent with this policy.

6. In the event of any question or complaint relating to this policy, employees may speak to the human resources manager.

Critical Issues in Religious Accommodation

When employer work schedules or policies conflict with employee religious beliefs, the results can be highly emotional. State and federal law prohibit discrimination on the basis of religion. The employer is required to make a reasonable accommodation, but not an accommodation that causes an undue hardship. Safety requirements will override religious dress concerns. Employ-

---

Sample Employee Notice: Religious Accommodation

It is the policy of XYZ Company to afford equal opportunity for employment. All employment decisions are made without regard to race, color, age, sex, religion, national origin, ancestry, physical or mental disability that can be reasonably accommodated, sexual orientation, type of military discharge, source of income, and parental or marital status.

---

ees' religious proselytizing can be controlled by solicitation and distribution policies, discussed in chapter 6.

Summary

Although employees resent employer intrusions into their personal lives, employers sometimes have good reason to be concerned about employees' off-duty activities, particularly when they have an adverse effect on job performance or business operations. Secondary employment may be allowable as long as there is no conflict of interest, no competition, and no effect on job performance. Criminal misconduct away from work will reflect badly on the company and may affect the employee's job performance. Employee dating is generally of no concern to the employer unless it creates a potential sexual harassment claim or conflict of interest. An individual's religious beliefs should be of no concern to the employer unless they conflict with a job schedule or assignment. And whether an employee stops off after work at the local pub for a beer and a cigarette should be of no concern to the employer. In fact, unless there is a job-related safety or health issue, such lawful off-duty activity may be protected by law in some states.

The bottom line message is this: An employer should respect the privacy of employees' personal time unless an employee's activities have a clear and direct effect on the business.

Appendix

Management Guidelines

Criminal Misconduct

▪ Obtain and evaluate facts of the criminal misconduct incident before making an employment decision or taking adverse action against an employee.

▪ Identify a job-performance issue as a basis for employment action that may be taken pursuant to criminal misconduct.

▪ Identify or be prepared to show how an individual's criminal misconduct has an adverse affect on the firm's business or reputation in the community.

▪ Show a relationship between the employee's job duties and the criminal misconduct in order to justify a job action.

▪ Recognize that an arrest is not necessarily an indication of guilt.

▪ Recognize that addressing an individual's violation of absence reporting procedures and absence control policies may be a valid alternative to dealing with off-the-job criminal misconduct.

▪ Prepare a policy guideline for responding to police investigations, subpoena service, and arrests.

When an investigation takes place in the workplace:

▪ Verify officers' identification and any search or arrest warrant.

▪ Arrange for an inconspicuous meeting between the law enforcement officers and the employee being investigated or arrested, such as in a conference room or private office away from coworkers.

▪ Avoid public release of information about criminal investigation or arrest of an employee.

Secondary Employment

▪ Identify job-related requirements for limiting or prohibiting secondary employment. Typical reasons include preventing conflict of interest, preventing work with a competitor, or ensuring employee availability for overtime or on-call work.

▪ Prepare a written policy or include the policy limiting or prohibiting secondary employment in an employee handbook for distribution to employees, an employment agreement, or a management personnel policy manual.

▪ Check the law in your state or area to ensure that there are no limits on policies relating to secondary employment or other lawful activities off the job.

- Emphasize job-related issues such as an employee's failure to perform or inability to work as scheduled when taking corrective action for secondary employment.

- Recognize that the strongest basis for dealing with secondary employment is focusing on the individual's job performance or specific real or potential threats to the business due to conflict of interest or competitive threats.

- Identify which employee, jobs, or job categories are covered by the policy and what work or activities are prohibited.

- Identify whether employees can accept other employment during a leave of absence.

Workplace Smoking

- Check state laws to determine whether your firm is subject to any state clean indoor air law.

- Check state laws to determine whether your firm is subject to a smokers' rights law.

- Evaluate safety requirements at your workplace and prohibit use of smoking materials in areas where flammable or combustible materials are used or stored.

- Evaluate sanitation issues at your workplace, and prohibit use of smoking materials in areas where food or medical products are handled, processed, or prepared.

- Generally, you are free to create a smoke-free workplace by prohibiting use of smoking materials on the job or on the premises, but if limited by law, you may not discriminate against smokers or individuals exercising rights protected by law.

- You may elect to permit employees to designate their work areas or offices as smoke free.

- You may elect to limit use of smoking materials on the job to designated areas and/or times.

- If your firm implements a smoke-free workplace, you may elect to offer stop smoking clinics or products as a way to help employees stop smoking.

Employee Dating and Other Nonwork Activities

- Check state laws to see whether there are limits or prohibitions on discrimination on the basis of lawful off-duty conduct or use of lawful products off the job.

- Identify a specific business purpose for limiting or prohibiting any off-duty conduct.

- Prepare a written policy guideline to employees and supervisors to outline the company's position on off-duty issues.

■ To minimize the likelihood of liability, address off-duty conduct when it directly affects an employee's on-the-job performance or clearly affects the company image or reputation in the community.

■ Dating or romantic relationships between a supervisor and a subordinate should be discouraged or prohibited; such conduct is unprofessional and could result in sexual harassment claims.

■ Define and communicate a sexual harassment policy to employees and management.

■ Implement your policy in a uniform and consistent manner.

Employee Sexual Preference

■ Check state and local laws to see whether sexual preference or sexual orientation is a protected-class category under equal employment opportunity laws.

■ Do not limit hiring or employee job assignments merely because a coworker or customer prefers not to deal with an employee because of his or her sexual orientation. The EEOC has stated that customer or coworker preferences are not adequate justification for a discriminatory employment practice.

■ Focus hiring decisions on an individual's ability to meet job qualifications.

■ Focus employment decisions on an individual's ability to meet job-related performance standards.

■ Apply employment and policy decisions uniformly for all employees.

Religious Accommodations

■ Become familiar with Title VII of the Civil Rights Act of 1964 and its provisions relating to religious discrimination and reasonable accommodations.

■ Check civil rights law in your state to identify limitations relating to religious discrimination.

■ Take care to avoid discriminatory or different employment practices due to an individual's religion when making hiring, promotion, disciplinary, benefits, and other employment decisions.

■ Avoid inquiries relating to employees' religious beliefs.

■ Avoid collection or retention of information that may relate to an individual's religious beliefs.

■ Train and instruct supervisory personnel on preventing and/or dealing with any form of religious discrimination or harassment.

■ Consider an employee's statement or complaint about work interference with religious beliefs.

- Make a reasonable accommodation when work interferes with an employee's religious beliefs.

- Document actions taken to accommodate an employee's religious beliefs.

- Identify clear business needs or safety requirements for dress codes, and carefully evaluate an employee's religious dress or grooming practices if there appears to be a conflict.

- Recognize that workplace safety takes precedence over religious dress or appearance that creates a safety hazard or violates safety rules.

- Define and uniformly enforce a no-solicitation policy to control religious proselytizing.

Q & A: Employee Rights Regarding Off-Duty Conduct

Q *What are an employee's privacy rights in the event of an arrest or other criminal misconduct?*

A Adult criminal records are public records, so when an employer gains access to an individual's criminal record for a job-related purpose, it is not an unlawful privacy invasion. An arrest or other criminal misconduct may result in a privacy invasion claim if an employer publicizes private information in an outrageous manner or releases false information about an employee. Consideration of an individual's arrest record is considered to be a discriminatory employment practice by the EEOC. A criminal conviction may be considered in an employment decision if it is reasonably related to job responsibilities.

Q *Can an employer regulate an individual's secondary employment?*

A An employer has justification to regulate an individual's secondary employment if it creates a conflict of interest, affects job performance, results in competition, or limits an employee's availability for on-call, overtime, or regular work. However, some states have laws prohibiting discrimination against an individual for lawful off-duty conduct. Such a law may limit adverse action against an employee because of secondary employment.

Q *What are smokers' rights? What are nonsmokers' rights?*

A Smokers' rights are protected in some states where a state law prohibits discrimination against individuals for off-the-job use of smoking materials or other lawful products. Nonsmokers are protected in some areas where state or local clean air laws prohibit use of smoking materials in public places or require restaurants to provide smoking and nonsmoking areas. Clean air laws generally do not apply to private workplaces that are not open to the public. Subject to these limits, private employers may elect to permit smoking or to designate the area smoke free. Keep in mind OSHA fire safety guidelines, which require employers to prohibit use of smoking materials or other open flames near areas where flammables or explosives are stored or used. And to keep peace in the workplace, define and publish a clear policy on smoking.

Q   *Can an employer regulate employee dating or other off-duty activities?*

A   An employee's dating practices, social or recreational activities, and intimate relationships are generally viewed by employees as private matters that should be of no concern to their employer. But under certain circumstances, employers have become involved in employee dating or social activities. One of the greatest concerns to employers is prevention of incidents that could be viewed as sexual harassment. Other areas of employer concern may include employee off-duty conduct that affects job performance or clearly affects the company's image in the community. Some states prohibit employer discrimination against employees because of lawful off-duty conduct such as dating.

Q   *Does an employee have any rights protecting against employer regulation of sexual preference, sexual orientation, or other alternative lifestyle?*

A   Some states or municipalities have laws prohibiting discrimination on the basis of sexual orientation or sexual preference. In those areas, an employment decision based on sexual orientation or preference would be in violation of the law. But there is no federal employment law that provides protection on this issue. An employer's outrageous surveillance into private aspects of an individual's life or publicizing private or false information could be grounds for a legal claim against the employer.

Q   *Does an employee have any rights providing protection for privacy of religious beliefs?*

A   Federal and state antibias laws provide protection for employees from discrimination on the basis of religion. This means that it is an illegal employment practice for an employer to make an employment decision or to treat an employee differently based on an employee's religion. The employer is required to make a reasonable accommodation if there is a conflict between work schedules and an individual's Sabbath observation or to make a reasonable accommodation for an individual's religious dress or appearance. An employer may enforce a no-solicitation policy to prevent or control religious proselytizing.

11

Emerging Issues in Workplace Privacy

As the 1990s draw to a close, conflicts over workplace privacy are exploding right and left. I believe that privacy concerns will continue to mushroom, especially in several emerging areas, the subject of this chapter. Some of these areas relate to the broader issue of personal privacy in society, as well as privacy concerns in the employer and employee relationship.

The Right to Medical Privacy

Mary Jones is a working mother with an active lifestyle who considers herself to be in good health. In the past year, Mary had occasion to receive medical treatment four times. As a result of an allergy flare-up in the spring, she saw her doctor and received an antihistamine prescription. During the summer, her doctor recommended precautionary removal of a skin blemish to prevent the likelihood of skin cancer. The procedure was performed at a local outpatient surgery center. In early fall, she sprained her wrist from a fall while roller blading in the park and received emergency room care. After experiencing a late period, she received pregnancy and pap tests at her gynecologist's office.

Each one of these instances created or added to medical records at her doctor's office, the local pharmacy, the outpatient surgery center, the hospital, and her gynecologist's office. When Mary filed insurance claims through her employer, medical information was routed to the firm's health insurance company, which created claims records for its files. Mary expected that these medical records would not be released to others or used in employment decisions. But without proper controls—especially in the case of computer records that are processed by an insurance company or a third-party administrator or handled by staff specialists—there is a real potential for unauthorized release of private medical information.

Computerized ordering systems known as electronic data interchange (EDI) provide a direct computer link through which a firm and its suppliers can purchase and order parts and supplies. EDI concepts are increasingly being applied to medical claims processing and other forms of data transfers involving private employee information. These processing procedures may put confidential medical information about individuals into E-mail type systems or centralized databases that health care providers, medical institutions, and insurance companies can use to share individual medical data.

Information stored in these databases creates the possibility of a cradle-to-grave look at an individual's health history—a boon for health care professionals who can use it for better evaluation, diagnosis, and care, and perhaps an unintentional boon for hackers and others to disclose or otherwise unscrupulously use medical data.

Although less than 5 percent of physicians and 25 percent of hospitals now store patient records electronically, this number is expected to increase as the fast-growing medical data industry develops computerized networks. Presently a $100 million industry, this industry is expected to grow to an estimated $1.5 billion by the year 2001.[1] As it grows, there will be a vital need to build in controls for access and use of data to protect medical records privacy.

Telecommuting from the Home Office

Thanks to personal computers, modems, facsimile machines, and E-mail, employees in certain jobs can work effectively from a home office rather than trekking to the office every day. But the use of these new communications tools also creates new questions affecting the employee's private life.

When does a telecommuter's work time end and personal time begin? Does the possession of a communications tool mean that the employee is continually on call? Does the employer's expectation on use of these tools represent a privacy invasion? How can the employer be sure that off-site or telecommuting employees are working the requisite hours? Does the employer

1. "The Right to Medical Privacy," *Workplace Visions* (SHRM), Jan./Feb. 1997, p. 2.

have a right to monitor employee activities in the home because the home office is now a company worksite? All of these questions and more must be answered when a firm begins using the new portable personal technologies.

One company's use of lap top computers led to a dispute about whether employees were required to perform routine projects over the weekend. In this firm, employees were given lap top computers with fax modems for full communication link to the computer systems at the firm's main office. With the consent of management, some employees decided to telecommute from home, coming into the office only when meetings were scheduled. One weekend, a manager called a staff worker to check the status of a pending but noncritical project. The employee returned the call from her vacation home. The manager insisted that the project be completed over the weekend, saying, ". . . that's why we gave you the mobile office." The employee was furious. She felt that the weekend was her own time and that after-hours work was only required in an emergency.[2]

Watch for new questions about the traditional employer-employee relationship to surface as new communications and data handling devices are introduced into the workplace.

Web Watching

While you are surfing the net, the web is watching you. New tools allow businesses that set up web site home pages to track who is visiting a web site and how often in order to identify potential or actual customers. At a very basic level, web site operators can accept E mail and track visitor inquiries, track down-loaded choices, and enter actual customer orders. These data can be analyzed just like other sales data.

Companies can also obtain data on web site visitors through registration procedures and questionnaires. Through registration, the web site operator asks the web visitor to provide information about name, address, telephone, employer, job, or other similar data. Questionnaires may in fact be marketing surveys asking about preferences, interests, and other business or personal data. Web site users can also purchase software that tracks and analyzes web visits. All these data can be classified, coded, and analyzed, resulting in the creation of valuable customer or prospect lists.

2. Ibid.

An alarming new trend emerged recently when Central Point Software, a firm that sells computer housekeeping programs called utilities, obtained data about customer computer systems without the knowledge or permission of customers. Alert customers who had purchased the PC Tools utilities software noticed an added text file had appeared on their hard drives. According to news reports, some 10,000 personal computers were scanned by an electronic registration form when the unwary owners clicked "send" to electronically register their purchase of the utilities software. After users squawked about their renegade file on E-mail bulletin boards, the utilities software firm stopped its practice of reading customers' systems features.[3]

Nonetheless, this appears to be a growing practice. For example, a recent notice in HR Magazine alerts SHRM members that its web page equips the user's web browser with a hidden file, called a "cookie" in computer parlance, that logs their visits and keeps inquiries to a specified limit.[4] The very thought that an outside computer can attach data to your hard drive or read your system configuration is alarming. While the SHRM cookie seems harmless, what's next? Can a web site operator or a hacker enter your computer system, read your checking account number or balance, or use personal data to electronically transfer funds from your account? Will an employer using similar technology be able to track E-mail messages and read data stored in files an employee believed to be private? The existing privacy laws do not fully address these new issues, particularly in relation to employer monitoring of private intranet communication systems within an organization.

The Encryption Debate

As the Internet becomes a communications medium, companies are beginning to recognize the need to protect confidentiality of messages. Royal Dutch Shell Group, a Netherlands-based oil and chemical conglomerate, now transmits business communications to its 120 far-flung companies through the Internet, using sophisticated encryption technology to protect company secrets from prying eyes.

Also called cryptography, encryption is a process of coding an electronic message so that only a designated receiver with a "key" to unlock the code can decipher the message. In a typical encryption process, a coding system

3. Nikchil Hutheesing, "Big Modem Is Watching," Forbes, Feb. 13, 1995, p. 156.
4. Mike Frost, "From the E-Mailbag," HR Magazine, May 1997, p. 34.

referred to as a public key is used to garble the message. Only the recipient with a private key can decipher the message. As long as the encryption keys are kept private, no one can intercept or read the message except for the designated recipient.

Because encryption creates a privacy expectation, it creates new privacy questions. Employees using the coded messages may feel that their messages are private and that there is a privacy invasion if the employer intercepts encrypted messages. But what happens if an employee loses or forgets an encryption key? And how will encryption be handled when an individual separates from employment? As with other lock, key, or security systems, the employer wants to have some sort of a master key or key recovery system.

Trusted Information Systems, a Glenwood, Maryland, company involved in setting up encryption systems, offers one solution to this issue. Rather than save messages on private keys, the encryption system gives the company the ability to recover the keys used to encrypt the message. If the need to access a message arises, the company can then decrypt the key and decode the relevant message.

Whatever system is used to encrypt messages on the Internet or even private intranets, employee privacy issues will also need to be defined and communicated.

Growing Government Regulation

Watch for increased government intervention as concerns about privacy grow. At a recent annual meeting of the Information Industry Association, FTC Commissioner Christine A. Varney warned employers and on-line businesses to restrict their collection of data, especially from children, or the government would increase its role to protect personal privacy.[5]

Expanded interest by government in privacy issues was reflected in the legislation proposed or considered in the U.S. Congress in 1996. Nine hundred thirty of the 7,945 bills introduced before the 104th Congress incorporated some privacy issues.[6] Among the issues under consideration were the following:

5. Stephen H. Wildstrom, "They're Watching You On-Line," *Business Week*, Nov. 11, 1996, p. 19.
6. Ibid.

- Proposed telecommunications reform legislation included restrictions on the collecting of customer preference information and use of tele-communications equipment.
- A credit reporting reform bill sought to address certain privacy-related issues.
- A medical records confidentiality act, proposed in 1995, seeks to replace local privacy laws with a federal standard on the issue of privacy of medical records.
- A health insurance reform act, which was passed into law, requires the secretary of health and human services to provide Congress with a report and recommendations to protect health information privacy.
- A privacy for consumers and workers act proposes federal standards relating to employer electronic monitoring of employees, telephone call monitoring, use of collected data, and certain privacy protections.

As the government gets into the business of privacy regulation, things get complicated and bureaucratic. Government regulation leads to restrictions, rules, and voluminous regulations. Consider, for example, the rules now in place under the Polygraph Protection Act of 1988. While there are conflicting opinions on the polygraph's value and accuracy, its use is subject to strict notification requirements, prohibited in preemployment screening, and permitted only for individuals who had access to property that is missing and who are suspect.

Consider too the Communications Decency Act passed by Congress in 1996. Intended to prevent and provide criminal penalties for the obscene or harassing use of telecommunication facilities, it prohibited the transmission of obscene or sexually oriented information via interactive computer service to persons under eighteen years of age. As a result of a legal challenge, a U.S. Appeals Court has held that the law is unconstitutional. The protections intended by this law are now on hold. At this writing, the constitutionality question is on appeal to the U.S. Supreme Court.[7]

Government becomes involved in social issues when there is an apparent need to correct a social wrong. When employer abuses of employee privacy rights come to light, the government is pressured to do something to protect "employee rights." However, government laws, regulations, and subsequent court decisions often complicate matters. If employers can exercise their right

7. Ibid.

to manage employee relations in a reasonable and nondiscriminatory manner, then there will be less pressure for government intervention.

High-Tech Tools Create New Privacy Questions

Personal technologies are highly portable new tools that can facilitate business communications and productivity—or become tools of surveillance and monitoring, as one company learned. The company obtained sophisticated handheld computer terminals to aid productivity and communications of field sales personnel who spent about 90 percent of their time in their sales territories. Whereas sales representatives previously had to call the office to place orders, check status or pricing, and update customer files, they could now use miniature communications terminals instead.

Besides allowing them to handle customer inquiries, enter orders, quote prices, check order status, view order history, and complete required reports, the terminals let sales representatives contact each other to arrange luncheon meetings. As the sales representatives became more familiar with the devices, they began to use them for personal communications. Initially, management took a hands-off approach to regulating communications with the devices. But later, sensing possible abuse of the devices, management began to use the system to monitor communications of one sales representative. When monitoring showed extensive use of the device for personal communications, management responded by taking away the communications terminal. Other sales personnel, now fearful of management surveillance, essentially stopped using the devices except to page another, following up with a conversation on a pay tele phone.[8]

In yet another example, a concrete company operating a fleet of cement mixing trucks encountered a dilemma related to use of personal cellular telephones by truck drivers. Even though the trucks were equipped with two-way radios, drivers complained that radio transmissions failed to get through to the dispatcher during peak periods. Transmission difficulties forced some drivers to use their personal cellular telephones to reach the dispatcher's office for directions, to report order changes, and even to report an accident. Management's dilemma arose when it learned that drivers were making personal tele-

---

8. H. Jefferson Smith and Keri E. Pearlson, "Drawing the Line," *Beyond Computing* (Northbook, IL), June 1996, p. 20.

phone calls while on the job and some other employees requested that the company reimburse them for cellular telephone use.

Personal portable technologies clearly aid productivity and communications, but their use creates new questions about the nature and privacy of employer and employee communications. Employees expect or assume that any personal communications are private and not the employer's business. But the employer who spent money on the communications device feels justified in monitoring communications to ensure productivity is maintained and assets are properly used. As a result, each new form of communication is likely to encounter the workplace privacy tug-of-war between employee privacy rights and management control.

In Conclusion

Privacy has been referred to as our shrinking right—a right that is being chipped away as employers undertake greater monitoring and surveillance of employees. But a growing body of regulations, state and federal statutes, and case law is giving guidance on what constitutes a privacy invasion. Also, many employers are weighing their priorities, deciding which will cost more: an occasional privacy claim or lost inventory due to a workplace that is not monitored. The ideal goal for employer and employee alike is to find a balance that respects individual dignity while protecting the safety, productivity, and profitability of the workplace.

Appendix

Model Privacy Code

- Use monitoring as a positive aid to employee training, to help improve customer services, and to help determine adequate staffing.

- Use monitoring as a means to ensure compliance with federal and state laws and regulations that protect consumers and businesses.

- Use monitoring to protect the security of employees, customers, and the general public and to safeguard financial assets and public funds.

- Use monitoring to assist in fairly evaluating employee performance.

- Limit the collection, review, and use of data about an individual employee, obtained through electronic monitoring, to information relevant to the employee's work.

- Provide prior disclosure in writing to employees that may be monitored, to provide reasons for such monitoring and to obtain the informed consent of employees to monitoring.

- Clearly designate telephones that are monitored and provide employees with access to alternative telephones for private conversations.

- Provide employees with an opportunity to review information obtained by electronic monitoring when such information is used as a basis for disciplinary action.

- Avoid disclosure of employee data obtained by electronic monitoring to third parties, except pursuant to law or the informed consent of the employee.

- Avoid engaging in visual surveillance of employees in dressing rooms, locker rooms, rest rooms, or showers, except pursuant to law or for security reasons

From "Privacy and American Business," reprinted from *HR News*, Nov. 1994, p. 9.

Abbreviations Used in Notes

ARB	*Labor Arbitration Awards* (Chicago: Commerce Clearing House)
BNA	Bureau of National Affairs, Washington, DC
CCH	Commerce Clearing House, Chicago
CFR	*Code of Federal Regulations*
EPD Cases	*Employment Practices Decisions Cases* (Chicago: Commerce Clearing House)
IER Cases	*Individual Employment Rights Cases* (Washington, DC: Bureau of National Affairs)
IERM	*Individual Employment Rights Manual* (Washington, DC: Bureau of National Affairs)
LRRM	*Labor Relations Reference Manual* (Washington, DC: Bureau of National Affairs)
SHRM	Society for Human Resource Management, Alexandria, VA
USCA	*United States Code Annotated*

Index

About the Author

William S. Hubbartt, president, is the principal and owner of HUBBARTT & ASSOCIATES, a human resources management consulting firm located in St. Charles, Illinois, specializing in personnel policy development, employee handbook preparation, employee compensation, and supervisory training.

Mr. Hubbartt has over 25 years of experience in human resource management, including positions in industry, corporate, government, and consulting. He was awarded a lifetime accreditation as a Senior Professional in Human Resources (SPHR), from the Human Resource Certification Institute, and in 1995, he received the Certified Compensation Professional (CCP) designation from the American Compensation Association. He earned an M.S. in industrial relations from Loyola University, Chicago. He is a member of the Society of Human Resource Management and was 1991 and 1992 chairman of the Human Resource Group of the Greater O'Hare Association.

A respected business writer, Mr. Hubbartt is author of *Performance Appraisal Manual for Managers and Supervisors* (Commerce Clearing House, 1992); *Personnel Policy Handbook: How to Prepare a Personnel Policy Manual That Works* (McGraw-Hill, 1993); *What Every Employee Ought to Know about Performance Appraisals* (CCH, 1994); and *What You Ought to Know about Participating in Employee Committees and Work Teams* (CCH, 1995). He is also author of the "Management Memo" column in the *Kane County Chronicle*, a newspaper published in Geneva, Illinois.